Made in the USA
Monee, IL
19 October 2022

ILLUSTRATED JOB
IN HEBREW

ILLUSTRATED JOB
IN HEBREW

Dominick S. Hernández

GlossaHouse
Wilmore, KY
www.GlossaHouse.com

Bible. Job. Hebrew. Westminster Theological Text. 2020.
Illustrated Job in Hebrew / Dominick S. Hernández; [Keith Neely, illustrator].
– Wilmore, KY : GlossaHouse, ©2020.

xix + 60 pages : color illustrations ; 28 cm. –
(GlossaHouse Illustrated Biblical Texts)

Summary: The Hebrew text of the Book of Job is set within colorful
illustrations to represent narration, dialogue, monologue, and scripture quotations,
together with a new English version by GlossaHouse translators.
Text in Hebrew and English.
ISBN 9781636630052 (paperback)

1. Bible. Job--Cartoons and comics.   2. Bible. Job--Picture Bibles.
I. Hernández, Dominick S.   II. Neely, Keith, 1943-   III. Title.   IV. Series.
V. Bible. Job. English. Hernández. 2020.

Library of Congress Control Number: 2020946513

GLOSSAHOUSE
ILLUSTRATED BIBLICAL TEXTS

SERIES EDITOR
Timothy C. McNinch

GlossaHouse
Wilmore, KY
www.GlossaHouse.com

ליאיר ויעל הרננדז אורנאלס

אני מקווה שהתמונות הפשוטות האלו יעזרו לכם להבין את התוכן המסובך
של ספר זה. אני מקווה שהתוכן המסובך של הספר יביא אתכם לידע
ולקשר עמוק עם האל המפואר שמוצג בספר.

To Yair and Yael Hernández Ornelas

*May the simple pictures of this book help you understand the complex text of
the book; may the complex text of the book bring you into a deeper knowledge
and relationship with the glorious God portrayed in the text.*

Table of Contents

x . . . . Series Introduction

xii . . . . Introduction to *Illustrated Job*

xviii . . . . . . Table of Hebrew Numbers (1–100)

xix . . . . Table of *Ketiv/Qere* Instances

1 . . . . Job Chapter 1 (פרק א)

4 . . . . Job Chapter 2 (פרק ב)

5 . . . . Job Chapter 3 (פרק ג)

6 . . . . Job Chapter 4 (פרק ד)

7 . . . . Job Chapter 5 (פרק ה)

8 . . . . Job Chapter 6 (פרק ו)

9 . . . . Job Chapter 7 (פרק ז)

9 . . . . Job Chapter 8 (פרק ח)

10 . . . . Job Chapter 9 (פרק ט)

11 . . . . Job Chapter 10 (פרק י)

12 . . . . Job Chapter 11 (פרק יא)

12 . . . . Job Chapter 12 (פרק יב)

13 . . . . Job Chapter 13 (פרק יג)

14 . . . . Job Chapter 14 (פרק יד)

14 . . . . Job Chapter 15 (פרק טו)

15 . . . . Job Chapter 16 (פרק טז)

16 . . . . Job Chapter 17 (פרק יז)

16 . . . . Job Chapter 18 (פרק יח)

17 . . . . Job Chapter 19 (פרק יט)

18 . . . . Job Chapter 20 (פרק כ)

19 . . . . Job Chapter 21 (פרק כא)

20 . . . . Job Chapter 22 (פרק כב)

21 . . . . Job Chapter 23 (פרק כג)

22 . . . . Job Chapter 24 (פרק כד)

23 . . . . Job Chapter 25 (פרק כה)

23 . . . . Job Chapter 26 (פרק כו)

24 . . . . Job Chapter 27 (פרק כז)

25 . . . . Job Chapter 28 (פרק כח)

25 . . . . Job Chapter 29 (פרק כט)

26 . . . . Job Chapter 30 (פרק ל)

27 . . . . Job Chapter 31 (פרק לא)

28 . . . . Job Chapter 32 (פרק לב)

29 . . . . Job Chapter 33 (פרק לג)

30 . . . . Job Chapter 34 (פרק לד)

31 . . . . Job Chapter 35 (פרק לה)

32 . . . . Job Chapter 36 (פרק לו)

33 . . . . Job Chapter 37 (פרק לז)

33 . . . . Job Chapter 38 (פרק לח)

35 . . . . Job Chapter 39 (פרק לט)

36 . . . . Job Chapter 40 (פרק מ)

37 . . . . Job Chapter 41 (פרק מא)

38 . . . . Job Chapter 42 (פרק מב)

41 . . . . Endnotes

Series Introduction

Timothy C. McNinch
series editor, GIBT (Hebrew Bible)

One evening, after my preschool daughter had finished reading her picture book, on a whim I tossed the thick novel I was reading into her lap. Her eyes widened and an innocent look of bewilderment crept across her face, as she turned over page after page of words, words, and more words.

"But where are all the pictures, Daddy?"

It is not an accident that children begin reading with picture books. Our brains first learn to read by seeing pictures and associating words on a page with the images they represent. Likewise, second-language classrooms are saturated with visual vocabulary. Why, then, do students of biblical Hebrew typically run to purchase a dictionary and a crisp copy of the *Biblia Hebraica Stuttgartensia* in order to slog through words, words, and more words—with no images to help build bridges in the language center of their brains?

GlossaHouse Illustrated Biblical Texts offer a different learning and reading experience. They embed the Hebrew text of the Bible in the context of Keith Neely's evocative, full-color illustrations. This innovative presentation helps students of biblical languages to distinguish narrative from dialogue at a glance, picking up on visual cues of action, tension, and emotion. They are the equivalent of my daughter's picture books, but for biblical language students of all ages and stages. With these books as a tool, our hope is that the languages of the Bible will no longer feel like "dead languages" in students' minds—merely ancient codes to be deciphered into usable English; rather, we anticipate that they will come alive as languages of actual communication, vehicles used by ancient authors to express their stories in the idiom of their own hearts! We hope that these books will help you hear their voices, thick with the accent of their ancient dialects. Whether you are a beginning student of biblical languages, or an accomplished scholar, our hope is that this fresh presentation of the ancient texts will ignite your imagination, and turn the world of these words into an expansive, multicolored landscape in your mind's eye.

(story flows from top-right to bottom-left)

About the Format

You will have discovered, by now, that this book is "backwards." Just as the Hebrew language runs from right to left, this immersive volume has been printed from the "back" to the "front" (from an English reader's perspective). As you read the stories within, keep in mind that the narrative flow of each illustration, each row of images, and each page runs from the top-right to the bottom-left. Even Keith Neely's original illustrations have been reversed for this book, in order to more closely mimic the perception of those whose interior world runs right-to-left.

On each page, spoken language is presented in white speech bubbles, as you might find in a comic book or graphic novel. Narration is presented in tan boxes, including little phrases like, "She said," or "Then Abraham spoke, saying." In the typical graphic novel, these minutiae are omitted, since the fact that a character is speaking is made self-evident by the use of a speech bubble. However, they are retained in the present book so that we may represent the complete biblical text.

The Hebrew text used in this series is adapted from the "Westminster Leningrad Codex" (known as the *WTT*, or *Westminster Theological Text*), a digitally transcribed text produced by the good people at the J. Alan Groves Center for Advanced Biblical Research at Westminster Theological Seminary. The "Leningrad Codex" itself, upon which the *WTT* is based, is the earliest complete manuscript of the Hebrew Bible we have so far discovered. It is the primary source behind most modern editions of the Hebrew Bible and a plethora of modern translations.

We have made only minor adaptations to the *WTT* for this presentation of the Hebrew Bible: We have retained the vowel points for the text, but have stripped away all the other cantillation marks, for the sake of simplicity and readability. In addition, the *WTT* (following Leningrad) highlights instances where the spelling or pronunciation (*Qere*) of a word was remembered differently by the Masoretic scribes from what was written (*Ketiv*) in the received text. In such cases, they wrote their traditions and corrections in the margin, leaving the received text intact. Because they often represent a more readable form of the text, we have sometimes used the Masoretes' corrections (the *Qere*) in our presentation of the Hebrew text. Finally, we have marked the beginning of each biblical chapter with the Hebrew letter or letters signifying its numeric value. If you are still learning the Hebrew number system, you may find it helpful to consult the Table of Contents to identify a particular chapter's number, or refer to the chart of Hebrew numbers (1–100) that follows the introductions.

About the Translation

At the bottom of each page, we have provided an original English translation. However, keep in mind that in this book, the primary tool to help you comprehend the text is the visual illustration that accompanies it. For the most immersive experience, try to glean the meaning of the text from the context of those images first, before looking to the English translation for help.

In our translation, we have attempted to preserve the general word order of the Hebrew sentences (with the exception that we usually put the subject before the verb, while the tendency in biblical Hebrew is the reverse). Additionally, to help give you a sense of the economy of the Hebrew language, we have tried to consistently translate each Hebrew word with the same English word throughout the book. However, due to the differences in the languages, this practice can make for some impossibly awkward sentences, and at times we have compromised in order to produce intelligible English.

Multiple names for the divine are used in the Hebrew Bible. Many English translations render the covenantal name of God as "Yahweh," "Jehovah," or "The LORD." Known as the Tetragrammaton, this four-letter Hebrew name is revered in both Jewish and Christian faith communities. In most religious Jewish communities, the name is not spoken aloud in Hebrew (nor even written, outside of the Bible) and is certainly not pronounced "Yahweh" or "Jehovah." Instead, when the divine name is encountered while reading the biblical text aloud, the word "Adonai" (meaning "lord") or "Ha-Shem" (meaning "the name") is substituted, so as not to pronounce the ineffable name. Respecting these tradtions of reverence for the divine name, in this series' English translations we use the word "Adonai" to render the Tetragrammaton, or leave it unvocalized as YHWH. Additionally, regarding the divine, we have retained masculine pronouns for God where the text uses them, though we do not intend to make a theological claim about the gender of God with this practice.

Please enjoy reading these innovative resources. May they deepen your love for the Scriptures as you endeavor to read them in their own language.

כל הכבוד לאלוהים!

Introduction to Illustrated Job

Dominick S. Hernández

A couple of years ago, while my family was living in Israel, we were invited to the first birthday party for a child of family friends in Tel Aviv. As an increasing number of guests arrived for the mid-summer event, breathing space turned into a premium in the compact apartment, causing a group of adults to find refuge on the host's balcony overlooking the beach. There, I found myself sitting in close proximity to another guest who was kind enough to introduce himself and strike up a conversation. Naturally, we reverted to small talk as we kept one eye on each other and the other on the multitude of potential hazards customary to children's parties, which are ironically fraught with danger:

"What do you do for a living?" I asked, defaulting to the initial question that every new acquaintance asks at one-year-olds' parties.

My new Israeli friend communicated that he was employed by one of the world's most well-known high-tech companies. Impressed, I anticipated the instinctive reciprocal question, and I was not disappointed:

"So, what do you do for a living?"

"I am a PhD student in Bible"—I expected complete apathy.

"What are you writing on?" he retorted, much to my surprise.

"The book of Job."

"Ahh, the one written in Aramaic."

"What do you mean? The book of Job was written in Hebrew," I responded.

"Nah, Job was written in Aramaic," he countered with near certainty.

Approximately two minutes into our conversation, I was faced with a decision that would forever affect the trajectory of our newfound friendship: Should I argue with this gentleman and risk harming our mutually-needed comradery at this unpredictable event over the language of the book of Job? After all, my friend was a native Israeli who had been speaking Hebrew his whole life; he had surely taken Bible classes in school while growing up; and, as his position of employment suggested, he was clearly very smart. I, on the other hand, was a Hebrew-language learner. Who was I to challenge him?

At first, I considered it imprudent to argue with him over such a specialized issue at a baby's birthday party. Why would I risk so much so soon? No, it was not worth it.

But he was wrong, and I *had* to do something.

Suddenly, I had an idea. I would do what most people who grew up in my generation would do: let my cell phone do the talking.

"Look," I said as I thrust my cell phone in his direction with the Bible application open. "Check it out for yourself."

My new friend took the phone and stared at it for a couple of seconds, apparently still not really sure of what he was reading. Then, in a bewildered manner that justified his confusion, he slowly returned the phone to me and stated, "You are right. That *is* Hebrew… but… I have no idea what that's saying!" My new friend's comment was humorous at the time and served as a suitable transition into a less polemical conversation topic.

As I reflect upon this conversation years later, I cannot help but ponder several unintended lessons that pertain to reading Job. On the one hand, my native Israeli friend surely *could* understand Job to a certain extent since, after a brief glance at my phone, he was able to quickly identify that he was reading Hebrew. His academic training in the act of reading permitted him to *essentially* recognize and *basically* understand the text that he had momentarily skimmed. On the other hand, my friend's unequivocal and hyperbolic response, asserting that he had entirely no idea what was going on in the passage, was just as true. He *could not really* understand what he was reading in that moment; the text was supremely difficult. His educational training in reading Hebrew, recognizing morphology and syntax, and intuitively grasping the meaning of Hebrew-language texts was of little use as he stared at Job on that Tel Aviv balcony.

Perhaps if my Hebrew-speaking buddy were to have the opportunity to expound upon his pithy response, he might elaborate by stating, "I *sort of* get what's going on in Job. I recognize the language system. If I read long enough, I might be able to get the main points of the entire composition, but… Wait! Why does the Biblical Hebrew language I think I *should* know look and feel so much different from the Hebrew that I *actually* know? I *pretty much* get Job, but—wait a minute—I do not *really* understand Job!"

The essence of this concocted explanation is ever so applicable to modern readers of Job: We surely are able to follow the basic movement of the composition and observe the most notable theological and literary motifs therein, but we likewise grapple with the peculiarities and intricacies of the text and the theological questions that arise by way of analyzing it. Readers of Job who engage with the Hebrew text or a quality translation appreciate the basic storyline of the drama, which can be generally encapsulated in a manner similar to the following sketch:

The book begins by presenting a divine contest in the heavenly realm, during which the story's protagonist, Job, becomes the focal point (chapters 1–2). The Satan contends that Job only honors God because God has protected him and caused him to prosper. In order to demonstrate that this accusation is false, God initially permits the Satan to traumatize Job through the destruction of his surroundings and demise of his loved ones, but later allows the Satan to even harm Job physically, insofar as Job's injuries do not bring about his death. Job's terrible plight moves his friends, Eliphaz, Bildad, and Zophar, to visit him with the intent of providing consolation.

At the beginning of their visit, Job's friends demonstrate empathy by weeping and sitting with him in silence for an entire week. Job eventually breaks the silence by emphatically cursing the day in which he was born (chapter 3). The unseemly manner in which Job expresses his vexation seems to compel his friends to respond and, at least initially, strive to persuade Job to change his way of reflecting upon his situation. They do this by taking turns communicating their outlook on his predicament. Job finds their speeches quite unhelpful; he responds critically to each of them in turn, mostly directing his complaints toward God (chapters 4–22). Throughout the first round of speeches, Job's friends *generally* agree that Job has committed some sort of offense against God, and that an act of genuine contrition would suffice in order to reap the blessings of God anew (chapters 4–11). However, Job continuously frustrates his friends by denying that he has committed any deed warranting the type of hardship he suffers, thus challenging their perception of God's system of just retribution. By the second time Job's friends speak, they more vehemently express their convictions by ultimately proposing the logical conclusion of their view of just retribution: Job is suffering the consequences of being wicked, which necessarily indicates that Job is a wicked person (chapters 15–20). Job's response to his companions' second speeches is a direct rebuttal of their view that evildoers always suffer by pointing out that the wicked frequently prosper (chapter 21).

Eliphaz continues harping on the traditional view of just retribution in his third speech (chapter 22). Job's response to this speech ushers in a portion of the composition in which interpretive dubiety abounds. Several of Job's statements in this section seem as if he impersonates his friends (perhaps sardonically or parodically) or legitimately changes his mind about topics that were mentioned in previous speeches (chapters 23–24). Be that as it may, Bildad momentarily interrupts Job's speech (chapter 25) prior to Job again making several questionable assertions, leading to further bewilderment concerning why Job sounds like his friends (chapters 26–27). These complicated chapters are followed by a beautiful poem that relates wisdom to the fear of the Lord (chapter 28). The speaker of the wisdom poem of chapter 28 is not overtly identified, leaving the reader to deduce the provenance of the discourse that portrays the wellspring of wisdom. Job, once again, is explicitly designated as the speaker of the ensuing monologue in which he depicts his life prior to his trials (chapters 29–31).

An unforeseen event comes to pass at this point in the composition with the introduction of the previously inconspicuous character, Elihu (chapter 32). Elihu self-identifies as the youngest of the friends and presumes to know the correct manner in which to respond to Job (chapters 33–37). There are numerous opinions concerning the emergence of the character Elihu as well as the merit of his speech in regard to the overall meaning(s) of Job. Nevertheless, after his speeches, Elihu effectively recedes from view upon God's emergence out of the whirlwind to confront Job. Throughout the whirlwind speeches, God repeatedly questions Job with regard to his role in, and understanding of, creation order (chapters 38–41). Job responds to God twice with language that turns out to be painfully ambiguous (40:4–5; 42:2–6). Yet, by the end of the book, Job is depicted as blessed once again with children, riches, and health (chapter 42).

Normal quibbles and minor diversions aside, students of the Bible—those who read the text in their native language as well as Biblical-Hebrew-language learners—understand the flow of the book of Job to be *something like* this summary. In this sense, everyone who is able to read Job can boast of understanding Job. Likewise, I think my Israeli friend would agree that he could understand Job.

Nonetheless, the honesty of my Israeli friend goes a long way in curbing scholastic elitism when it comes to the book of Job. The reality is that *everyone* struggles with Job. Those who read translations of Job into their native language still wonder about the surrealness of the heavenly scene; they strive to develop creative interpretations of the puzzling issues of the third round of speeches; they question if Job actually does "repent" and what the answer to this debate implies concerning the book's theology. Similarly, Hebrew-language specialists throughout the ages—including native Modern Hebrew speakers and Biblical-Hebrew experts—have been stupefied by the language of Job and, ironically, revert to asking many of the same unsettled questions related to perplexing texts, which, in essence, are: "What in the world is going on here? Why does the text look like that? What does that word mean?"—and the like. From the novice reader who is learning the basics of biblical poetry to the Hebrew grammarians and biblical philologists whose livelihoods are practically based upon their ability to develop reasonable solutions to difficult textual issues, reading Job is commensurate with learning humility.

This modest disposition is fundamental to learning more about the text of Job as well as learning from the book of Job. Reading Job is similar to gazing into a clear night sky through a high-powered telescope; the longer and more intently one looks, the more striking the observation that there is much more in the panorama than could ever have been previously realized or expected. Regardless of how high-powered one's telescope (e.g., level of language skills, academic training) is, and irrespective of the angle toward which one is looking at the sky (e.g., philological, theological, literary), as the observer gazes, the nature of the cosmos emerges to be increasingly beautiful as well as complex. The intricate nature of Job continuously facilitates refinements in understanding and a heightened appreciation of the composition for all who are willing to engage in the joy and labor of reading it.

Over the years, scholars have developed an ever-growing corpus of literature that has assisted in understanding Job in its ancient Near Eastern literary and linguistic contexts. This has come by way of advancements in diverse areas of study including: Cuneiform studies (which brought to light the comparable ancient Near Eastern "pious sufferer" compositions), Semitic philology, cognitive metaphor theory, poetics, and other academic disciplines. Accordingly, there is no shortage of helps when it comes to reading Job. This translation can serve as an asset to all types of people that are interested in Job—irrespective of where one is in the process of Hebrew-language learning. Children can pick up the volume and basically understand the storyline of the text through looking at the pictures; people who are proficient in reading English can understand the flow of the book through the translation and helpful illustrations; students of Biblical Hebrew can read along in Hebrew, while using the pictures for context and the English translation as a gloss for unknown words; skilled Hebrew readers will refer to the English translation less frequently and will likely be interested in the translation notes in the appendix that attend to grammatical peculiarities and other translation issues.

The Task of Translating Job

Translations of the Bible are rendered on a continuum between "text-oriented" and "audience-oriented" approaches. The method of translation and the character of the final product are dependent upon the goal(s) of the translator and intended readers. Edward L. Greenstein explains that in utilizing the "text-oriented approach, the translator must somehow confront the audience with the strangeness of the language, anthropology, and world-view of the source. In the contemporizing or audience-oriented approach, the translator must transform the source into an idiom and conceptual framework that will resonate with the readership. In bringing the audience to the source, there is a likelihood of losing comprehension. In bringing the text to the audience, there is a likelihood of losing the sense and/or its impact."[1] Greenstein clearly articulates the discernment process of translators who struggle with how to render a source composition into the target language.

Translators are conscious of the fact that something always has to give in translation; the translator is forced to relinquish the advantages of one type of translation to benefit from others. In this manner, translations intrinsically demonstrate the goal(s) of the translator, the intended audience, and, conversely, the characteristics of a rendering that the translator considers dispensable for the objectives of that particular work. Since Job is a unique book written in sophisticated Hebrew, translating the text necessarily dispossesses this magnificent artwork of some of the attributes that make it so aesthetically pleasing. A major question that prevails when translating Job is: "How much of the aesthetics of the original composition does the translator strive to maintain?" Correspondingly, "What is the translator willing to 'sacrifice' in order to 'redeem' other desired results?"

This volume of the *GlossaHouse Illustrated Biblical Texts* series markedly participates in this game of give and take and can be likened to a forceful swing of the pendulum to the text-oriented side of the translation continuum. This rendering brings the readership as close as possible to the source material, with a specific focus on word-for-word translation of the language that makes up the uncanny text of Job. This approach to translating is certainly not the only way of translating Job—nor, in my opinion, can it be argued that this is invariably the "best" way of translating the book. Nevertheless, in the game of give-and-take translation, this rendering has distinctly sacrificed the aesthetic grandeur of the book of Job for the sake of the pedagogical benefits of learning Hebrew with a gloss that closely mirrors the underlying Hebrew text (i.e., The Westminster Leningrad Codex [www.tanach.us])—even striving to imitate the word order, when possible. These pedagogical benefits deserve a bit more explanation.

Much of the book of Job was written in poetry. Poetry, by nature, employs unique language. The poetic sections of Job, however, are exquisite Hebrew poetry that consist of dozens of *hapax legomena*, numerous rare words (i.e., morphologically and phonologically distinctive) that are intended to be

---

[1] "Challenges in Translating the Book of Job," in *Found in Translation: Essays on Jewish Biblical Translation in Honor of Leonard J. Greenspoon*, eds. James W. Barker, Anthony Le Donne, Joel N. Lohr (West Lafayette, IN: Purdue University Press, 2018), 180.

understood in derivative meanings, and Hebraicized words from other languages, among other peculiarities. Additionally, Job is replete with literary techniques that are difficult to translate with the same richness and clarity (e.g., parody, hyperbole, metaphors, imagery, and other rhetorical devices). Add to this equation that there is no shortage of text-critical issues in the book, and the sum of all of these parts synergistically presents Job as most unaccommodating to the pretense of translation. Upon glancing at the Hebrew text of Job, it seems that anyone who would dare to translate the book should be a gifted poet in their own right, not to mention a linguist who is trained in Semitics and biblical textual criticism. Even under these idealistic translation circumstances, the notion of an English-language equivalent of Job is a questionable objective, if not a presumptuous one. Taking this into consideration, studying—let alone translating—the text of Job could strike beginning and advanced students of Biblical Hebrew alike as a crippling task.

Welcome the stringent-text-oriented approach. Through this type of translation of Job, readers are able to toil with the difficult text until they come across an unknown word or phrase. By glancing at the strict translation at the bottom of the page, readers are aided by the English text with a straightforward translation of the unfamiliar word or phrase. Upon receiving the information needed from the English translation, students are encouraged to continue reading the Hebrew text that is accompanied by the helpful pictures in the top portion of the page.

A translation that strictly resembles the underlying Hebrew text is most helpful under these circumstances. This translation is not intended to be read as a standalone composition and should not be judged as such. Rather, the translation should be viewed in terms of how it facilitates reader engagement with the Hebrew text, and thereby, increases their academic learning time (i.e., pedagogical value). Encouraging Biblical-Hebrew students to continue reading upon encountering difficulties is no inconsequential matter; getting bogged down with unknown words or phrases hardly expedites a deeper understanding of the language and most certainly does not encourage the type of passion that is necessary to continuously increase in knowledge of the subject material throughout one's lifetime.

For some experienced readers of Job, this exceedingly text-oriented translation might *feel* like violence is being executed upon the book. Furthermore, a strict adherence to the Westminster Leningrad Codex has curbed the investigation of legitimate textual and philological questions in Job (e.g., potential emendations, textual dislocation, clues from other Semitic languages) for the sake of the translation being based upon one stable source text. This has led to a fair bit of awkwardness and repetition (i.e., lack of stylistic variation) in some parts of the translation. I have deliberately left this unusual language in the translation when English-language grammar rules permit (though, sometimes even these conventions were stretched). Despite the fact that skilled readers of Hebrew might consider this translation to be an affront to the beauty of Job, I have tried to balance my choice of words on the tightrope between a precise rendering of the Hebrew of Job and intelligibility of the English translation. In numerous cases, I admittedly defaulted to precision at the expense of clarity.

I trust that the notes in the appendix of this volume will be particularly helpful for readers with further questions concerning critical issues. Most of the notes address wording that was added to the translation in order to make sense of the text, hypotheses as to the meanings of rare words, and other grammatical, morphological, and syntactical oddities. I have not been completely consistent in following either the *Ketiv* or *Qere*. When they occur in the Westminster Leningrad Codex, I have chosen the option which made most sense to me in each particular context (see the *Table of Ketiv/Qere Instances* on p. xix). I have included notes concerning these decisions, though not always. The hundreds of translation notes in the appendix is by no stretch of the imagination comprehensive—as if it were ever really possible to create such a set of notes on Job. I have tried to keep the notes concise so as not to ensnare readers in the appendix instead of redirecting them to the Hebrew text.

In your hands, you have one translation of Job on a continuum in which many legitimate renderings can coexist and even complement each other. My hope is to someday participate in a more contemporized translation and try my hand at bringing the text to the audience. However, I recognize that even then, the principle of give and take will still apply; I will give up the helpfulness of a literal gloss for a more aesthetically pleasing translation; I will forfeit the simplicity of immediately knowing the dictionary meaning of individual Hebrew words for the enjoyment of discovering the synergistic meaning of the component parts of Hebrew poetry. Reading different types of translations might, ironically, be one of the ways by which readers of Job develop a stronger appreciation of the Hebrew text. In doing so, we are able to learn important lessons through our struggle to decipher that which is going on behind the scenes—not dissimilar to the protagonist of the book at hand.

Acknowledgments

Many people contributed to this project and deserve to be recognized for their assistance in bringing it to fruition.

Primeramente, le quisiera agradecer a mi esposa Gaby por haber tenido el mismo tipo de paciencia conmigo durante nuestros 18 años de casados que Dios tuvo con Job durante sus sufrimientos. Tú, Gaby, has sido el pilar de nuestra familia y jamás podría lograr mis metas si no las adaptaras como las tuyas también y si no me apoyaras durante el proceso de llevarlas a cabo.

I would like to thank Catherine Merrifield for painstakingly reading the entire translation and appendix. Mrs. Merrifield provided numerous helpful comments on grammar and punctuation which helped bring about the final form of this project.

I am grateful to Charles Loder who is responsible for all of the typesetting. Without the work of Mr. Loder, this book would not have been completed in a timely manner or be nearly as aesthetically pleasing as it is in its current form.

Gratitude is in order for the GlossaHouse team. Special thanks are due to Michael Halcomb for securing me as an author. I would like to thank Tim McNinch for his patience in waiting for the manuscript and for his assistance in the editorial process.

I am greatly indebted to Professor Ed Greenstein of Bar-Ilan University who served as my doctoral advisor during my PhD studies on the book of Job. He has influenced me beyond what I could reasonably footnote. I highly recommend his recent translation of the book of Job for readers who are interested in pursuing further philological and textual issues: Edward L. Greenstein. *Job: A New Translation*. New Haven: Yale University Press, 2019.

Table of Hebrew Numbers (1–100)

ט 9	ח 8	ז 7	ו 6	ה 5	ד 4	ג 3	ב 2	א 1
יט 19	יח 18	יז 17	טז 16	טו 15	יד 14	יג 13	יב 12	יא 11	י 10
כט 29	כח 28	כז 27	כו 26	כה 25	כד 24	כג 23	כב 22	כא 21	כ 20
לט 39	לח 38	לז 37	לו 36	לה 35	לד 34	לג 33	לב 32	לא 31	ל 30
מט 49	מח 48	מז 47	מו 46	מה 45	מד 44	מג 43	מב 42	מא 41	מ 40
נט 59	נח 58	נז 57	נו 56	נה 55	נד 54	נג 53	נב 52	נא 51	נ 50
סט 69	סח 68	סז 67	סו 66	סה 65	סד 64	סג 63	סב 62	סא 61	ס 60
עט 79	עח 78	עז 77	עו 76	עה 75	עד 74	עג 73	עב 72	עא 71	ע 70
פט 89	פח 88	פז 87	פו 86	פה 85	פד 84	פג 83	פב 82	פא 81	פ 80
צט 99	צח 98	צז 97	צו 96	צה 95	צד 94	צג 93	צב 92	צא 91	צ 90
									ק 100

* Note that 15 (טו) and 16 (טז) break the pattern. This is done in order to avoid using combinations of letters that are within the divine name.

Table of Ketiv/Qere Instances

The Hebrew text of this volume usually follows the Masoretic *Qere*, but occasionally follows the *Ketiv* when it has been judged to be the more helpful reading. Below is a table of all *Ketiv/Qere* instances in Job. The unshaded words are those found in the Hebrew text of this volume.

Qere (קרי)	*Ketiv* (כתיב)	Reference	*Qere* (קרי)	*Ketiv* (כתיב)	Reference
דְּרָכָיו	דְּרָכוֹ	26:14a	אֲחִיוֹתֵיהֶם	אֲחִיָתֵיהֶם	1:4
גְּבוּרוֹתָיו	גְּבוּרָתוֹ	26:14b	אַתָּה	אַתְּ	1:10
שְׂרִידָיו	שְׂרִידוֹ	27:15	יָצָאתִי	יָצָתִי	1:21
יִתְרִי	יִתְרוֹ	30:11	וְעַד	עַד	2:7
תּוּשִׁיָּה	תְּשֻׁוָה	30:22	וְיָדָיו	וְיָדוֹ	5:18
הִיא	הוּא	31:11a	וְהַוָּתִי	וְהַוָּתִי	6:2
וְהִיא	וְהוּא	31:11b	לוֹ	לֹא	6:21
חֲלָצָיו	חֲלָצוֹ	31:20	וְשֻׁבוּ	וְשֻׁבִי	6:29
וָרֹב	וְרִיב	33:19	עֲלֵי	עַל	7:1
וְשֻׁפּוּ	וּשְׁפִי	33:21	וָגוּשׁ	וְגִישׁ	7:5
נַפְשׁוֹ	נַפְשִׁי	33:28a	תַּחְתָּיו	תַּחְתּוֹ	9:13
וְחַיָּתוֹ	וְחַיָּתִי	33:28b	בְּמֵי	בְּמוֹ	9:30
בְּתַחְבּוּלוֹתָיו	בְּתַחְבּוּלֹתוֹ	37:12	וַחֲדָל	יֶחְדָּל	10:20a
מִן	מִנ	38:1	וְשִׁית	יָשִׁית	10:20b
יָדַעְתָּ הַשַּׁחַר	יִדַּעְתָּה שַּׁחַר	38:12	לוֹ	לֹא	13:15
יְלָדָיו	יְלָדוֹ	38:41	חֻקָּיו	חֻקּוֹ	14:5
יָשִׁיב	יָשׁוּב	39:12	בִּקְדֹשָׁיו	בִּקְדֹשׁוֹ	15:15
כְּנָפָיו	כְּנָפוֹ	39:26	וְצָפוּי	וְצָפוּ	15:22
וְאֶפְרֹחָיו	וְאֶפְרֹחוֹ	39:30	בַּשְׂיוֹ	בַּשְׂוֹ	15:31
מִן	מִנ	40:6	חֳמַרְמְרוּ	חֳמַרְמְרָה	16:16
פְּחָדָיו	פְּחָדוֹ	40:17	שַׁדּוּן	שַׁדּוֹן	19:29
לוֹ	לֹא	41:4	עֲלוּמָיו	עֲלוּמָו	20:11
יָדַעְתִּי	יָדַעְתָּ	42:2	יִכָּלוּ	יָבֹלוּ	21:13
שְׁבוּת	שְׁבִית	42:10	עֵינָיו	עֵינוֹ	21:20
אֲחִיוֹתָיו	אֲחִיתָיו	42:11	וְיֹדְעָיו	וְיֹדְעוֹ	24:1
וַיִּרְאֶה	וַיַּרְא	42:16	יִקְצוֹרוּ	יַקְצִירוּ	24:6
			וּבִתְבוּנָתוֹ	וּבִתְבוּנָתוֹ	26:12

איוב פרק א

1 אִישׁ הָיָה בְאֶרֶץ־עוּץ אִיּוֹב שְׁמוֹ וְהָיָה הָאִישׁ הַהוּא תָּם וְיָשָׁר וִירֵא אֱלֹהִים וְסָר מֵרָע 2 וַיִּוָּלְדוּ לוֹ שִׁבְעָה בָנִים וְשָׁלוֹשׁ בָּנוֹת 3 וַיְהִי מִקְנֵהוּ שִׁבְעַת אַלְפֵי־צֹאן וּשְׁלֹשֶׁת אַלְפֵי גְמַלִּים וַחֲמֵשׁ מֵאוֹת צֶמֶד־בָּקָר וַחֲמֵשׁ מֵאוֹת אֲתוֹנוֹת וַעֲבֻדָּה רַבָּה מְאֹד וַיְהִי הָאִישׁ הַהוּא גָּדוֹל מִכָּל־בְּנֵי־קֶדֶם

4 וְהָלְכוּ בָנָיו וְעָשׂוּ מִשְׁתֶּה בֵּית אִישׁ יוֹמוֹ וְשָׁלְחוּ וְקָרְאוּ לִשְׁלֹשֶׁת אַחְיֹתֵיהֶם לֶאֱכֹל וְלִשְׁתּוֹת עִמָּהֶם

5 וַיְהִי כִּי הִקִּיפוּ יְמֵי הַמִּשְׁתֶּה וַיִּשְׁלַח אִיּוֹב וַיְקַדְּשֵׁם וְהִשְׁכִּים בַּבֹּקֶר וְהֶעֱלָה עֹלוֹת מִסְפַּר כֻּלָּם כִּי אָמַר אִיּוֹב

אוּלַי חָטְאוּ בָנַי וּבֵרְכוּ אֱלֹהִים בִּלְבָבָם

כָּכָה יַעֲשֶׂה אִיּוֹב כָּל־הַיָּמִים

1:1 There was a man in the land of Utz. Job was his name. That man was blameless and upright. He feared God[1] and turned away from evil. 2 There were born to him seven sons and three daughters. 3 His cattle were[2] seven thousand sheep, three thousand camels, five hundred yoke of oxen, five hundred female donkeys, and he had a very great labor force. That man was the greatest[3] of all the sons of the east. 4 His sons went and held a feast in the house of each one on his birthday.[4] They sent and called for their three sisters to eat and to drink with them. 5 When[5] the days of a feast came around, Job sent and sanctified them. He rose up early in the morning and offered up burnt offerings according to the number of them all because Job said, "It may be that my sons have sinned, and cursed[6] God in their hearts." Thus Job did every day.

1

6 The day[7] came to pass when the divine beings[8] came to present themselves before Adonai. The Satan[9] also came among them. 7 Adonai said to the Satan, "From where have you come?" The Satan answered Adonai and said, "From roaming in the land, and from walking around in it." 8 Adonai said to the Satan, "Have you paid attention[10] to my servant, Job? For there is no one like him in the land, a blameless and an upright man. He fears God, and turns away from evil." 9 Then the Satan answered Adonai, and said, "Does Job fear God for free? 10 Have you not placed a fence about him, and about his house, and about all that is his,[11] from every side? You have blessed the work of his hands, and his cattle has increased[12] in the land. 11 However, send out your hand, and touch all that is his. He will surely[13] curse you to your face. 12 Adonai said to the Satan, "Look, all that is his is in your hand. Only toward him, do not send out your hand." The Satan went out from the presence[14] of Adonai. 13 The day came to pass when both his sons and his daughters were eating and drinking wine in their oldest brother's house, 14 and there came a messenger to Job. He said, "The oxen were plowing, and the donkeys grazing alongside them,[15] 15 and the Sabeans[16] fell upon and took them. They struck the attendants with the edge of the sword.[17] Only I escaped alone to tell you."

16 While this one was still speaking, another[18] came and said, "A fire of God fell from the sky, and burned the sheep and the attendants, and consumed them. Only I escaped alone to tell you." 17 While this one was still speaking, another came and said, "The Chaldeans formed three bands, and made a raid against the camels, and took them. They struck the attendants with the edge of the sword. Only I alone escaped to tell you." 18 While this one was still speaking, another came and said, "Your sons and your daughters were eating and drinking wine in their oldest brother's house, 19 and suddenly,[19] there came a great wind from across the wilderness and struck the four corners of the house. It fell on the youths, and they died. Only I alone escaped to tell you." 20 Job arose, and tore his robe, and sheared his head, and fell to the ground, and prostrated himself. 21 He said, "Naked I came out[20] of my mother's womb, and naked will I return there. Adonai gave, and Adonai took away. May the name of Adonai be blessed." 22 In all this, Job did not sin, and did not attribute impropriety[21] to God.

2:1 The day came to pass when the divine beings came to present themselves before Adonai. The Satan also came among them to present himself before Adonai. 2 Adonai said to the Satan, "From where have you come?" The Satan answered Adonai, and said, "From roaming in the land, and from walking around in it." 3 Adonai said to the Satan, "Have you paid attention to my servant, Job? For there is no one like him in the land, a blameless and an upright man. He fears God and turns away from evil. He still holds on to his integrity although you incited me[1] against him, to consume him for nothing." 4 Satan answered Adonai, and said, "Skin for skin.[2] All that a man has he will give up for the sake of his life. 5 However, send out your hand now, and touch his bone and his flesh, and he will surely curse you to your face." 6 Adonai said to the Satan, "Here, he is in your hand! Only preserve his life."[4] 7 Then the Satan went out from the presence of Adonai and struck Job with a severe inflammation[5] from the sole of his foot to the crown of his head. 8 He took for himself a potsherd to scratch himself with it, and he sat among the ashes. 9 Then his wife said to him, "You still hold on to your integrity. Curse God and die!"

10 But he said to her, "You are speaking as one of the godless women⁶ would speak.⁷ Will we receive the good from God, and not receive the evil?" In all this, Job did not sin with his lips. 11 When Job's three friends heard of all this distress which⁸ came upon him, they came—each man from his place:⁹ Eliphaz the Temanite, Bildad the Shuhite, and Zophar the Naamathite. They met together to come to show sympathy for him and to comfort him. 12 They lifted up their eyes from afar, and they did not recognize him. They raised their voices and wept. Each man tore his robe,¹⁰ and threw dust on their heads toward the sky. 13 They sat with him on the ground¹¹ seven days and seven nights, and none spoke a word to him, because they saw that his pain had become very great. 3:1 After this, Job opened his mouth and cursed the day of his birth.¹ 2 Job answered and said, 3 "May the day in which I was born be damned,² and the night that said, 'A man has been conceived.' 4 May that day be darkness. May God not seek it from above and may light not shine upon it.

5 May darkness and deep gloom desecrate it. May a cloud dwell on it. May deep darkness of the day terrify it. 6 That night—may darkness take it. May it not rejoice among the days of the year. Into the number of the months, may it not come. 7 Behold! May that night be sterile. May no joyful sound come into it. 8 May the cursers of the day curse it—those who are ready to arouse Leviathan. 9 May the stars of its twilight grow dark. May it hope for light, and there be none, and may it not see the break of dawn. 10 Because it did not close the doors of my womb and did not hide trouble from my eyes. 11 Why did I not die from the womb and expire when I came out from the belly? 12 Why did the knees meet me? And why the two breasts that I sucked? 13 For now, I would have lain down and been quiet. I would have slept, then it would have rested for me; 14 With kings and counselors of the land, the builders of ruins for themselves, 15 or with princes who have gold—those who fill their houses with silver. 16 Or why was I not as a buried stillborn? Why was I not as babies who never saw light? 17 There the restless cease troubling and there the weary rest. 18 There prisoners are altogether at ease. They do not hear the voice of the taskmaster. 19 Small and great are there. And a servant is free from his master there. 20 Why does he give light to the sufferer, and life to the bitter of soul, 21 those who wait for death, but it is nonexistent; and those who dig for it more than hidden treasures; 22 those who are glad unto rejoicing. They exult because they find the grave. 23 Why does God give light to a man whose way is hidden, and whom God has placed a screen around? 24 For before my food comes my groaning. My roars pour forth like water. 25 For a fear that I feared has come upon me, and that which I dreaded has come to me. 26 I am not at ease, and I am not quiet, I do not rest; but turmoil came." 4:1 Eliphaz the Temanite answered and said, 2 "If someone attempts a word with you, will you be weary? But restrain words—who can do this? 3 Behold, you have instructed many, and weak hands you have strengthened.

‎4 כּוֹשֵׁל יְקִימוּן מִלֶּיךָ וּבִרְכַּיִם כֹּרְעוֹת תְּאַמֵּץ 5 כִּי עַתָּה תָּבוֹא אֵלֶיךָ וַתֵּלֶא תִּגַּע עָדֶיךָ וַתִּבָּהֵל 6 הֲלֹא יִרְאָתְךָ כִּסְלָתֶךָ תִּקְוָתְךָ וְתֹם דְּרָכֶיךָ 7 זְכָר־נָא מִי הוּא נָקִי אָבָד וְאֵיפֹה יְשָׁרִים נִכְחָדוּ 8 כַּאֲשֶׁר רָאִיתִי חֹרְשֵׁי אָוֶן וְזֹרְעֵי עָמָל יִקְצְרֻהוּ 9 מִנִּשְׁמַת אֱלוֹהַּ יֹאבֵדוּ וּמֵרוּחַ אַפּוֹ יִכְלוּ 10 שַׁאֲגַת אַרְיֵה וְקוֹל שָׁחַל וְשִׁנֵּי כְפִירִים נִתָּעוּ 11 לַיִשׁ אֹבֵד מִבְּלִי־טָרֶף וּבְנֵי לָבִיא יִתְפָּרָדוּ 12 וְאֵלַי דָּבָר יְגֻנָּב וַתִּקַּח אָזְנִי שֵׁמֶץ מֶנְהוּ 13 בִּשְׂעִפִּים מֵחֶזְיֹנוֹת לָיְלָה בִּנְפֹל תַּרְדֵּמָה עַל־אֲנָשִׁים 14 פַּחַד קְרָאַנִי וּרְעָדָה וְרֹב עַצְמוֹתַי הִפְחִיד 15 וְרוּחַ עַל־פָּנַי יַחֲלֹף תְּסַמֵּר שַׂעֲרַת בְּשָׂרִי 16 יַעֲמֹד וְלֹא־אַכִּיר מַרְאֵהוּ תְּמוּנָה לְנֶגֶד עֵינָי דְּמָמָה וָקוֹל אֶשְׁמָע 17 הַאֱנוֹשׁ מֵאֱלוֹהַּ יִצְדָּק אִם מֵעֹשֵׂהוּ יִטְהַר־גָּבֶר 18 הֵן בַּעֲבָדָיו לֹא יַאֲמִין וּבְמַלְאָכָיו יָשִׂים תָּהֳלָה 19 אַף שֹׁכְנֵי בָתֵּי־חֹמֶר אֲשֶׁר־בֶּעָפָר יְסוֹדָם יְדַכְּאוּם לִפְנֵי־עָשׁ 20 מִבֹּקֶר לָעֶרֶב יֻכַּתּוּ מִבְּלִי מֵשִׂים לָנֶצַח יֹאבֵדוּ 21 הֲלֹא־נִסַּע יִתְרָם בָּם יָמוּתוּ וְלֹא בְחָכְמָה

פרק ה

1 קְרָא־נָא הֲיֵשׁ עוֹנֶךָּ וְאֶל־מִי מִקְּדֹשִׁים תִּפְנֶה 2 כִּי־לֶאֱוִיל יַהֲרָג־כָּעַשׂ וּפֹתֶה תָּמִית קִנְאָה 3 אֲנִי־רָאִיתִי אֱוִיל מַשְׁרִישׁ וָאֶקּוֹב נָוֵהוּ פִתְאֹם 4 יִרְחֲקוּ בָנָיו מִיֶּשַׁע וְיִדַּכְּאוּ בַשַּׁעַר וְאֵין מַצִּיל 5 אֲשֶׁר קְצִירוֹ רָעֵב יֹאכֵל וְאֶל־מִצִּנִּים יִקָּחֵהוּ וְשָׁאַף צַמִּים חֵילָם 6 כִּי לֹא־יֵצֵא מֵעָפָר אָוֶן וּמֵאֲדָמָה לֹא־יִצְמַח עָמָל 7 כִּי־אָדָם לְעָמָל יוּלָּד וּבְנֵי־רֶשֶׁף יַגְבִּיהוּ עוּף 8 אוּלָם אֲנִי אֶדְרֹשׁ אֶל־אֵל וְאֶל־אֱלֹהִים אָשִׂים דִּבְרָתִי 9 עֹשֶׂה גְדֹלוֹת וְאֵין חֵקֶר נִפְלָאוֹת עַד־אֵין מִסְפָּר 10 הַנֹּתֵן מָטָר עַל־פְּנֵי־אָרֶץ וְשֹׁלֵחַ מַיִם עַל־פְּנֵי חוּצוֹת 11 לָשׂוּם שְׁפָלִים לְמָרוֹם וְקֹדְרִים שָׂגְבוּ יֶשַׁע 12 מֵפֵר מַחְשְׁבוֹת עֲרוּמִים וְלֹא־תַעֲשֶׂינָה יְדֵיהֶם תּוּשִׁיָּה 13 לֹכֵד חֲכָמִים בְּעָרְמָם וַעֲצַת נִפְתָּלִים נִמְהָרָה 14 יוֹמָם יְפַגְּשׁוּ־חֹשֶׁךְ וְכַלַּיְלָה יְמַשְׁשׁוּ בַצָּהֳרָיִם 15 וַיֹּשַׁע מֵחֶרֶב מִפִּיהֶם וּמִיַּד חָזָק אֶבְיוֹן 16 וַתְּהִי לַדַּל תִּקְוָה וְעֹלָתָה קָפְצָה פִּיהָ 17 הִנֵּה אַשְׁרֵי אֱנוֹשׁ יוֹכִחֶנּוּ אֱלוֹהַּ וּמוּסַר שַׁדַּי אַל־תִּמְאָס 18 כִּי הוּא יַכְאִיב וְיֶחְבָּשׁ יִמְחַץ וְיָדָיו תִּרְפֶּינָה

---

4 Your words lifted up the stumbling. You have made firm the feeble knees. 5 But now it has come to you, and you are impatient. It touches you, and you are terrified. 6 Is not your fear of God your confidence? Is not your hope the integrity of your ways? 7 Remember, now, who is[1] innocent that has perished? And where are the upright that have been destroyed? 8 As I have seen, those who plow iniquity, and those who sow mischief, will reap it. 9 From the breath of God they will perish and from the breath of his nose they will be consumed. 10 The roar of the lion, and the voice of the lion, the teeth of the young lions are broken.[2] 11 The old lion dies for lack of prey and the sons of the lion are scattered. 12 A word that was stolen away was brought to me and my ear received a whisper of it. 13 In disquieting thoughts from the visions of the night, when deep sleep falls on men,[3] 14 dread befell me (and trembling) and it made many of my bones tremble. 15 But then, a spirit passed before me.[4] The hair of my flesh bristled.[5] 16 It stood, but I did not recognize its appearance. A form was before my eyes. Silence, and then I heard a voice:[6] 17 'Can mankind be more just than God? Can a man be pure more than his maker? 18 If he does not trust in his servants and charges his angels with error,[7] 19 indeed he does the same with dwellers of clay houses,[8] whose foundations are in the dust. They are crushed[9] before the moth. 20 From morning to the evening they are beaten into pieces. Without paying attention,[10] they perish forever. 21 Is not their cord[11] pulled out from within them?[12] They die, and not in wisdom.' 5:1 Call now! Is there anyone who answers you? To whom of the holy ones will you turn? 2 For anger[1] kills the foolish,[2] and a simple person, jealousy puts to death. 3 I have seen a foolish person taking root, and I cursed his habitation suddenly. 4 His children are distanced[3] from salvation. They are crushed[4] in the gate and there is no deliverer. 5 Hunger[5] eats that which is his harvest,[6] and takes it to thorns.[7] Yet, he[8] craves for their wealth, but is a snare. 6 For disaster does not come out of dust, and trouble does not sprout from the ground. 7 Surely,[9] man is born[10] for trouble, and the sons of Resheph[11] are exalted to fly. 8 However, I would make a supplication to God; and unto God, I would commit my plea. 9 God does great things and, without investigation, marvelous things to the point where there is no number; 10 He is the giver of rain on the face of the land, and sender of waters on[12] fields,[13] 11 setting[14] lowly ones in a high place and mourners[15] are exalted[16] to safety. 12 He frustrates the thoughts of the crafty, so that their hands cannot produce success. 13 He catches the wise in their craftiness and the counsel of the twisted is carried out rashly. 14 They encounter darkness by day, and, as in the night, they grope in the midday. 15 He saves from the sword of their mouth, and from the hand of the strong, he saves the needy. 16 There will be hope for the poor, and injustice shuts its mouth. 17 Behold, blessed is the man whom God corrects. Thus, the discipline of Shaddai, do not reject. 18 For he causes pain, and he comforts. He smites, and his hands heal.

פרק ו

¹⁹ בְּשֵׁשׁ צָרוֹת יַצִּילֶךָּ וּבְשֶׁבַע לֹא־יִגַּע בְּךָ רָע ²⁰ בְּרָעָב פָּדְךָ מִמָּוֶת וּבְמִלְחָמָה מִידֵי חָרֶב ²¹ בְּשׁוֹט לָשׁוֹן תֵּחָבֵא וְלֹא־תִירָא מִשֹּׁד כִּי יָבוֹא ²² לְשֹׁד וּלְכָפָן תִּשְׂחָק וּמֵחַיַּת הָאָרֶץ אַל־תִּירָא ²³ כִּי עִם־אַבְנֵי הַשָּׂדֶה בְרִיתֶךָ וְחַיַּת הַשָּׂדֶה הָשְׁלְמָה־לָךְ ²⁴ וְיָדַעְתָּ כִּי־שָׁלוֹם אָהֳלֶךָ וּפָקַדְתָּ נָוְךָ וְלֹא תֶחֱטָא ²⁵ וְיָדַעְתָּ כִּי־רַב זַרְעֶךָ וְצֶאֱצָאֶיךָ כְּעֵשֶׂב הָאָרֶץ ²⁶ תָּבוֹא בְכֶלַח אֱלֵי־קָבֶר כַּעֲלוֹת גָּדִישׁ בְּעִתּוֹ ²⁷ הִנֵּה־זֹאת חֲקַרְנוּהָ כֶּן־הִיא שְׁמָעֶנָּה וְאַתָּה דַע־לָךְ

¹ וַיַּעַן אִיּוֹב וַיֹּאמַר ² לוּ שָׁקוֹל יִשָּׁקֵל כַּעְשִׂי וְהַוָּתִי בְּמֹאזְנַיִם יִשְׂאוּ־יָחַד ³ כִּי־עַתָּה מֵחוֹל יַמִּים יִכְבָּד עַל־כֵּן דְּבָרַי לָעוּ ⁴ כִּי חִצֵּי שַׁדַּי עִמָּדִי אֲשֶׁר חֲמָתָם שֹׁתָה רוּחִי בִּעוּתֵי אֱלוֹהַּ יַעַרְכוּנִי ⁵ הֲיִנְהַק־פֶּרֶא עֲלֵי־דֶשֶׁא אִם יִגְעֶה־שּׁוֹר עַל־בְּלִילוֹ ⁶ הֲיֵאָכֵל תָּפֵל מִבְּלִי־מֶלַח אִם־יֶשׁ־טַעַם בְּרִיר חַלָּמוּת ⁷ מֵאֲנָה לִנְגּוֹעַ נַפְשִׁי הֵמָּה כִּדְוֵי לַחְמִי ⁸ מִי־יִתֵּן תָּבוֹא שֶׁאֱלָתִי וְתִקְוָתִי יִתֵּן אֱלוֹהַּ ⁹ וְיֹאֵל אֱלוֹהַּ וִידַכְּאֵנִי יַתֵּר יָדוֹ וִיבַצְּעֵנִי ¹⁰ וּתְהִי עוֹד נֶחָמָתִי וַאֲסַלְּדָה בְחִילָה לֹא יַחְמוֹל כִּי־לֹא כִחַדְתִּי אִמְרֵי קָדוֹשׁ ¹¹ מַה־כֹּחִי כִי־אֲיַחֵל וּמַה־קִּצִּי כִּי־אַאֲרִיךְ נַפְשִׁי ¹² אִם־כֹּחַ אֲבָנִים כֹּחִי אִם־בְּשָׂרִי נָחוּשׁ ¹³ הַאִם אֵין עֶזְרָתִי בִי וְתֻשִׁיָּה נִדְּחָה מִמֶּנִּי ¹⁴ לַמָּס מֵרֵעֵהוּ חָסֶד וְיִרְאַת שַׁדַּי יַעֲזוֹב ¹⁵ אַחַי בָּגְדוּ כְמוֹ־נָחַל כַּאֲפִיק נְחָלִים יַעֲבֹרוּ ¹⁶ הַקֹּדְרִים מִנִּי־קָרַח עָלֵימוֹ יִתְעַלֶּם־שָׁלֶג ¹⁷ בְּעֵת יְזֹרְבוּ נִצְמָתוּ בְּחֻמּוֹ נִדְעֲכוּ מִמְּקוֹמָם ¹⁸ יִלָּפְתוּ אָרְחוֹת דַּרְכָּם יַעֲלוּ בַתֹּהוּ וְיֹאבֵדוּ ¹⁹ הִבִּיטוּ אָרְחוֹת תֵּמָא הֲלִיכֹת שְׁבָא קִוּוּ־לָמוֹ ²⁰ בֹּשׁוּ כִּי־בָטָח בָּאוּ עָדֶיהָ וַיֶּחְפָּרוּ ²¹ כִּי־עַתָּה הֱיִיתֶם לֹא תִּרְאוּ חֲתַת וַתִּירָאוּ ²² הֲכִי־אָמַרְתִּי הָבוּ לִי וּמִכֹּחֲכֶם שִׁחֲדוּ בַעֲדִי ²³ וּמַלְּטוּנִי מִיַּד־צָר וּמִיַּד עָרִיצִים תִּפְדּוּנִי

19 He will save you in six troubles; and in seven, evil will not touch you. 20 In famine he ransoms you from death, and in war, from the power[17] of the sword. 21 You will be hidden from the scourge of the tongue,[18] and you will not be afraid of violence when it comes. 22 You will laugh at violence and at famine; and of the animals[19] of the land, you will not be afraid.[20] 23 For your covenant will be with the stones of the field, and the animals of the field will be at peace with you.[21] 24 You will know that your tent will be in peace. You will visit your habitation, and you will not go astray. 25 You will know that your seed will be great, and that your offspring will be as the herbage of the land. 26 You will come to the grave in vigor, like the piling[22] of a heap in its season. 27 Behold this! We have examined it. It is so. Hear it and know it."[23] 6:1 Job answered and said, 2 "If only my anger were surely weighed, and together my destruction[1] and my anger were set in the balances.[2] 3 Because now, it would be heavier than the sand of the seas! Therefore, my words have expressed carelessness.[4] 4 For the arrows of Shaddai are within me, and their poison is that which my spirit drinks. The terrors[5] of God set themselves in order[6] against me. 5 Does the wild donkey bray when he is upon grass, or does the ox low concerning his fodder?[7] 6 Can a tasteless thing be eaten without salt, or is there taste in a white of an egg?[8] 7 My soul refuses to overcome them.[9] They[10] are like illnesses of my flesh.[11] 8 Oh that[12] my request would come to pass; and that God would grant my hope, 9 and that God would acquiesce, and that he would crush me! That he would set his hand free and cut me off! 10 It[13] will yet be my comfort that I may rejoice in my anguish.[14] He does not spare, but I have not denied the words of the Holy One. 11 What is my strength, that I should hope; and what is my end, that I should be patient?[15] 12 Is the strength of stones my strength? Is my flesh bronze?[16] 13 Is my help not existent in me? Yet, success is driven away from me. 14 To the despairing one—lovingkindess comes from his friend; and to him who forsakes—the fear of Shaddai. 15 My brothers have rebelled as a stream, as the channel of streams that cross over from one side to another; 16 Those[17] who mourn[18] from ice; upon them snow hides itself. 17 In a time of heat, they are scorched; they are annihilated. In its heat, they dwindle out of their place. 18 The ways of their path are twisted. They go up into nothingness and they perish. 19 The caravans of Tema looked. The travelers of Sheba waited for them. 20 They were embarrassed because he trusted.[19] They came unto it[20] and were ashamed. 21 For now, you all are nothing. You see a terror and fear. 22 Did I say, 'Give to me?' or, 'Give a bribe on my behalf from your wealth?' 23 or, 'Deliver me from the hand of a foe?' or, 'Redeem me from the hand of adversaries?'

24 Teach me, and I will be silent. Also, in what did I err? Cause me to understand it. 25 How grievous are words of uprightness! But what does the reproof[21] from you all prove? 26 Do you plan to reprove words, and chide[22] the words of a despairing man as[23] wind? 27 Indeed, you would cast lots over an orphan, and bargain over your friend. 28 But now, be willing to look at me, and see if I will lie to[24] your faces. 29 Return now. There will not be injustice; But, return because my righteousness is still in it.[25] 30 Is there injustice with[26] my tongue? Can my palate[27] not understand destruction?[28] 7:1 Isn't hard work for humankind who lives upon the land, and aren't his days like the days of a hired laborer? 2 As a servant longs for a shadow, and as a hired laborer hopes for his wages, 3 so am I made to possess, for me, months of worthlessness, and nights of trouble are appointed[1] to me. 4 If I lie down, then I say, 'When will I arise?' but the night continues, and I excessively toss and turn[2] until twilight. 5 He has clothed[3] my flesh with worms[4] and lumps of dirt. My skin hardens up and then flows.[5] 6 My days run faster than a loom, and they end with no hope.[6] 7 Remember! My life is a breath.[7] My eye[8] will not return to seeing good. 8 The eye of my observer will not behold me. Your eyes will be upon me,[9] but I will not exist. 9 Just as the cloud fades and departs, so he who goes down to Sheol will not come up. 10 He will not return again to his house, and his place will not recognize him again.[10] 11 Even I will not refrain from my mouth—oh, that I may speak in the distress of my spirit; that I may complain in the bitterness of my soul. 12 Am I Yamm or Tannin that you put a watch over me? 13 If I say, 'My couch will comfort me, my couch will lift up my complaint,'[11] 14 then you scare me with dreams, and from visions you terrify me. 15 My soul chooses strangling;[12] death rather than my bones. 16 I am fed up.[13] I will not live forever. Leave me alone[14] because my days are breath. 17 What is man, that you should make him great, and that you should pay attention[15] to him? 18 And do you visit him every morning;[16] and test him at every moment?[17] 19 How much will you not look away from me? Will you not leave me alone until my swallowing of my spit? 20 Have[18] I have sinned? What have I done to you, watcher of humankind? Why did you set me as a target for you, and I have become a burden upon myself? 21 And what? You do not take away my transgression and remove away my iniquity. For now, will I lie down in the dust.[19] You will seek me, and I will not exist." 8:1 Then Bildad the Shuhite answered and said, 2 "Until when will you speak these things? Also, a great wind are the sayings of your mouth!

9

פרק ט

וַיַּעַן אִיּוֹב וַיֹּאמַר ׃1 אָמְנָם יָדַעְתִּי כִי־כֵן וּמַה־יִּצְדַּק² אֱנוֹשׁ עִם־אֵל ׃ אִם־יַחְפֹּץ לָרִיב עִמּוֹ³ לֹא־יַעֲנֶנּוּ אַחַת מִנִּי־אָלֶף ׃ חֲכַם⁴ לֵבָב וְאַמִּיץ כֹּחַ מִי־הִקְשָׁה אֵלָיו וַיִּשְׁלָם ׃ הַמַּעְתִּיק הָרִים וְלֹא יָדָעוּ אֲשֶׁר⁵ הֲפָכָם בְּאַפּוֹ ׃ הַמַּרְגִּיז אֶרֶץ מִמְּקוֹמָהּ⁶ וְעַמּוּדֶיהָ יִתְפַלָּצוּן ׃ הָאֹמֵר לַחֶרֶס וְלֹא⁷ יִזְרָח וּבְעַד כּוֹכָבִים יַחְתֹּם ׃ נֹטֶה⁸ שָׁמַיִם לְבַדּוֹ וְדוֹרֵךְ עַל־בָּמֳתֵי יָם ׃ עֹשֶׂה־עָשׁ כְּסִיל וְכִימָה⁹ וְחַדְרֵי תֵמָן ׃ עֹשֶׂה גְדֹלוֹת עַד־אֵין חֵקֶר וְנִפְלָאוֹת עַד־אֵין¹⁰ מִסְפָּר ׃ הֵן יַעֲבֹר עָלַי וְלֹא אֶרְאֶה וְיַחֲלֹף וְלֹא־אָבִין לוֹ ׃ הֵן¹¹ יַחְתֹּף מִי יְשִׁיבֶנּוּ מִי־יֹאמַר אֵלָיו מַה־תַּעֲשֶׂה ׃ אֱלוֹהַּ¹³ לֹא־יָשִׁיב אַפּוֹ תַּחְתָּיו שָׁחֲחוּ עֹזְרֵי רָהַב ׃ אַף כִּי־אָנֹכִי¹⁴ אֶעֱנֶנּוּ אֶבְחֲרָה דְבָרַי עִמּוֹ ׃ אֲשֶׁר אִם־צָדַקְתִּי לֹא אֶעֱנֶה¹⁵ לִמְשֹׁפְטִי אֶתְחַנָּן ׃ אִם־קָרָאתִי וַיַּעֲנֵנִי לֹא־אַאֲמִין כִּי־יַאֲזִין¹⁶ קוֹלִי ׃ אֲשֶׁר־בִּשְׂעָרָה יְשׁוּפֵנִי וְהִרְבָּה פְצָעַי חִנָּם ׃ לֹא־יִתְּנֵנִי¹⁸ הָשֵׁב רוּחִי כִּי יַשְׂבִּעַנִי מַמְּרֹרִים

הַאֵל יְעַוֵּת מִשְׁפָּט וְאִם־שַׁדַּי יְעַוֵּת־צֶדֶק ׃3 אִם־בָּנֶיךָ חָטְאוּ־לוֹ וַיְשַׁלְּחֵם בְּיַד־פִּשְׁעָם ׃4 אִם־אַתָּה תְּשַׁחֵר אֶל־אֵל וְאֶל־שַׁדַּי⁵ תִּתְחַנָּן ׃ אִם־זַךְ וְיָשָׁר אָתָּה כִּי־עַתָּה יָעִיר⁶ עָלֶיךָ וְשִׁלַּם נְוַת צִדְקֶךָ ׃ וְהָיָה רֵאשִׁיתְךָ⁷ מִצְעָר וְאַחֲרִיתְךָ יִשְׂגֶּה מְאֹד ׃ כִּי־שְׁאַל־נָא⁸ לְדֹר רִישׁוֹן וְכוֹנֵן לְחֵקֶר אֲבוֹתָם ׃ כִּי־תְמוֹל⁹ אֲנַחְנוּ וְלֹא נֵדָע כִּי צֵל יָמֵינוּ עֲלֵי־אָרֶץ ׃ הֲלֹא־הֵם יוֹרוּךָ יֹאמְרוּ לָךְ וּמִלִּבָּם יוֹצִאוּ¹⁰ מִלִּים ׃ הֲיִגְאֶה־גֹּמֶא בְּלֹא בִצָּה¹¹ יִשְׂגֶּה־אָחוּ בְלִי־מָיִם ׃ עֹדֶנּוּ בְאִבּוֹ לֹא¹² יִקָּטֵף וְלִפְנֵי כָל־חָצִיר יִיבָשׁ ׃ כֵּן אָרְחוֹת¹³ כָּל־שֹׁכְחֵי אֵל וְתִקְוַת חָנֵף תֹּאבֵד ׃ אֲשֶׁר־יָקוֹט כִּסְלוֹ וּבֵית עַכָּבִישׁ מִבְטַחוֹ ׃ יִשָּׁעֵן עַל־בֵּיתוֹ וְלֹא יַעֲמֹד יַחֲזִיק בּוֹ וְלֹא¹⁵ יָקוּם ׃ רָטֹב הוּא לִפְנֵי־שָׁמֶשׁ וְעַל גַּנָּתוֹ¹⁶ יֹנַקְתּוֹ תֵצֵא ׃ עַל־גַּל שָׁרָשָׁיו יְסֻבָּכוּ בֵּית¹⁷ אֲבָנִים יֶחֱזֶה ׃ אִם־יְבַלְּעֶנּוּ מִמְּקוֹמוֹ וְכִחֶשׁ¹⁸ בּוֹ לֹא רְאִיתִיךָ ׃ הֶן־הוּא מְשׂוֹשׂ דַּרְכּוֹ¹⁹ וּמֵעָפָר אַחֵר יִצְמָחוּ ׃ הֶן־אֵל לֹא יִמְאַס²⁰ תָּם וְלֹא־יַחֲזִיק בְּיַד־מְרֵעִים ׃ עַד־יְמַלֵּה²¹ שְׂחוֹק פִּיךָ וּשְׂפָתֶיךָ תְרוּעָה ׃ שֹׂנְאֶיךָ²² יִלְבְּשׁוּ־בֹשֶׁת וְאֹהֶל רְשָׁעִים אֵינֶנּוּ ׃

---

3 Will God pervert justice? Will Shaddai pervert righteousness? 4 If your children sinned against him, he has delivered them on account of[1] their transgression. 5 If you seek God,[2] and supplicate to Shaddai; 6 If you are pure and upright, surely now he will bring protection[3] upon you, and make safe the habitation of your righteousness. 7 Your beginning was a small thing, but your end will greatly prosper.[4] 8 For inquire now of the first generation. Pay attention to the searching out of their fathers. 9 For we are yesterday, and we do not know. For our days on the land are a shadow. 10 Will they not teach you? Will they not[5] tell you and bring words out of their hearts? 11 Will a reed rise up without a swamp? Will rushes[6] grow without water? 12 While still in its shoot it will not be plucked, and before all grass, it dries up. 13 Thus are the paths of all forgetters of God. The hope of the godless will perish—14 whose confidence is gossamer, and a spider's web is his trust. 15 He will lean himself upon his house, but it will not stand up. He will take hold of it, but it will not stand. 16 He[7] is moist before the sun, and upon his garden, his shoot goes out. 17 On a heap of stones his roots are interwoven. He sees a house of stones. 18 If it destroys him from his place and then denies him, saying, 'I do not see you…'[8] 19 Indeed, this is the joy of his way: out of dust, others[9] will sprout. 20 Indeed, God will not reject a blameless person, and will not strengthen the hand of evildoers. 21 Yet, he will fill your mouth with laughter, and your lips with a shout of joy. 22 Your haters will clothe themselves with shame, and the tent of the wicked is no more." **9:1** Job answered and said, 2 "Truly I know that it is so, but how can humankind be righteous with God? 3 If he desires to dispute with him,[1] he will not respond to him one time in a thousand.[2] 4 He is wise of heart,[3] and mighty of strength. Who is stubborn[4] toward him and will be whole? 5 He is the remover of mountains and they do not know that he overturns them in his anger. 6 He is the shaker of the land from its place, and its pillars tremble.[5] 7 The one who speaks to the sun[6] and it does not rise, and who seals up[7] the stars. 8 He alone spreads out the heavens, and treads on the back of Yamm.[8] 9 He makes the Great Bear,[9] Orion, and the Pleiades, and the Rooms of the South. 10 He does great things beyond[10] searching out and marvelous things beyond number. 11 Behold,[11] he passes over me, but I do not see him. He passes through, but I do not perceive him. 12 Behold, he snatches away. Who can turn him back? Who will say to him, 'What are you doing?' 13 God will not turn back his anger. The helpers of Rahab bow beneath him. 14 Will I even respond to him? Will I choose my words with him? 15 Which—even if I were righteous, I would not respond to him. Even if[12] I implore my legal opponent; 16 If I called and he answered me, I would not believe that he would listen to my voice. 17 For he would bruise[13] me with a hair, and multiply my wounds for nothing. 18 He would not permit me to return my breath; for he gorges me[14] with bitter things.[15]

פרק ט

19 אִם־לְכֹחַ אַמִּיץ הִנֵּה וְאִם־לְמִשְׁפָּט מִי יוֹעִידֵנִי׃ 20 אִם־אֶצְדָּק פִּי יַרְשִׁיעֵנִי תָּם־אָנִי וַיַּעְקְשֵׁנִי׃ 21 תָּם־אָנִי לֹא־אֵדַע נַפְשִׁי אֶמְאַס חַיָּי׃ 22 אַחַת הִיא עַל־כֵּן אָמַרְתִּי תָּם וְרָשָׁע הוּא מְכַלֶּה׃ 23 אִם־שׁוֹט יָמִית פִּתְאֹם לְמַסַּת נְקִיִּם יִלְעָג׃ 24 אֶרֶץ נִתְּנָה בְיַד־רָשָׁע פְּנֵי־שֹׁפְטֶיהָ יְכַסֶּה אִם־לֹא אֵפוֹא מִי־הוּא׃ 25 וְיָמַי קַלּוּ מִנִּי־רָץ בָּרְחוּ לֹא־רָאוּ טוֹבָה׃ 26 חָלְפוּ עִם־אֳנִיּוֹת אֵבֶה כְּנֶשֶׁר יָטוּשׂ עֲלֵי־אֹכֶל׃ 27 אִם־אָמְרִי אֶשְׁכְּחָה שִׂיחִי אֶעֶזְבָה פָנַי וְאַבְלִיגָה׃ 28 יָגֹרְתִּי כָל־עַצְּבֹתָי יָדַעְתִּי כִּי־לֹא תְנַקֵּנִי׃ 29 אָנֹכִי אֶרְשָׁע לָמָּה־זֶּה הֶבֶל אִיגָע׃ 30 אִם־הִתְרָחַצְתִּי בְמֵי־שָׁלֶג וַהֲזִכּוֹתִי בְּבֹר כַּפָּי׃ 31 אָז בַּשַּׁחַת תִּטְבְּלֵנִי וְתִעֲבוּנִי שַׂלְמוֹתָי׃ 32 כִּי־לֹא־אִישׁ כָּמֹנִי אֶעֱנֶנּוּ נָבוֹא יַחְדָּו בַּמִּשְׁפָּט׃ 33 לֹא יֵשׁ־בֵּינֵינוּ מוֹכִיחַ יָשֵׁת יָדוֹ עַל־שְׁנֵינוּ׃ 34 יָסֵר מֵעָלַי שִׁבְטוֹ וְאֵמָתוֹ אַל־תְּבַעֲתַנִּי׃ 35 אֲדַבְּרָה וְלֹא אִירָאֶנּוּ כִּי לֹא־כֵן אָנֹכִי עִמָּדִי׃

פרק י

1 נָקְטָה נַפְשִׁי בְּחַיָּי אֶעֶזְבָה עָלַי שִׂיחִי אֲדַבְּרָה בְּמַר נַפְשִׁי׃ 2 אֹמַר אֶל־אֱלוֹהַּ אַל־תַּרְשִׁיעֵנִי הוֹדִיעֵנִי עַל מַה־תְּרִיבֵנִי׃ 3 הֲטוֹב לְךָ כִּי־תַעֲשֹׁק כִּי־תִמְאַס יְגִיעַ כַּפֶּיךָ וְעַל־עֲצַת רְשָׁעִים הוֹפָעְתָּ׃ 4 הַעֵינֵי בָשָׂר לָךְ אִם־כִּרְאוֹת אֱנוֹשׁ תִּרְאֶה׃ 5 הֲכִימֵי אֱנוֹשׁ יָמֶיךָ אִם־שְׁנוֹתֶיךָ כִּימֵי גָבֶר׃ 6 כִּי־תְבַקֵּשׁ לַעֲוֹנִי וּלְחַטָּאתִי תִדְרוֹשׁ׃ 7 עַל־דַּעְתְּךָ כִּי־לֹא אֶרְשָׁע וְאֵין מִיָּדְךָ מַצִּיל׃ 8 יָדֶיךָ עִצְּבוּנִי וַיַּעֲשׂוּנִי יַחַד סָבִיב וַתְּבַלְּעֵנִי׃ 9 זְכָר־נָא כִּי־כַחֹמֶר עֲשִׂיתָנִי וְאֶל־עָפָר תְּשִׁיבֵנִי׃ 10 הֲלֹא כֶחָלָב תַּתִּיכֵנִי וְכַגְּבִנָּה תַּקְפִּיאֵנִי׃ 11 עוֹר וּבָשָׂר תַּלְבִּישֵׁנִי וּבַעֲצָמוֹת וְגִידִים תְּסֹכְכֵנִי׃ 12 חַיִּים וָחֶסֶד עָשִׂיתָ עִמָּדִי וּפְקֻדָּתְךָ שָׁמְרָה רוּחִי׃ 13 וְאֵלֶּה צָפַנְתָּ בִלְבָבֶךָ יָדַעְתִּי כִּי־זֹאת עִמָּךְ׃ 14 אִם־חָטָאתִי וּשְׁמַרְתָּנִי וּמֵעֲוֹנִי לֹא תְנַקֵּנִי׃ 15 אִם־רָשַׁעְתִּי אַלְלַי לִי וְצָדַקְתִּי לֹא־אֶשָּׂא רֹאשִׁי שְׂבַע קָלוֹן וּרְאֵה עָנְיִי׃ 16 וְיִגְאֶה כַּשַּׁחַל תְּצוּדֵנִי וְתָשֹׁב תִּתְפַּלָּא־בִי׃

---

19 If it relates to strength, behold, he is mighty; and if it is of a legal judgment, who will summon me? 20 If I were righteous, my mouth would condemn me. I am blameless, but he declares me perverted.[16] 21 I am blameless. I do not know myself. I am fed up[17] with my life. 22 It is one. Therefore, I declare: the blameless and the wicked he brings to an end! 23 If scourging kills suddenly, he mocks at the trial of the innocent. 24 The earth is given into the hand of the wicked. He covers the faces of its judges. If not he, then who is it? 25 But my days run faster than a runner. They flee. They see no good. 26 They pass with ships of reed, like an eagle descends on food. 27 If I say,[18] 'Let me forget my complaint, let me forget my face,[19] and let me cheer up;' 28 I will fear all my pains. I know that you will not acquit me. 29 I will be guilty. Why do I toil for this in vain? 30 If I wash myself with the water of snow, and cleanse my palms with lye, 31 then you will plunge me in the pit and my clothes will abhor me. 32 For he is not a man, as I am, that I might respond to him. 33 There is no judge between us that he might lay his hand on both of us. 34 May he turn away his rod from upon me, and may his terror not terrify me; 35 That I may speak and not fear him, because I am not right with myself. 10:1 My soul hates itself in my life. I will let my complaint loose upon myself. I will speak in the bitterness of my soul. 2 I will say to God, 'Do not condemn me! Inform me about what charge you bring against me. 3 Is it good for you that you do wrong; that you reject the product of your hands and shine upon the counsel of the wicked? 4 Do you have eyes of flesh? Will you see as humankind sees?[1] 5 Are your days as the days of humankind? Are your years like the days of a man 6 that you seek my iniquity, and you investigate my sin?[2] 7 in addition to[3] your understanding that I am not wicked? Yet, there is no deliverer from your hand. 8 Your hands have shaped me and made me together, all about—and you destroy me. 9 Remember now that you made me like clay and to dust you will return me? 10 Have you not poured me out like milk, and made me congeal like cheese? 11 You dressed me with skin and flesh and wove me together with bones and sinews. 12 Life and lovingkindness you have done with me and your providence has kept my spirit. 13 But these things you have hidden in your heart. I know that this is with you: 14 if I sin, you watch me and will not acquit me from my iniquity. 15 If I am wicked, woe to me! And if I am righteous, I will not lift up my head. Be filled[4] with dishonor and see my affliction. 16 If it rises up,[5] you hunt me like the lion, and you return[6] and you show yourself wonderful against me.[7]

פרק יא

¹⁷ תְּחַדֵּשׁ עֵדֶיךָ נֶגְדִּי וְתֶרֶב כַּעַשְׂךָ עִמָּדִי חֲלִיפוֹת וְצָבָא עִמִּי ¹⁸ וְלָמָּה מֵרֶחֶם הֹצֵאתָנִי אֶגְוַע וְעַיִן לֹא־תִרְאֵנִי ¹⁹ כַּאֲשֶׁר לֹא־הָיִיתִי אֶהְיֶה מִבֶּטֶן לַקֶּבֶר אוּבָל ²⁰ הֲלֹא־מְעַט יָמַי יֶחְדָּל יָשִׁית מִמֶּנִּי וְאַבְלִיגָה מְּעָט ²¹ בְּטֶרֶם אֵלֵךְ וְלֹא אָשׁוּב אֶל־אֶרֶץ חֹשֶׁךְ וְצַלְמָוֶת ²² אֶרֶץ עֵיפָתָה כְּמוֹ אֹפֶל צַלְמָוֶת וְלֹא סְדָרִים וַתֹּפַע כְּמוֹ־אֹפֶל

פרק יא

¹ וַיַּעַן צֹפַר הַנַּעֲמָתִי וַיֹּאמַר ² הֲרֹב דְּבָרִים לֹא יֵעָנֶה וְאִם־אִישׁ שְׂפָתַיִם יִצְדָּק ³ בַּדֶּיךָ מְתִים יַחֲרִישׁוּ וַתִּלְעַג וְאֵין מַכְלִם ⁴ וַתֹּאמֶר זַךְ לִקְחִי וּבַר הָיִיתִי בְעֵינֶיךָ ⁵ וְאוּלָם מִי־יִתֵּן אֱלוֹהַּ דַּבֵּר וְיִפְתַּח שְׂפָתָיו עִמָּךְ ⁶ וְיַגֶּד־לְךָ תַּעֲלֻמוֹת חָכְמָה כִּי־כִפְלַיִם לְתוּשִׁיָּה וְדַע כִּי־יַשֶּׁה לְךָ אֱלוֹהַּ מֵעֲוֺנֶךָ ⁷ הַחֵקֶר אֱלוֹהַּ תִּמְצָא אִם עַד־תַּכְלִית שַׁדַּי תִּמְצָא ⁸ גָּבְהֵי שָׁמַיִם מַה־תִּפְעָל עֲמֻקָּה מִשְּׁאוֹל מַה־תֵּדָע ⁹ אֲרֻכָּה מֵאֶרֶץ מִדָּהּ וּרְחָבָה מִנִּי־יָם ¹⁰ אִם־יַחֲלֹף וְיַסְגִּיר וְיַקְהִיל וּמִי יְשִׁיבֶנּוּ ¹¹ כִּי־הוּא יָדַע מְתֵי־שָׁוְא וַיַּרְא־אָוֶן וְלֹא יִתְבּוֹנָן ¹² וְאִישׁ נָבוּב יִלָּבֵב וְעַיִר פֶּרֶא אָדָם יִוָּלֵד ¹³ אִם־אַתָּה הֲכִינוֹתָ לִבֶּךָ וּפָרַשְׂתָּ אֵלָיו כַּפֶּךָ ¹⁴ אִם־אָוֶן בְּיָדְךָ הַרְחִיקֵהוּ וְאַל־תַּשְׁכֵּן בְּאֹהָלֶיךָ עַוְלָה ¹⁵ כִּי־אָז תִּשָּׂא פָנֶיךָ מִמּוּם וְהָיִיתָ מֻצָק וְלֹא תִירָא ¹⁶ כִּי־אַתָּה עָמָל תִּשְׁכָּח כְּמַיִם עָבְרוּ תִזְכֹּר ¹⁷ וּמִצָּהֳרַיִם יָקוּם חָלֶד תָּעֻפָה כַּבֹּקֶר תִּהְיֶה ¹⁸ וּבָטַחְתָּ כִּי־יֵשׁ תִּקְוָה וְחָפַרְתָּ לָבֶטַח תִּשְׁכָּב ¹⁹ וְרָבַצְתָּ וְאֵין מַחֲרִיד וְחִלּוּ פָנֶיךָ רַבִּים ²⁰ וְעֵינֵי רְשָׁעִים תִּכְלֶינָה וּמָנוֹס אָבַד מִנְהֶם וְתִקְוָתָם מַפַּח־נָפֶשׁ

פרק יב

¹ וַיַּעַן אִיּוֹב וַיֹּאמַר ² אָמְנָם כִּי אַתֶּם־עָם וְעִמָּכֶם תָּמוּת חָכְמָה ³ גַּם־לִי לֵבָב כְּמוֹכֶם לֹא־נֹפֵל אָנֹכִי מִכֶּם וְאֶת־מִי־אֵין כְּמוֹ־אֵלֶּה ⁴ שְׂחֹק לְרֵעֵהוּ אֶהְיֶה קֹרֵא לֶאֱלוֹהַּ וַיַּעֲנֵהוּ שְׂחוֹק צַדִּיק תָּמִים

17 You renew your witnesses against me and increase your anger with me. Replacements and an army are with me. 18 And why have you brought me out of the womb?' I should have died, and an eye would not have seen me. 19 Would I had been just as if I never was! Would I had been carried from the womb to the grave.[8] 20 Are not my days few and it will cease? May he set his attention[9] away from me so that I may brighten up a little, 21 before I go and I will not return, to the land of darkness and gloom; 22 a land whose darkness is like the darkness of gloom and disorder.[10] The land that shines like darkness." 11:1 Then Zophar, the Naamathite, answered and said, 2 "Will an abundance of words not be answered and will a boaster[1] be justified? 3 Your boasting silences men. You mock, but there is no one to rebuke. 4 You say, 'My doctrine is pure. I am clean in your eyes.' 5 However, if only[2] God would speak, and open his lips with you, 6 and declare to you the secrets of wisdom. For there are two sides[3] to wisdom. And know that God causes you to forget your iniquity.[4] 7 Will you find the deep inquiries of God? Will you explore until the limit of Shaddai? 8 The heights of the heavens—What can you do? It[5] is deeper than Sheol—What can you know? 9 Its measure is longer than the land, and wider than the sea. 10 If he passes by, or delivers up, or causes an assembly to gather, then who will turn him back? 11 For he knows men of no worth. He sees iniquity, but he does not show consideration. 12 But a hollow man is given a heart[6] and the colt of a donkey is born a human. 13 If you establish your heart and spread your palms toward him—14 if iniquity is in your hand, put it far away. May injustice not dwell in your tents. 15 For then you will lift up your face without blemish. You will be established, and you will not fear 16 because you will forget trouble. You will remember it like water that passed by. 17 And more than noon your duration of life will rise. It will be dark;[7] you will be like the morning. 18 You will trust because there is hope. You will search for security and will lie down. 19 You will lie down, and there will be nothing that will cause you to fear. Many will entreat your favor. 20 However, the eyes of the wicked will waste away. Also, a refuge will vanish from before them, and their hope is the breathing out of the spirit."[8] 12:1 Job answered and said, 2 "Indeed you are people, and wisdom will die with you. 3 I have a heart like you. I do not fall from among you all.[1] And with whom are there not words like these? 4 I am one who is a laughingstock to his friend—who calls to God and he answers him. Righteous, blameless—a laughingstock!

לַפִּיד בּוּז לְעַשְׁתּוּת שַׁאֲנָן נָכוֹן לְמוֹעֲדֵי רָגֶל ⁶ יִשְׁלָיוּ אֹהָלִים לְשֹׁדְדִים וּבַטֻּחוֹת לְמַרְגִּיזֵי אֵל לַאֲשֶׁר הֵבִיא אֱלוֹהַּ בְּיָדוֹ ⁷ וְאוּלָם שְׁאַל־נָא בְהֵמוֹת וְתֹרֶךָּ וְעוֹף הַשָּׁמַיִם וְיַגֶּד־לָךְ ⁸ אוֹ שִׂיחַ לָאָרֶץ וְתֹרֶךָּ וִיסַפְּרוּ לְךָ דְּגֵי הַיָּם ⁹ מִי לֹא־יָדַע בְּכָל־אֵלֶּה כִּי יַד־יְהוָה עָשְׂתָה זֹּאת ¹⁰ אֲשֶׁר בְּיָדוֹ נֶפֶשׁ כָּל־חָי וְרוּחַ כָּל־בְּשַׂר־אִישׁ ¹¹ הֲלֹא־אֹזֶן מִלִּין תִּבְחָן וְחֵךְ אֹכֶל יִטְעַם־לוֹ ¹² בִּישִׁישִׁים חָכְמָה וְאֹרֶךְ יָמִים תְּבוּנָה ¹³ עִמּוֹ חָכְמָה וּגְבוּרָה לוֹ עֵצָה וּתְבוּנָה ¹⁴ הֵן יַהֲרוֹס וְלֹא יִבָּנֶה יִסְגֹּר עַל־אִישׁ וְלֹא יִפָּתֵחַ ¹⁵ הֵן יַעְצֹר בַּמַּיִם וְיִבָשׁוּ וִישַׁלְּחֵם וְיַהַפְכוּ אָרֶץ ¹⁶ עִמּוֹ עֹז וְתוּשִׁיָּה לוֹ שֹׁגֵג וּמַשְׁגֶּה ¹⁷ מוֹלִיךְ יוֹעֲצִים שׁוֹלָל וְשֹׁפְטִים יְהוֹלֵל ¹⁸ מוּסַר מְלָכִים פִּתֵּחַ וַיֶּאְסֹר אֵזוֹר בְּמָתְנֵיהֶם ¹⁹ מוֹלִיךְ כֹּהֲנִים שׁוֹלָל וְאֵתָנִים יְסַלֵּף ²⁰ מֵסִיר שָׂפָה לְנֶאֱמָנִים וְטַעַם זְקֵנִים יִקָּח ²¹ שׁוֹפֵךְ בּוּז עַל־נְדִיבִים וּמְזִיחַ אֲפִיקִים רִפָּה ²² מְגַלֶּה עֲמֻקוֹת מִנִּי־חֹשֶׁךְ וַיֹּצֵא לָאוֹר צַלְמָוֶת ²³ מַשְׂגִּיא לַגּוֹיִם וַיְאַבְּדֵם שֹׁטֵחַ לַגּוֹיִם וַיַּנְחֵם ²⁴ מֵסִיר לֵב רָאשֵׁי עַם־הָאָרֶץ וַיַּתְעֵם בְּתֹהוּ לֹא־דָרֶךְ ²⁵ יְמַשְׁשׁוּ־חֹשֶׁךְ וְלֹא־אוֹר וַיַּתְעֵם כַּשִּׁכּוֹר

פרק יג

¹ הֶן־כֹּל רָאֲתָה עֵינִי שָׁמְעָה אָזְנִי וַתָּבֶן לָהּ ² כְּדַעְתְּכֶם יָדַעְתִּי גַם־אָנִי לֹא־נֹפֵל אָנֹכִי מִכֶּם ³ אוּלָם אֲנִי אֶל־שַׁדַּי אֲדַבֵּר וְהוֹכֵחַ אֶל־אֵל אֶחְפָּץ ⁴ וְאוּלָם אַתֶּם טֹפְלֵי־שָׁקֶר רֹפְאֵי אֱלִל כֻּלְּכֶם ⁵ מִי־יִתֵּן הַחֲרֵשׁ תַּחֲרִישׁוּן וּתְהִי לָכֶם לְחָכְמָה ⁶ שִׁמְעוּ־נָא תוֹכַחְתִּי וְרִבוֹת שְׂפָתַי הַקְשִׁיבוּ ⁷ הַלְאֵל תְּדַבְּרוּ עַוְלָה וְלוֹ תְּדַבְּרוּ רְמִיָּה ⁸ הֲפָנָיו תִּשָּׂאוּן אִם־לָאֵל תְּרִיבוּן ⁹ הֲטוֹב כִּי־יַחְקֹר אֶתְכֶם אִם־כְּהָתֵל בֶּאֱנוֹשׁ תְּהָתֵלּוּ בוֹ ¹⁰ הוֹכֵחַ יוֹכִיחַ אֶתְכֶם אִם־בַּסֵּתֶר פָּנִים תִּשָּׂאוּן ¹¹ הֲלֹא שְׂאֵתוֹ תְּבַעֵת אֶתְכֶם וּפַחְדּוֹ יִפֹּל עֲלֵיכֶם ¹² זִכְרֹנֵיכֶם מִשְׁלֵי־אֵפֶר לְגַבֵּי־חֹמֶר גַּבֵּיכֶם ¹³ הַחֲרִישׁוּ מִמֶּנִּי וַאֲדַבְּרָה־אָנִי וְיַעֲבֹר עָלַי מָה ¹⁴ עַל־מָה אֶשָּׂא בְשָׂרִי בְשִׁנָּי וְנַפְשִׁי אָשִׂים בְּכַפִּי ¹⁵ הֵן יִקְטְלֵנִי לֹא אֲיַחֵל אַךְ־דְּרָכַי אֶל־פָּנָיו אוֹכִיחַ ¹⁶ גַּם־הוּא־לִי לִישׁוּעָה כִּי־לֹא לְפָנָיו חָנֵף יָבוֹא ¹⁷ שִׁמְעוּ שָׁמוֹעַ מִלָּתִי וְאַחֲוָתִי בְּאָזְנֵיכֶם ¹⁸ הִנֵּה־נָא עָרַכְתִּי מִשְׁפָּט יָדַעְתִּי כִּי־אֲנִי אֶצְדָּק ¹⁹ מִי־הוּא יָרִיב עִמָּדִי כִּי־עַתָּה אַחֲרִישׁ וְאֶגְוָע

---

5 There is contempt for calamity;[2] For a thought,[3] there is ease. He is prepared for slips of the foot. 6 The tents of robbers are at ease, and there is security[4] for the agitators of God—for those who bring God in their hand. 7 However,[5] ask Behemoth, now, and it will teach you; and fowl of the heavens will declare to you. 8 Or speak to the land, and it will teach you; and the fish of the sea will recount to you. 9 Who does not know, in all these things, that Adonai's hand did this? 10 Which in his hand is the soul of all living things and the breath of all mankind?[6] 11 Does an ear not examine words, as a palate tastes its food?[7] 12 With the aged is wisdom; and the length of days is understanding. 13 With him are wisdom and might. His[8] are counsel and understanding. 14 Behold, he destroys, and it is not built again. He closes a man in,[9] and it will not be opened. 15 Behold, he restrains the waters, and they dry up; and he sends them out, and they overturn the earth. 16 With him are strength and wisdom. His[10] are the misled and the misleader. 17 He leads counselors away barefoot;[11] and judges, he turns into fools. 18 He loosens the discipline of kings and binds a girdle at their loins. 19 He leads priests away barefoot, and the enduring ones, he ruins. 20 He removes the speech of the faithful, and the judgment of the elders, he takes. 21 He pours out contempt on nobles and loosens the belt[12] of the strong.[13] 22 He uncovers deep things from darkness and brings gloom to the light. 23 He makes nations great, and he destroys them. He expands nations, and he leads them.[14] 24 He removes the heart of the leaders of the people of the land and causes them to wander in chaos without a way. 25 They grope the darkness without light.[15] He causes them to wander like a drunk man. **13:1** Behold, all my eye has seen, my ear has heard and understands it. 2 I also know your knowledge[1] I do not fall from among you all.[2] 3 However, I will speak to Shaddai, and I desire to argue with God.[3] 4 But[4] you are smearers of deception. You all are physicians of worthlessness. 5 If only you would be utterly silent, it would be wisdom for you.[5] 6 Hear now my argument and pay attention to the pleadings of my lips. 7 Will you speak injustice to God, and to him will you speak deceit? 8 Will you show partiality to him?[6] Will you plead for God? 9 Is it good that he examines you? Will you deceive him like deceiving a man? 10 He will definitely reprove you if in secret you show partiality. 11 Will his majesty not terrify you, and his fear fall upon you? 12 Your remembrances are proverbs of ash. Your bosses are bosses[7] of clay. 13 Be silent[8] that I may speak and come upon me what may.[9] 14 For what should I lift up my flesh with my teeth and place my life in my palm? 15 Behold, he will kill me. I will not hope. Yet, I will prove my ways to his face. 16 Also he is my salvation,[10] for a godless person cannot come before him. 17 You must hear my speech, and my declaration[11] will be in your ears. 18 Behold now, I have set forth my case. I know I am in the right.[12] 19 Who is he who will contend with me? For then[13] I would be silent and die.

13

פרק יג

20 אַךְ־שְׁתַּיִם אַל־תַּעַשׂ עִמָּדִי אָז מִפָּנֶיךָ לֹא אֶסָּתֵר: 21 כַּפְּךָ מֵעָלַי הַרְחַק וְאֵמָתְךָ אַל־תְּבַעֲתַנִּי: 22 וּקְרָא וְאָנֹכִי אֶעֱנֶה אוֹ־אֲדַבֵּר וַהֲשִׁיבֵנִי: 23 כַּמָּה לִי עֲוֹנוֹת וְחַטָּאוֹת פִּשְׁעִי וְחַטָּאתִי הֹדִיעֵנִי: 24 לָמָּה־פָנֶיךָ תַסְתִּיר וְתַחְשְׁבֵנִי לְאוֹיֵב לָךְ: 25 הֶעָלֶה נִדָּף תַּעֲרוֹץ וְאֶת־קַשׁ יָבֵשׁ תִּרְדֹּף: 26 כִּי־תִכְתֹּב עָלַי מְרֹרוֹת וְתוֹרִישֵׁנִי עֲוֹנוֹת נְעוּרָי: 27 וְתָשֵׂם בַּסַּד רַגְלַי וְתִשְׁמוֹר כָּל־אָרְחוֹתָי עַל־שָׁרְשֵׁי רַגְלַי תִּתְחַקֶּה: 28 וְהוּא כְּרָקָב יִבְלֶה כְּבֶגֶד אֲכָלוֹ עָשׁ:

פרק יד

1 אָדָם יְלוּד אִשָּׁה קְצַר יָמִים וּשְׂבַע־רֹגֶז: 2 כְּצִיץ יָצָא וַיִּמָּל וַיִּבְרַח כַּצֵּל וְלֹא יַעֲמוֹד: 3 אַף־עַל־זֶה פָּקַחְתָּ עֵינֶךָ וְאֹתִי תָבִיא בְמִשְׁפָּט עִמָּךְ: 4 מִי־יִתֵּן טָהוֹר מִטָּמֵא לֹא אֶחָד: 5 אִם חֲרוּצִים יָמָיו מִסְפַּר־חֳדָשָׁיו אִתָּךְ חֻקָּיו עָשִׂיתָ וְלֹא יַעֲבוֹר: 6 שְׁעֵה מֵעָלָיו וְיֶחְדָּל עַד־יִרְצֶה כְּשָׂכִיר יוֹמוֹ: 7 כִּי יֵשׁ לָעֵץ תִּקְוָה אִם־יִכָּרֵת וְעוֹד יַחֲלִיף וְיֹנַקְתּוֹ לֹא תֶחְדָּל: 8 אִם־יַזְקִין בָּאָרֶץ שָׁרְשׁוֹ וּבֶעָפָר יָמוּת גִּזְעוֹ: 9 מֵרֵיחַ מַיִם יַפְרִחַ וְעָשָׂה קָצִיר כְּמוֹ־נָטַע: 10 וְגֶבֶר יָמוּת וַיֶּחֱלָשׁ וַיִּגְוַע אָדָם וְאַיּוֹ: 11 אָזְלוּ־מַיִם מִנִּי־יָם וְנָהָר יֶחֱרַב וְיָבֵשׁ: 12 וְאִישׁ שָׁכַב וְלֹא־יָקוּם עַד־בִּלְתִּי שָׁמַיִם לֹא יָקִיצוּ וְלֹא־יֵעֹרוּ מִשְּׁנָתָם: 13 מִי יִתֵּן בִּשְׁאוֹל תַּצְפִּנֵנִי תַּסְתִּירֵנִי עַד־שׁוּב אַפְּךָ תָּשִׁית לִי חֹק וְתִזְכְּרֵנִי: 14 אִם־יָמוּת גֶּבֶר הֲיִחְיֶה כָּל־יְמֵי צְבָאִי אֲיַחֵל עַד־בּוֹא חֲלִיפָתִי: 15 תִּקְרָא וְאָנֹכִי אֶעֱנֶךָּ לְמַעֲשֵׂה יָדֶיךָ תִכְסֹף: 16 כִּי־עַתָּה צְעָדַי תִּסְפּוֹר לֹא־תִשְׁמוֹר עַל־חַטָּאתִי: 17 חָתֻם בִּצְרוֹר פִּשְׁעִי וַתִּטְפֹּל עַל־עֲוֹנִי: 18 וְאוּלָם הַר־נוֹפֵל יִבּוֹל וְצוּר יֶעְתַּק מִמְּקֹמוֹ: 19 אֲבָנִים שָׁחֲקוּ מַיִם תִּשְׁטֹף־סְפִיחֶיהָ עֲפַר־אָרֶץ וְתִקְוַת אֱנוֹשׁ הֶאֱבַדְתָּ: 20 תִּתְקְפֵהוּ לָנֶצַח וַיַּהֲלֹךְ מְשַׁנֶּה פָנָיו וַתְּשַׁלְּחֵהוּ: 21 יִכְבְּדוּ בָנָיו וְלֹא יֵדָע וְיִצְעֲרוּ וְלֹא־יָבִין לָמוֹ: 22 אַךְ־בְּשָׂרוֹ עָלָיו יִכְאָב וְנַפְשׁוֹ עָלָיו תֶּאֱבָל:

פרק טו

1 וַיַּעַן אֱלִיפַז הַתֵּימָנִי וַיֹּאמַר: 2 הֶחָכָם יַעֲנֶה דַעַת־רוּחַ וִימַלֵּא קָדִים בִּטְנוֹ: 3 הוֹכֵחַ בְּדָבָר לֹא יִסְכּוֹן וּמִלִּים לֹא־יוֹעִיל בָּם: 4 אַף־אַתָּה תָּפֵר יִרְאָה וְתִגְרַע שִׂיחָה לִפְנֵי־אֵל: 5 כִּי יְאַלֵּף עֲוֹנְךָ פִיךָ וְתִבְחַר לְשׁוֹן עֲרוּמִים: 6 יַרְשִׁיעֲךָ פִיךָ וְלֹא־אָנִי וּשְׂפָתֶיךָ יַעֲנוּ־בָךְ: 7 הֲרִאישׁוֹן אָדָם תִּוָּלֵד וְלִפְנֵי גְבָעוֹת חוֹלָלְתָּ: 8 הַבְסוֹד אֱלוֹהַּ תִּשְׁמָע וְתִגְרַע אֵלֶיךָ חָכְמָה: 9 מַה־יָּדַעְתָּ וְלֹא נֵדָע תָּבִין וְלֹא־עִמָּנוּ הוּא: 10 גַּם־שָׂב גַּם־יָשִׁישׁ בָּנוּ כַּבִּיר מֵאָבִיךָ יָמִים:

20 Only two things do not do with me. Then I will not hide myself from your face: 21 distance your hand from upon me, and may your terror not make me afraid. 22 Call and I will answer, or I will speak, and you answer me. 23 How many are my iniquities and sins?[14] Make known to me my transgression and my sin. 24 Why do you hide your face, and consider me an enemy to you? 25 Will you cause a driven leaf to tremble and pursue dry chaff? 26 For you write poisonous things[15] about me, and you make me inherit the iniquities of my youth. 27 You put my feet in the stocks and watch all of my ways. You engrave upon the roots of my feet.[16] 28 And he[17] wears away like decay; like a garment that a moth has eaten.[18] 14:1 A man is born of a woman, is short of days and sated with agitation.[1] 2 He comes forth like a flower and withers. He flees like a shadow and does not stand. 3 Even upon this[2] have you opened your eye, and will you bring me into a legal case with you? 4 Who will grant clean from unclean? Not one. 5 If his days are fixed,[3] the number of his months is with you; you made his boundaries, and he cannot cross over. 6 Gaze away from him, and he will cease, until he satisfies his day as a hireling. 7 For there is hope for the tree if it is cut down. It will replace itself again,[4] and its shoot will not cease. 8 If its root grows old into the land, and its stump dies in the dust, 9 from the scent of water it will bud, and will make branches like a plant. 10 But a man dies and grows weak. A man perishes, and where is he? 11 Waters go from the sea, and the river drains[5] and is dry. 12 A man[6] lies down and does not rise. Until there are no more heavens, they will not awake, and they will not be awoken from their sleep. 13 If only you would hide me in Sheol and hide me until the turning back of your wrath. You will set a limit for me and remember me. 14 If a man dies, will he be revived? I will await all of the days of my service, until the coming of my replacement. 15 You will call, and I will answer you. You will long for the work of your hands. 16 For now you count my steps. You do not watch over my sin. 17 My transgression is sealed in a bag. You will plaster over my transgression. 18 However, the mountain falls—it sinks—and a rock moves from its place. 19 The waters rub away stones. Its torrents wash off[7] the dust of the earth, and you destroy the hope of humankind. 20 You overpower him forever, and he departs. You change his face and send him away. 21 His sons may be honored, but he will not know. They may be insignificant, but he will not perceive them. 22 But his flesh on him hurts, and his soul mourns over him." 15:1 Then Eliphaz the Temanite answered and said, 2 "Does a wise man respond with knowledge of wind and fill his belly with the east wind, 3 arguing with a word that is not beneficial, and words with which he can do them[1] no good? 4 Even you break fear,[2] and withdraw mediation before God. 5 For your iniquity teaches your mouth, and you choose a crafty tongue.[3] 6 Your mouth condemns you, and not I; And your lips testify against you. 7 Were you the first man born, and were you brought forth before the hills? 8 Did you hear the council of God and withdraw wisdom unto yourself? 9 What do you know that we do not know—that you understand which is not with us?[4] 10 Both gray-haired and aged[5] are among us;[6] greater in days than your father.[7]

פרק טז

וַיַּעַן אִיּוֹב וַיֹּאמַר

11 הַמְעַט מִמְּךָ תַּנְחֻמוֹת אֵל וְדָבָר לָאַט עִמָּךְ׃ 12 מַה־יִּקָּחֲךָ לִבֶּךָ וּמַה־יִּרְזְמוּן עֵינֶיךָ׃ 13 כִּי־תָשִׁיב אֶל־אֵל רוּחֶךָ וְהֹצֵאתָ מִפִּיךָ מִלִּין׃ 14 מָה־אֱנוֹשׁ כִּי־יִזְכֶּה וְכִי־יִצְדַּק יְלוּד אִשָּׁה׃ 15 הֵן בִּקְדֹשָׁיו לֹא יַאֲמִין וְשָׁמַיִם לֹא־זַכּוּ בְעֵינָיו׃ 16 אַף כִּי־נִתְעָב וְנֶאֱלָח אִישׁ־שֹׁתֶה כַמַּיִם עַוְלָה׃ 17 אֲחַוְךָ שְׁמַע־לִי וְזֶה־חָזִיתִי וַאֲסַפֵּרָה׃ 18 אֲשֶׁר־חֲכָמִים יַגִּידוּ וְלֹא כִחֲדוּ מֵאֲבוֹתָם׃ 19 לָהֶם לְבַדָּם נִתְּנָה הָאָרֶץ וְלֹא־עָבַר זָר בְּתוֹכָם׃ 20 כָּל־יְמֵי רָשָׁע הוּא מִתְחוֹלֵל וּמִסְפַּר שָׁנִים נִצְפְּנוּ לֶעָרִיץ׃ 21 קוֹל־פְּחָדִים בְּאָזְנָיו בַּשָּׁלוֹם שׁוֹדֵד יְבוֹאֶנּוּ׃ 22 לֹא־יַאֲמִין שׁוּב מִנִּי־חֹשֶׁךְ וְצָפוּי הוּא אֱלֵי־חָרֶב׃ 23 נֹדֵד הוּא לַלֶּחֶם אַיֵּה יָדַע כִּי־נָכוֹן בְּיָדוֹ יוֹם־חֹשֶׁךְ׃ 24 יְבַעֲתֻהוּ צַר וּמְצוּקָה תִּתְקְפֵהוּ כְּמֶלֶךְ עָתִיד לַכִּידוֹר׃ 25 כִּי־נָטָה אֶל־אֵל יָדוֹ וְאֶל־שַׁדַּי יִתְגַּבָּר׃ 26 יָרוּץ אֵלָיו בְּצַוָּאר בַּעֲבִי גַּבֵּי מָגִנָּיו׃ 27 כִּי־כִסָּה פָנָיו בְּחֶלְבּוֹ וַיַּעַשׂ פִּימָה עֲלֵי־כָסֶל׃ 28 וַיִּשְׁכּוֹן עָרִים נִכְחָדוֹת בָּתִּים לֹא־יֵשְׁבוּ לָמוֹ אֲשֶׁר הִתְעַתְּדוּ לְגַלִּים׃ 29 לֹא־יֶעְשַׁר וְלֹא־יָקוּם חֵילוֹ וְלֹא־יִטֶּה לָאָרֶץ מִנְלָם׃ 30 לֹא־יָסוּר מִנִּי־חֹשֶׁךְ יֹנַקְתּוֹ תְּיַבֵּשׁ שַׁלְהָבֶת וְיָסוּר בְּרוּחַ פִּיו׃ 31 אַל־יַאֲמֵן בַּשָּׁו נִתְעָה כִּי־שָׁוְא תִּהְיֶה תְמוּרָתוֹ׃ 32 בְּלֹא־יוֹמוֹ תִּמָּלֵא וְכִפָּתוֹ לֹא רַעֲנָנָה׃ 33 יַחְמֹס כַּגֶּפֶן בִּסְרוֹ וְיַשְׁלֵךְ כַּזַּיִת נִצָּתוֹ׃ 34 כִּי־עֲדַת חָנֵף גַּלְמוּד וְאֵשׁ אָכְלָה אָהֳלֵי־שֹׁחַד׃ 35 הָרֹה עָמָל וְיָלֹד אָוֶן וּבִטְנָם תָּכִין מִרְמָה׃

2 שָׁמַעְתִּי כְאֵלֶּה רַבּוֹת מְנַחֲמֵי עָמָל כֻּלְּכֶם׃ 3 הֲקֵץ לְדִבְרֵי־רוּחַ אוֹ מַה־יַּמְרִיצְךָ כִּי תַעֲנֶה׃ 4 גַּם אָנֹכִי כָּכֶם אֲדַבֵּרָה לוּ־יֵשׁ נַפְשְׁכֶם תַּחַת נַפְשִׁי אַחְבִּירָה עֲלֵיכֶם בְּמִלִּים וְאָנִיעָה עֲלֵיכֶם בְּמוֹ רֹאשִׁי׃ 5 אֲאַמִּצְכֶם בְּמוֹ־פִי וְנִיד שְׂפָתַי יַחְשֹׂךְ׃ 6 אִם־אֲדַבְּרָה לֹא־יֵחָשֵׂךְ כְּאֵבִי וְאַחְדְּלָה מַה־מִנִּי יַהֲלֹךְ׃ 7 אַךְ־עַתָּה הֶלְאָנִי הֲשִׁמּוֹתָ כָּל־עֲדָתִי׃ 8 וַתִּקְמְטֵנִי לְעֵד הָיָה וַיָּקָם בִּי כַחֲשִׁי בְּפָנַי יַעֲנֶה׃

11 Are the consolations of God too few for you,[8] and a gentle word[9] with you? 12 How does your heart take you away, and how does your eye wink[10] 13 that you turn your breath against God, and bring forth words from your mouth? 14 What is man that he would be pure and that one born of a woman should be righteous? 15 Behold, he does not trust in his holy ones, and the heavens are not clean in his eyes; 16 even less the abhorred and corrupt—a man who drinks injustice like water! 17 I will declare to you. Listen to me, and this that[11] I have seen, I will tell you, 18 which wise men declared, and did not conceal from their fathers—19 to them, only them, the land was given, and no stranger passed among them. 20 All of the days of the wicked he writhes, and the number of years for the ruthless is hidden.[12] 21 A sound of terrors is in his ears. In peace, an assailant comes upon him. 22 He does not believe in his return from darkness, and is spied out for a sword. 23 He wanders for bread—'Where is it?' He knows that the day of darkness is established in his hand. 24 Distress and anguish terrify him. It overpowers him[13] like a king ready for battle.[14] 25 Because he stretched out his hand against God, and against Shaddai he became mighty. 26 He runs at him with a stiff neck,[15] with the thickness of the bosses of his shields, 27 because he has covered his face with his fat and produced fat on his sinews. 28 He dwells in destroyed cities—houses in which no one dwells,[16] which are ready for heaps. 29 He will not be rich, and his substance will not endure,[17] and their gain[18] will not be extended on the land.[19] 30 He will not depart from darkness. A flame will dry up his branch. He will depart by the breath of his mouth. 31 May he not trust in emptiness, leading himself astray; for emptiness will be his exchange. 32 Before its day, it will be filled.[20] Its foliage will not be luxuriant. 33 He will shed[21] unripe grapes as the vine and will cast off[22] his blossom as the olive tree. 34 For the company of the godless is barren, and fire consumes the tents of bribery.[23] 35 Conceiving trouble, birthing iniquity—their womb prepares deceit." 16:1 Then Job answered and said, 2 "I have heard many words like these. You are all comforters of trouble. 3 Is there an end to the words of wind or what provokes you that you respond? 4 Even I could speak like you. If your soul were in the place of my soul, I could unite words against you,[1] and could shake my head at you.[2] 5 Yet, I would strengthen you with my mouth, and movement[3] of my lips would withhold trouble. 6 If I speak, my pain will not be withheld. If[4] I cease, what from me will go? 7 Surely, he has made me weary. You have made desolate all my company. 8 You shriveled me up. It has become a witness. My leanness has risen up against me. It testifies in my face.

פרק יז

1 רוּחִי חֻבָּלָה יָמַי נִזְעָכוּ קְבָרִים לִי 2 אִם־לֹא הֲתֻלִים עִמָּדִי וּבְהַמְּרוֹתָם תָּלַן עֵינִי 3 שִׂימָה־נָּא עָרְבֵנִי עִמָּךְ מִי הוּא לְיָדִי יִתָּקֵעַ 4 כִּי־לִבָּם צָפַנְתָּ מִּשָּׂכֶל עַל־כֵּן לֹא תְרֹמֵם 5 לְחֵלֶק יַגִּיד רֵעִים וְעֵינֵי בָנָיו תִּכְלֶנָה 6 וְהִצִּגַנִי לִמְשֹׁל עַמִּים וְתֹפֶת לְפָנִים אֶהְיֶה 7 וַתֵּכַהּ מִכַּעַשׂ עֵינִי וִיצֻרַי כַּצֵּל כֻּלָּם 8 יָשֹׁמּוּ יְשָׁרִים עַל־זֹאת וְנָקִי עַל־חָנֵף יִתְעֹרָר 9 וְיֹאחֵז צַדִּיק דַּרְכּוֹ וּטְהָר־יָדַיִם יֹסִיף אֹמֶץ 10 וְאוּלָם כֻּלָּם תָּשֻׁבוּ וּבֹאוּ נָא וְלֹא־אֶמְצָא בָכֶם חָכָם 11 יָמַי עָבְרוּ זִמֹּתַי נִתְּקוּ מוֹרָשֵׁי לְבָבִי 12 לַיְלָה לְיוֹם יָשִׂימוּ אוֹר קָרוֹב מִפְּנֵי־חֹשֶׁךְ 13 אִם־אֲקַוֶּה שְׁאוֹל בֵּיתִי בַּחֹשֶׁךְ רִפַּדְתִּי יְצוּעָי 14 לַשַּׁחַת קָרָאתִי אָבִי אָתָּה אִמִּי וַאֲחֹתִי לָרִמָּה 15 וְאַיֵּה אֵפוֹ תִקְוָתִי וְתִקְוָתִי מִי יְשׁוּרֶנָּה 16 בַּדֵּי שְׁאֹל תֵּרַדְנָה אִם־יַחַד עַל־עָפָר נָחַת

9 אַפּוֹ טָרַף וַיִּשְׂטְמֵנִי חָרַק עָלַי בְּשִׁנָּיו צָרִי יִלְטוֹשׁ עֵינָיו לִי 10 פָּעֲרוּ עָלַי בְּפִיהֶם בְּחֶרְפָּה הִכּוּ לְחָיָי יַחַד עָלַי יִתְמַלָּאוּן 11 יַסְגִּירֵנִי אֵל אֶל עֲוִיל וְעַל־יְדֵי רְשָׁעִים יִרְטֵנִי 12 שָׁלֵו הָיִיתִי וַיְפַרְפְּרֵנִי וְאָחַז בְּעָרְפִּי וַיְפַצְפְּצֵנִי וַיְקִימֵנִי לוֹ לְמַטָּרָה 13 יָסֹבּוּ עָלַי רַבָּיו יְפַלַּח כִּלְיוֹתַי וְלֹא יַחְמוֹל יִשְׁפֹּךְ לָאָרֶץ מְרֵרָתִי 14 יִפְרְצֵנִי פֶרֶץ עַל־פְּנֵי־פָרֶץ יָרֻץ עָלַי כְּגִבּוֹר 15 שַׂק תָּפַרְתִּי עֲלֵי גִלְדִּי וְעֹלַלְתִּי בֶעָפָר קַרְנִי 16 פָּנַי חֳמַרְמְרוּ מִנִּי־בֶכִי וְעַל עַפְעַפַּי צַלְמָוֶת 17 עַל לֹא־חָמָס בְּכַפָּי וּתְפִלָּתִי זַכָּה 18 אֶרֶץ אַל־תְּכַסִּי דָמִי וְאַל־יְהִי מָקוֹם לְזַעֲקָתִי 19 גַּם־עַתָּה הִנֵּה־בַשָּׁמַיִם עֵדִי וְשָׂהֲדִי בַּמְּרוֹמִים 20 מְלִיצַי רֵעָי אֶל־אֱלוֹהַּ דָּלְפָה עֵינִי 21 וְיוֹכַח לְגֶבֶר עִם־אֱלוֹהַּ וּבֶן־אָדָם לְרֵעֵהוּ 22 כִּי־שְׁנוֹת מִסְפָּר יֶאֱתָיוּ וְאֹרַח לֹא־אָשׁוּב אֶהֱלֹךְ

פרק יח

1 וַיַּעַן בִּלְדַּד הַשֻּׁחִי וַיֹּאמַר 2 עַד־אָנָה תְּשִׂימוּן קִנְצֵי לְמִלִּין תָּבִינוּ וְאַחַר נְדַבֵּר 3 מַדּוּעַ נֶחְשַׁבְנוּ כַבְּהֵמָה נִטְמִינוּ בְּעֵינֵיכֶם

9 His anger tears apart. He harasses me. He gnashes his teeth at me.[5] My adversary sharpens his eyes at me. 10 They gaped upon me with their mouth. Shamefully, they strike my cheeks. They gather together against me.[6] 11 God delivers me to the unjust, and casts me[7] into the hands of the wicked. 12 I was at ease, and he broke me apart. He seized me by my neck and shattered me. He has set me up as a target for himself. 13 His archers surround me. He cleaves my kidneys and does not have compassion. He pours out my gall to the ground. 14 He breaks me up with breach upon breach.[8] He runs at me[9] like a warrior. 15 I sewed sackcloth upon my skin,[10] and thrust my horn in the dust. 16 My face burns[11] from weeping, and upon my eyelids is gloom—17 upon no violence by my hand, and my prayer is pure. 18 Earth, do not cover my blood, and may it not be the place for my cry. 19 Even now, behold, my witness is in the heavens, and my witness is in the heights.[12] 20 My friends are my scorners. My eye weeps[13] for God. 21 With God, he judges for a man,[14] and a son of man proves for his friend. 22 For a number of years[15] will come, and I will go the path of no return.[16] 17:1 My spirit has been ruined. My days are extinguished.[1] Graves are for me. 2 Surely,[2] mockers are with me, and upon their contentiousness[3] my eye remains. 3 Set it down. Make a pledge for me with yourself. Who is he that will be thrust to my hand? 4 For you have hidden their heart from understanding. Therefore, you will not exalt them.[4] 5 He tells friends of a portion, and the eyes of his children will waste away.[5] 6 He has set me up to rule[6] peoples, but I have become like spit on the face.[7] 7 My eye grows dim from grief and my members are all like the shadow. 8 Upright men are astonished about this, and an innocent man rouses himself upon the godless. 9 Yet a righteous man takes hold of his way, and the clean of hands adds strength. 10 However, everyone,[8] return[9] and come now, and I will not find a wise person among you.[10] 11 My days have passed. My plans have been torn apart—the wishes[11] of my heart. 12 They change night into day.[12] Light is nearer than the presence of darkness. 13 If I hope for Sheol, my home, in the darkness I spread out my bed.[13] 14 I have called to the pit, 'You are my father' and to the worm, 'My mother,' and 'My sister.' 15 And where, where is my hope? And my hope, who will see it? 16 It will go down to the bars of Sheol; together on the dust of rest. 18:1 Bildad the Shuhite answered and said, 2 "How long will you put an end to words?[1] Understand, and afterwards, we will speak. 3 Why are we considered as the animal and have become unclean[2] in your eyes?[3]

16

4 He tears his soul in his anger. For your sake, will the earth be abandoned, and will a rock move from its place? 5 Yes, the light of the wicked will wane. The flame of his fire will not gleam. 6 Light will darken in his tent, and his lamp will wane on him. 7 His steps of strength will be restricted. His counsel will cast him down. 8 For he is cast into a net by his feet, and upon a net he walks. 9 He catches onto a trap with a heel. A snare seizes him. 10 His cord is hidden in the ground, and his trap[4] on a path. 11 Terrors terrify him all around and are scattered for him at his feet.[5] 12 His strength will be hungry, and calamity will be ready at his side. 13 It will consume the members of his skin. The firstborn of death will consume his members. 14 He is torn away from his tent—from his security—and it[6] marches him to a king of terrors. 15 It will dwell in his tent—it is not his.[7] Sulfur will be scattered[8] on his habitation. 16 His roots will dry up from below, and from above his branch will wither. 17 His memory vanishes from the earth, and he will not have a name in the open country.[9] 18 He will be driven from light into darkness, and from the world he will be banished.[10] 19 He has no progeny and no posterity among his people, and there is no survivor in his dwelling place. 20 Westerners will be astonished about his day, and Easterners take hold of horror. 21 Surely these are the dwellings of the unjust, and this is the place of the one who does not know God." 19:1 Job answered and said, 2 "How long will you grieve my soul, and crush me with words? 3 This is ten times you rebuke me. You are not ashamed that you disparage me.[1] 4 For even if[2] I have erred, my error[3] abides with me. 5 If indeed you will do terrible things against me,[4] and reprove me because of my shame,[5] 6 know then that God has subverted me, and with his net, he surrounded me. 7 Behold, I cry out, 'Violence!' but I am not answered. I cry out for help, but there is no justice. 8 He has walled up my path, and I cannot cross over, and over my paths he has set darkness. 9 He has stripped my honor from upon me and removed the crown of my head. 10 He has altogether[6] broken me down, and I depart. He has uprooted my hope like the tree. 11 His anger burns against me, and he considers me as one of his adversaries.[7] 12 His troops come together, build up their way against me, and they encamp on all sides of my tent. 13 He has distanced my brothers from me[8] and my acquaintances are estranged from me. 14 My close ones have ceased. My familiar ones have forgotten me. 15 Dwellers of my house and my maidservants consider me[9] a stranger. I am a stranger in their eyes. 16 I call to my servant and he does not answer. With my mouth I implore him for favor.

פרק כ

17 רוּחִי זָרָה לְאִשְׁתִּי וְחַנֹּתִי לִבְנֵי בִטְנִי
18 גַּם־עֲוִילִים מָאֲסוּ בִי אָקוּמָה
וַיְדַבְּרוּ־בִי 19 תִּעֲבוּנִי כָּל־מְתֵי סוֹדִי
וְזֶה־אָהַבְתִּי נֶהְפְּכוּ־בִי 20 בְּעוֹרִי
וּבִבְשָׂרִי דָּבְקָה עַצְמִי וָאֶתְמַלְּטָה בְּעוֹר
שִׁנָּי 21 חָנֻּנִי חָנֻּנִי אַתֶּם רֵעָי כִּי יַד־אֱלוֹהַּ
נָגְעָה בִּי 22 לָמָּה תִּרְדְּפֻנִי כְמוֹ־אֵל
וּמִבְּשָׂרִי לֹא תִשְׂבָּעוּ 23 מִי־יִתֵּן אֵפוֹ
וְיִכָּתְבוּן מִלָּי מִי־יִתֵּן בַּסֵּפֶר וְיֻחָקוּ
24 בְּעֵט־בַּרְזֶל וְעֹפָרֶת לָעַד בַּצּוּר
יֵחָצְבוּן 25 וַאֲנִי יָדַעְתִּי גֹּאֲלִי חָי וְאַחֲרוֹן
עַל־עָפָר יָקוּם 26 וְאַחַר עוֹרִי
נִקְּפוּ־זֹאת וּמִבְּשָׂרִי אֶחֱזֶה אֱלוֹהַּ
27 אֲשֶׁר אֲנִי אֶחֱזֶה־לִּי וְעֵינַי רָאוּ
וְלֹא־זָר כָּלוּ כִלְיֹתַי בְּחֵקִי 28 כִּי תֹאמְרוּ
מַה־נִּרְדָּף־לוֹ וְשֹׁרֶשׁ דָּבָר נִמְצָא־בִי
29 גּוּרוּ לָכֶם מִפְּנֵי־חֶרֶב כִּי־חֵמָה עֲוֺנוֹת
חָרֶב לְמַעַן תֵּדְעוּן שַׁדּוּן

1 וַיַּעַן צֹפַר הַנַּעֲמָתִי וַיֹּאמַר
2 לָכֵן שְׂעִפַּי יְשִׁיבוּנִי וּבַעֲבוּר חוּשִׁי בִי 3 מוּסַר
כְּלִמָּתִי אֶשְׁמָע וְרוּחַ מִבִּינָתִי יַעֲנֵנִי 4 הֲזֹאת
יָדַעְתָּ מִנִּי־עַד מִנִּי שִׂים אָדָם עֲלֵי־אָרֶץ 5 כִּי
רִנְנַת רְשָׁעִים מִקָּרוֹב וְשִׂמְחַת חָנֵף עֲדֵי־רָגַע
6 אִם־יַעֲלֶה לַשָּׁמַיִם שִׂיאוֹ וְרֹאשׁוֹ לָעָב יַגִּיעַ
7 כְּגֶלֲלוֹ לָנֶצַח יֹאבֵד רֹאָיו יֹאמְרוּ אַיּוֹ 8 כַּחֲלוֹם
יָעוּף וְלֹא יִמְצָאוּהוּ וְיֻדַּד כְּחֶזְיוֹן לָיְלָה 9 עַיִן
שְׁזָפַתּוּ וְלֹא תוֹסִיף וְלֹא־עוֹד תְּשׁוּרֶנּוּ מְקוֹמוֹ
10 בָּנָיו יְרַצּוּ דַלִּים וְיָדָיו תָּשֵׁבְנָה אוֹנוֹ
11 עַצְמוֹתָיו מָלְאוּ עֲלוּמָיו וְעִמּוֹ עַל־עָפָר
תִּשְׁכָּב 12 אִם־תַּמְתִּיק בְּפִיו רָעָה יַכְחִידֶנָּה
תַּחַת לְשׁוֹנוֹ 13 יַחְמֹל עָלֶיהָ וְלֹא יַעַזְבֶנָּה
וְיִמְנָעֶנָּה בְּתוֹךְ חִכּוֹ 14 לַחְמוֹ בְּמֵעָיו נֶהְפָּךְ
מְרוֹרַת פְּתָנִים בְּקִרְבּוֹ 15 חַיִל בָּלַע וַיְקִאֶנּוּ
מִבִּטְנוֹ יוֹרִשֶׁנּוּ אֵל 16 רֹאשׁ־פְּתָנִים יִינָק
תַּהַרְגֵהוּ לְשׁוֹן אֶפְעֶה 17 אַל־יֵרֶא בִפְלַגּוֹת
נַהֲרֵי נַחֲלֵי דְּבַשׁ וְחֶמְאָה 18 מֵשִׁיב יָגָע וְלֹא
יִבְלָע כְּחֵיל תְּמוּרָתוֹ וְלֹא יַעֲלֹס

17 My breath stinks to my wife and I am loathsome to the children of my womb. 18 Even young people reject me. I arise and they speak against me. 19 All of the men of my council[10] abhor me, and those whom[11] I have loved have turned against me. 20 My bone has stuck to my skin and to my flesh and I have been mortared[12] to the skin of my teeth. 21 Show favor unto me, show favor unto me—you my friends!—because the hand of God has touched me. 22 Why do you persecute me like God,[13] and of my flesh you are not satisfied? 23 If only, then, my words were written![14] If only in a scroll[15] they were decreed; 24 with a stylus of iron and lead they were engraved forever in the rock! 25 For I know that my Redeemer lives, and at last he will rise upon the dust. 26 And after they flayed my skin with this,[16] then from my flesh[17] I will behold God, 27 whom I will behold for myself, and my eyes will see, and not a stranger. My kidneys waste away in my bosom. 28 If you say, 'For what will we persecute him?' and the root of the matter is found in me, 29 be afraid of the presence of the sword for yourselves. For wrath is like the iniquities of the sword, so that you may know that there is a judgment."[18] 20:1 Zophar the Naamathite answered and said, 2 "Therefore my disquieting thoughts cause me to respond, for the sake of my feeling that is in me. 3 I hear a correction of my reproach, and the spirit of my understanding causes me to answer. 4 Do you know this[1] from forever—from the putting of humankind upon the land—5 that the joy of the wicked is short,[2] and the joy of the godless is during a moment? 6 If his height goes up to the heavens, and his head reaches to the clouds, 7 like his dung he will perish forever. Those looking at him will say, 'Where is he?' 8 Like a dream he will fly away, and they will not find him. He will be chased away like a vision of the night. 9 An eye saw him and will not do it again, and no longer will his place[3] see him. 10 His children will seek the favor of the poor, and his hands will give back his wealth. 11 His bones are full of his youthful vigor, but with him it will lie down on the dust. 12 Though[4] evil is sweet in his mouth—though[5] he hides it under his tongue, 13 though he spare it, and does not loose it, and withholds it within his palate—14 his food in his bowels is turned. The venom of serpents is within him. 15 He swallowed wealth, and he will vomit it. From his belly, God will dispossess it. 16 He will suck the venom of a cobra. The tongue of a viper will kill him. 17 He will not look at[6] the channels of rivers of streams[7] of honey and butter. 18 He will restore gain and will not swallow it, and he will not rejoice according to the wealth of his transaction.

18

19 כִּי־רִצַּץ עָזַב דַּלִּים בַּיִת גָּזַל וְלֹא יִבְנֵהוּ 20 כִּי לֹא־יָדַע שָׁלֵו בְּבִטְנוֹ בַּחֲמוּדוֹ לֹא יְמַלֵּט 21 אֵין־שָׂרִיד לְאָכְלוֹ עַל־כֵּן לֹא־יָחִיל טוּבוֹ 22 בִּמְלֹאות שִׂפְקוֹ יֵצֶר לוֹ כָּל־יַד עָמֵל תְּבוֹאֶנּוּ 23 יְהִי לְמַלֵּא בִטְנוֹ יְשַׁלַּח־בּוֹ חֲרוֹן אַפּוֹ וְיַמְטֵר עָלֵימוֹ בִּלְחוּמוֹ 24 יִבְרַח מִנֵּשֶׁק בַּרְזֶל תַּחְלְפֵהוּ קֶשֶׁת נְחוּשָׁה 25 שָׁלַף וַיֵּצֵא מִגֵּוָה וּבָרָק מִמְּרֹרָתוֹ יַהֲלֹךְ עָלָיו אֵמִים 26 כָּל־חֹשֶׁךְ טָמוּן לִצְפּוּנָיו תְּאָכְלֵהוּ אֵשׁ לֹא־נֻפָּח יֵרַע שָׂרִיד בְּאָהֳלוֹ 27 יְגַלּוּ שָׁמַיִם עֲוֹנוֹ וְאֶרֶץ מִתְקוֹמָמָה לוֹ 28 יִגֶל יְבוּל בֵּיתוֹ נִגָּרוֹת בְּיוֹם אַפּוֹ 29 זֶה חֵלֶק־אָדָם רָשָׁע מֵאֱלֹהִים וְנַחֲלַת אִמְרוֹ מֵאֵל

פרק כא

1 וַיַּעַן אִיּוֹב וַיֹּאמַר
2 שִׁמְעוּ שָׁמוֹעַ מִלָּתִי וּתְהִי־זֹאת תַּנְחוּמֹתֵיכֶם 3 שָׂאוּנִי וְאָנֹכִי אֲדַבֵּר וְאַחַר דַּבְּרִי תַלְעִיג

19 For he oppressed and abandoned the poor. He seized a house, but he will not rebuild it. 20 Because he knows no peace in his belly, he does not save any desired thing.[8] 21 There is no survivor for his eating. Therefore, his prosperity will not endure. 22 In the fullness of his sufficiency, he is distressed.[9] Every hand of a sufferer will come on him. 23 If filling his belly, God's[10] burning wrath is sent upon him, then it will rain on him[11]—in his flesh. 24 He will flee from an iron weapon. A bronze bow will pierce through him. 25 He draws it out, and it comes out of his back; and the glitter of the weapon[12] comes out[13] of his gall. Wherever he goes, terrors are upon him. 26 All darkness is reserved for his treasures. An unfanned fire[14] devours him. It will feed on the survivor in his tent. 27 The heavens will reveal his iniquity and earth will rise up against him. 28 The produce of his house will depart. They are poured out in the day of his wrath. 29 This is the portion of a wicked man from God and the inheritance of his decree from God." 21:1 Job answered and said, 2 "You must listen, listen to my words, and may this be your consolation.[1] 3 Endure me, and I will speak; and after my speaking, you can mock.

> ⁴הָאָנֹכִי לְאָדָם שִׂיחִי וְאִם־מַדּוּעַ לֹא־תִקְצַר רוּחִי ⁵פְּנוּ־אֵלַי וְהָשַׁמּוּ וְשִׂימוּ יָד עַל־פֶּה ⁶וְאִם־זָכַרְתִּי וְנִבְהָלְתִּי וְאָחַז בְּשָׂרִי פַּלָּצוּת ⁷מַדּוּעַ רְשָׁעִים יִחְיוּ עָתְקוּ גַּם־גָּבְרוּ חָיִל ⁸זַרְעָם נָכוֹן לִפְנֵיהֶם עִמָּם וְצֶאֱצָאֵיהֶם לְעֵינֵיהֶם ⁹בָּתֵּיהֶם שָׁלוֹם מִפָּחַד וְלֹא שֵׁבֶט אֱלוֹהַּ עֲלֵיהֶם ¹⁰שׁוֹרוֹ עִבַּר וְלֹא יַגְעִל תְּפַלֵּט פָּרָתוֹ וְלֹא תְשַׁכֵּל ¹¹יְשַׁלְּחוּ כַצֹּאן עֲוִילֵיהֶם וְיַלְדֵיהֶם יְרַקֵּדוּן ¹²יִשְׂאוּ כְּתֹף וְכִנּוֹר וְיִשְׂמְחוּ לְקוֹל עוּגָב ¹³יְכַלּוּ בַטּוֹב יְמֵיהֶם וּבְרֶגַע שְׁאוֹל יֵחָתּוּ ¹⁴וַיֹּאמְרוּ לָאֵל סוּר מִמֶּנּוּ וְדַעַת דְּרָכֶיךָ לֹא חָפָצְנוּ ¹⁵מַה־שַּׁדַּי כִּי־נַעַבְדֶנּוּ וּמַה־נּוֹעִיל כִּי נִפְגַּע־בּוֹ ¹⁶הֵן לֹא בְיָדָם טוּבָם עֲצַת רְשָׁעִים רָחֲקָה מֶנִּי ¹⁷כַּמָּה נֵר־רְשָׁעִים יִדְעָךְ וְיָבֹא עָלֵימוֹ אֵידָם חֲבָלִים יְחַלֵּק בְּאַפּוֹ ¹⁸יִהְיוּ כְּתֶבֶן לִפְנֵי־רוּחַ וּכְמֹץ גְּנָבַתּוּ סוּפָה ¹⁹אֱלוֹהַּ יִצְפֹּן־לְבָנָיו אוֹנוֹ יְשַׁלֵּם אֵלָיו וְיֵדָע ²⁰יִרְאוּ עֵינָיו כִּידוֹ וּמֵחֲמַת שַׁדַּי יִשְׁתֶּה ²¹כִּי מַה־חֶפְצוֹ בְּבֵיתוֹ אַחֲרָיו וּמִסְפַּר חֳדָשָׁיו חֻצָּצוּ ²²הַלְאֵל יְלַמֶּד־דָּעַת וְהוּא רָמִים יִשְׁפּוֹט ²³זֶה יָמוּת בְּעֶצֶם תֻּמּוֹ כֻּלּוֹ שַׁלְאֲנַן וְשָׁלֵיו ²⁴עֲטִינָיו מָלְאוּ חָלָב וּמֹחַ עַצְמוֹתָיו יְשֻׁקֶּה ²⁵וְזֶה יָמוּת בְּנֶפֶשׁ מָרָה וְלֹא־אָכַל בַּטּוֹבָה ²⁶יַחַד עַל־עָפָר יִשְׁכָּבוּ וְרִמָּה תְּכַסֶּה עֲלֵיהֶם ²⁷הֵן יָדַעְתִּי מַחְשְׁבוֹתֵיכֶם וּמְזִמּוֹת עָלַי תַּחְמֹסוּ ²⁸כִּי תֹאמְרוּ אַיֵּה בֵית־נָדִיב וְאַיֵּה אֹהֶל מִשְׁכְּנוֹת רְשָׁעִים ²⁹הֲלֹא שְׁאֶלְתֶּם עוֹבְרֵי דָרֶךְ וְאֹתֹתָם לֹא תְנַכֵּרוּ ³⁰כִּי לְיוֹם אֵיד יֵחָשֶׂךְ רָע לְיוֹם עֲבָרוֹת יוּבָלוּ ³¹מִי־יַגִּיד עַל־פָּנָיו דַּרְכּוֹ וְהוּא־עָשָׂה מִי יְשַׁלֶּם־לוֹ ³²וְהוּא לִקְבָרוֹת יוּבָל וְעַל־גָּדִישׁ יִשְׁקוֹד ³³מָתְקוּ־לוֹ רִגְבֵי נָחַל וְאַחֲרָיו כָּל־אָדָם יִמְשׁוֹךְ וּלְפָנָיו אֵין מִסְפָּר ³⁴וְאֵיךְ תְּנַחֲמוּנִי הָבֶל וּתְשׁוּבֹתֵיכֶם נִשְׁאַר־מָעַל

פרק כב

> ¹וַיַּעַן אֱלִיפַז הַתֵּימָנִי וַיֹּאמַר ²הַלְאֵל יִסְכָּן־גָּבֶר כִּי־יִסְכֹּן עָלֵימוֹ מַשְׂכִּיל ³הַחֵפֶץ לְשַׁדַּי כִּי תִצְדָּק וְאִם־בֶּצַע כִּי־תַתֵּם דְּרָכֶיךָ

4 Is my own complaint² to a man? And, why should I not grow impatient?³ 5 Turn to me, and be appalled, and put your hand on your mouth.⁴ 6 And if I remember, I am terrified. My flesh seizes trembling. 7 Why do the wicked live on, grow old, and also become mighty in wealth? 8 Their seed is established before them—with them their offspring before their eyes. 9 Their houses are at peace—without fear—and the rod of God is not upon them. 10 His bull impregnates and does not fail. His cow calves and does not miscarry. 11 They send out young ones like a flock,⁵ and their children dance. 12 They lift up⁶ like a tambourine and lyre, and take pleasure at the sound of the flute. 13 They complete their days in prosperity,⁷ and in a moment, they descend to Sheol. 14 They say to God, 'Depart from us' and, 'We do not delight in the knowledge of your ways. 15 What is Shaddai, that we should serve him, and what does it profit that we should entreat him?' 16 Behold, their prosperity is not in their hand. The counsel of the wicked is far from me. 17 How often does the lamp of the wicked wane, and their calamity comes on them? How often⁸ does God⁹ distribute pains¹⁰ in his anger? 18 How often are they as stubble before the wind, and like chaff that a strong wind steals away?¹¹ 19 How often does God store up his iniquity for his children? Let God¹² pay him, and he will know it. 20 May his eyes see his destruction,¹³ and from the anger of Shaddai may he drink. 21 For what is his delight in his household after him, when the number of his months¹⁴ are cut in half?¹⁵ 22 Can anyone teach God knowledge, since he¹⁶ judges the exalted?¹⁷ 23 This one dies in the essence of his physical fullness—entirely¹⁸ at ease¹⁹ and prosperous. 24 His pails²⁰ are full of milk, and the marrow of his bones is invigorated.²¹ 25 This one dies in a bitter soul and does not taste of good. 26 Together they lie down upon the dust, and the worm covers them. 27 Behold, I know your thoughts, and the evil thoughts about me with which you do wrong. 28 For you say, 'Where is the house of the nobleman?' and 'Where is the tent of the dwelling places of the wicked?' 29 Have you not asked travelers of the way?²² And their signs, do you not recognize? 30 That is, the wicked is withheld on the day of calamity.²³ They are led away on the day of indignation.²⁴ 31 Who will declare his way to his face, and for what he has done, who will recompense him? 32 Yet, he will be carried to the grave,²⁵ and over his tomb one will keep watch. 33 The clods of the wadi are sweet to him. Also, after him every man is drawn, and before him are innumerable people. 34 Then how can you comfort me with breath, while faithlessness remains in your answers?"²⁶ 22:1 Eliphaz the Temanite answered and said, 2 "Can a man be of benefit to God? For can a prudent man be of benefit to him?¹ 3 Is it a pleasure to Shaddai that you are righteous, and is it a profit for him that you make your ways whole?

פרק כג

⁴ הַמִיִּרְאָתְךָ יֹכִיחֶךָ יָבוֹא עִמְּךָ בַּמִּשְׁפָּט ⁵ הֲלֹא רָעָתְךָ רַבָּה וְאֵין־קֵץ לַעֲוֺנֹתֶיךָ ⁶ כִּי־תַחְבֹּל אַחֶיךָ חִנָּם וּבִגְדֵי עֲרוּמִּים תַּפְשִׁיט ⁷ לֹא־מַיִם עָיֵף תַּשְׁקֶה וּמֵרָעֵב תִּמְנַע־לָחֶם ⁸ וְאִישׁ זְרוֹעַ לוֹ הָאָרֶץ וּנְשׂוּא פָנִים יֵשֶׁב בָּהּ ⁹ אַלְמָנוֹת שִׁלַּחְתָּ רֵיקָם וּזְרֹעוֹת יְתֹמִים יְדֻכָּא ¹⁰ עַל־כֵּן סְבִיבוֹתֶיךָ פַחִים וִיבַהֶלְךָ פַּחַד פִּתְאֹם ¹¹ אוֹ־חֹשֶׁךְ לֹא־תִרְאֶה וְשִׁפְעַת־מַיִם תְּכַסֶּךָּ ¹² הֲלֹא־אֱלוֹהַּ גֹּבַהּ שָׁמָיִם וּרְאֵה רֹאשׁ כּוֹכָבִים כִּי־רָמּוּ ¹³ וְאָמַרְתָּ מַה־יָּדַע אֵל הַבְעַד עֲרָפֶל יִשְׁפּוֹט ¹⁴ עָבִים סֵתֶר־לוֹ וְלֹא יִרְאֶה וְחוּג שָׁמַיִם יִתְהַלָּךְ ¹⁵ הַאֹרַח עוֹלָם תִּשְׁמֹר אֲשֶׁר דָּרְכוּ מְתֵי־אָוֶן ¹⁶ אֲשֶׁר־קֻמְּטוּ וְלֹא־עֵת נָהָר יוּצַק יְסוֹדָם ¹⁷ הָאֹמְרִים לָאֵל סוּר מִמֶּנּוּ וּמַה־יִּפְעַל שַׁדַּי לָמוֹ ¹⁸ וְהוּא מִלֵּא בָתֵּיהֶם טוֹב וַעֲצַת רְשָׁעִים רָחֲקָה מֶנִּי ¹⁹ יִרְאוּ צַדִּיקִים וְיִשְׂמָחוּ וְנָקִי יִלְעַג־לָמוֹ ²⁰ אִם־לֹא נִכְחַד קִימָנוּ וְיִתְרָם אָכְלָה אֵשׁ ²¹ הַסְכֶּן־נָא עִמּוֹ וּשְׁלָם בָּהֶם תְּבוֹאַתְךָ טוֹבָה ²² קַח־נָא מִפִּיו תּוֹרָה וְשִׂים אֲמָרָיו בִּלְבָבֶךָ ²³ אִם־תָּשׁוּב עַד־שַׁדַּי תִּבָּנֶה תַּרְחִיק עַוְלָה מֵאָהֳלֶךָ ²⁴ וְשִׁית־עַל־עָפָר בָּצֶר וּבְצוּר נְחָלִים אוֹפִיר ²⁵ וְהָיָה שַׁדַּי בְּצָרֶיךָ וְכֶסֶף תּוֹעָפוֹת לָךְ ²⁶ כִּי־אָז עַל־שַׁדַּי תִּתְעַנָּג וְתִשָּׂא אֶל־אֱלוֹהַּ פָּנֶיךָ ²⁷ תַּעְתִּיר אֵלָיו וְיִשְׁמָעֶךָּ וּנְדָרֶיךָ תְשַׁלֵּם ²⁸ וְתִגְזַר־אוֹמֶר וְיָקָם לָךְ וְעַל־דְּרָכֶיךָ נָגַהּ אוֹר ²⁹ כִּי־הִשְׁפִּילוּ וַתֹּאמֶר גֵּוָה וְשַׁח עֵינַיִם יוֹשִׁעַ ³⁰ יְמַלֵּט אִי־נָקִי וְנִמְלַט בְּבֹר כַּפֶּיךָ

¹ וַיַּעַן אִיּוֹב וַיֹּאמַר ² גַּם־הַיּוֹם מְרִי שִׂחִי יָדִי כָּבְדָה עַל־אַנְחָתִי ³ מִי־יִתֵּן יָדַעְתִּי וְאֶמְצָאֵהוּ אָבוֹא עַד־תְּכוּנָתוֹ ⁴ אֶעֶרְכָה לְפָנָיו מִשְׁפָּט וּפִי אֲמַלֵּא תוֹכָחוֹת ⁵ אֵדְעָה מִלִּים יַעֲנֵנִי וְאָבִינָה מַה־יֹּאמַר לִי ⁶ הַבְּרָב־כֹּחַ יָרִיב עִמָּדִי לֹא אַךְ־הוּא יָשִׂם בִּי ⁷ שָׁם יָשָׁר נוֹכָח עִמּוֹ וַאֲפַלְּטָה לָנֶצַח מִשֹּׁפְטִי ⁸ הֵן קֶדֶם אֶהֱלֹךְ וְאֵינֶנּוּ וְאָחוֹר וְלֹא־אָבִין לוֹ

4 Is it from your fear that he reproves you; that he comes with you into the judgment? 5 Is not your evil great? But there is no end to your iniquities. 6 For you bind your brothers to a pledge for free, and the clothes of the naked you strip off. 7 You do not give a drink of water to the weary,[2] and from the hungry you withhold bread. 8 And a man of the arm[3]—to him is the earth. And the raised of face[4] live in it. 9 Widows you sent away empty, and the arms of the fatherless have been broken.[5] 10 Therefore, traps are all around you and sudden fear terrifies you—11 or darkness you will not see—and an abundance of water covers you. 12 Is not God in the height of the heavens? See! At the top of the stars that are on high. 13 You say, 'What does God know? Through a thick cloud, can he judge? 14 Dark clouds are a covering for him, and he does not see; and he walks around in the vault of the heavens.'[6] 15 Will you keep the way of antiquity, which men of iniquity have trodden, 16 who were seized before their time[7]—their foundation was poured like a stream—17 the ones who say to God, 'Turn away from us;' and, 'What can Shaddai do for us?' 18 Yet he filled their houses with good, but the counsel of the wicked is far from me.[8] 19 The righteous see it and rejoice, and the innocent mock them: 20 'Truly, our adversary[9] is destroyed, and their remnant, fire has consumed.' 21 Be reconciled, now, with him, and be complete. By this,[10] prosperity will come to you.[11] 22 Take, now, instruction from his mouth, and place his utterances in your heart. 23 If you return to Shaddai, you will be built up—if[12] you distance injustice from your tents[13] 24 and lay gold upon the dust, and the gold of Ophir[14] among the rock of the streams,[15] 25 and if Shaddai will be your gold[16] and the grandeurs[17] of silver to you, 26 for then you will delight yourself in Shaddai, and you will lift up your face to God. 27 You will make a supplication to him, and he will hear you. You will pay your vows. 28 You will decree a command, and it will stand for you; and upon your paths, light will shine. 29 For when they bring low, you will say, 'Pride!'[18] and the lowly of eyes he will save. 30 He delivers the unclean,[19] and he will be delivered by the cleanness of your hands." 23:1 Job answered and said, 2 "Also today my complaint is bitter. My hand[1] is heavy upon my groaning. 3 If only I knew that I could find him![2] I would come even to his dwelling place! 4 I would set out a case before him, and my mouth I would fill with arguments. 5 I would know the words that he would answer me, and I would understand what he would tell me. 6 In great power will he contend with me? No, but he would place[3] it against me. 7 There, the upright person reasons with him, and I could be delivered forever from my judge. 8 Behold, forward I go, and he is not there; and backwards, but I do not perceive him.

21

שְׂמֹאול בַּעֲשֹׂתוֹ וְלֹא־אָחַז יַעְטֹף יָמִין וְלֹא אֶרְאֶה׃ 10 כִּי־יָדַע דֶּרֶךְ עִמָּדִי בְּחָנַנִי כַּזָּהָב אֵצֵא׃ 11 בַּאֲשֻׁרוֹ אָחֲזָה רַגְלִי דַּרְכּוֹ שָׁמַרְתִּי וְלֹא־אָט׃ 12 מִצְוַת שְׂפָתָיו וְלֹא אָמִישׁ מֵחֻקִּי צָפַנְתִּי אִמְרֵי־פִיו׃ 13 וְהוּא בְאֶחָד וּמִי יְשִׁיבֶנּוּ וְנַפְשׁוֹ אִוְּתָה וַיָּעַשׂ׃ 14 כִּי יַשְׁלִים חֻקִּי וְכָהֵנָּה רַבּוֹת עִמּוֹ׃ 15 עַל־כֵּן מִפָּנָיו אֶבָּהֵל אֶתְבּוֹנֵן וְאֶפְחַד מִמֶּנּוּ׃ 16 וְאֵל הֵרַךְ לִבִּי וְשַׁדַּי הִבְהִילָנִי׃ 17 כִּי־לֹא נִצְמַתִּי מִפְּנֵי־חֹשֶׁךְ וּמִפָּנַי כִּסָּה־אֹפֶל׃

פרק כד

1 מַדּוּעַ מִשַּׁדַּי לֹא־נִצְפְּנוּ עִתִּים וְיֹדְעָיו לֹא־חָזוּ יָמָיו׃ 2 גְּבֻלוֹת יַשִּׂיגוּ עֵדֶר גָּזְלוּ וַיִּרְעוּ׃ 3 חֲמוֹר יְתוֹמִים יִנְהָגוּ יַחְבְּלוּ שׁוֹר אַלְמָנָה׃ 4 יַטּוּ אֶבְיוֹנִים מִדָּרֶךְ יַחַד חֻבְּאוּ עֲנִיֵּי־אָרֶץ׃ 5 הֵן פְּרָאִים בַּמִּדְבָּר יָצְאוּ בְּפָעֳלָם מְשַׁחֲרֵי לַטָּרֶף עֲרָבָה לוֹ לֶחֶם לַנְּעָרִים׃ 6 בַּשָּׂדֶה בְּלִילוֹ יִקְצוֹרוּ וְכֶרֶם רָשָׁע יְלַקֵּשׁוּ׃ 7 עָרוֹם יָלִינוּ מִבְּלִי לְבוּשׁ וְאֵין כְּסוּת בַּקָּרָה׃ 8 מִזֶּרֶם הָרִים יִרְטָבוּ וּמִבְּלִי מַחְסֶה חִבְּקוּ־צוּר׃ 9 יִגְזְלוּ מִשֹּׁד יָתוֹם וְעַל־עָנִי יַחְבֹּלוּ׃ 10 עָרוֹם הִלְּכוּ בְּלִי לְבוּשׁ וּרְעֵבִים נָשְׂאוּ עֹמֶר׃ 11 בֵּין־שׁוּרֹתָם יַצְהִירוּ יְקָבִים דָּרְכוּ וַיִּצְמָאוּ׃ 12 מֵעִיר מְתִים יִנְאָקוּ וְנֶפֶשׁ־חֲלָלִים תְּשַׁוֵּעַ וֶאֱלוֹהַּ לֹא־יָשִׂים תִּפְלָה׃ 13 הֵמָּה הָיוּ בְּמֹרְדֵי־אוֹר לֹא־הִכִּירוּ דְרָכָיו וְלֹא יָשְׁבוּ בִּנְתִיבֹתָיו׃ 14 לָאוֹר יָקוּם רוֹצֵחַ יִקְטָל־עָנִי וְאֶבְיוֹן וּבַלַּיְלָה יְהִי כַגַּנָּב׃ 15 וְעֵין נֹאֵף שָׁמְרָה נֶשֶׁף לֵאמֹר לֹא־תְשׁוּרֵנִי עָיִן וְסֵתֶר פָּנִים יָשִׂים׃ 16 חָתַר בַּחֹשֶׁךְ בָּתִּים יוֹמָם חִתְּמוּ־לָמוֹ לֹא־יָדְעוּ אוֹר׃ 17 כִּי יַחְדָּו בֹּקֶר לָמוֹ צַלְמָוֶת כִּי־יַכִּיר בַּלְהוֹת צַלְמָוֶת׃ 18 קַל־הוּא עַל־פְּנֵי־מַיִם תְּקֻלַּל חֶלְקָתָם בָּאָרֶץ לֹא־יִפְנֶה דֶּרֶךְ כְּרָמִים׃

9 He turns[4] left in his working, but I do not behold him; he turns right, but I do not see him. 10 Because he knows the way with me. If he tests me, I will come out like gold. 11 On his footstep, my foot has grasped. His path I have kept and not turned aside. 12 And I have not departed from the commandment of his lips; More than my portion, I treasured up the words of his mouth. 13 But he is altogether unique,[5] and who can turn him back? His soul desires something, and he does it. 14 For he completes my portion—and many things like these are with him. 15 Therefore, before his face, I fear. I consider and I am afraid of him. 16 For God has made my heart timid, and Shaddai has terrified me. 17 Yet, I have not been annihilated because of the darkness; and neither from the darkness that covers my face.[6] 24:1 Why are times not stored up from Shaddai, and why have the ones who know him not seen his days? 2 They overtake borders; They seize a flock and pasture it. 3 They drive away the donkey of orphans, and they hold the ox of a widow for a pledge. 4 They turn the needy from the way. The poor of the land are hidden. 5 Behold, as wild donkeys go out in the desert, in their work they are seekers of prey.[1] The steppe is the place for them where they find food for their children.[2] 6 They reap in the field; in his fodder. And from the field of the wicked, they take the spring crop.[3] 7 Naked[4] they spend the night without clothing and have no covering in the cold. 8 From the downpour of the mountains they are wet, and without a cover they embrace a rock. 9 They tear away the orphan from the breast, and over the poor they take a pledge. 10 They walk about naked[5] without clothing, and while they are hungry, they carry sheaves.[6] 11 Between their rows they press olive oil. They tread wine presses and are thirsty. 12 From a city, men groan, and a soul of wounded men cries out for help. Yet, God does not pay attention[7] to impropriety.[8] 13 They are among the rebels against light.[9] They do not know its ways and they do not dwell in its paths.[10] 14 At dawn a murderer rises. He will kill the poor and needy. And in the night, he will be like[11] a thief. 15 And the eye of the adulterer keeps watch for twilight, saying, 'An eye will not see me,' and a cover he puts over his face. 16 He digs into houses in the dark. They seal themselves up[12] in the daytime. They do not know the light. 17 For all of them[13]—morning for them is deep darkness, because he recognizes[14] the terrors of deep darkness. 18 He is light upon the face of the waters.[15] Their portion is cursed in the land. He does not turn the way of the vineyards.

פרק כה

19 צִיָּה גַם־חֹם יִגְזְלוּ מֵימֵי־שֶׁלֶג שְׁאוֹל חָטָאוּ 20 יִשְׁכָּחֵהוּ רֶחֶם מְתָקוֹ רִמָּה עוֹד לֹא־יִזָּכֵר וַתִּשָּׁבֵר כָּעֵץ עַוְלָה 21 רֹעֶה עֲקָרָה לֹא תֵלֵד וְאַלְמָנָה לֹא יְיֵטִיב 22 וּמָשַׁךְ אַבִּירִים בְּכֹחוֹ יָקוּם וְלֹא־יַאֲמִין בַּחַיִּין 23 יִתֶּן־לוֹ לָבֶטַח וְיִשָּׁעֵן וְעֵינֵיהוּ עַל־דַּרְכֵיהֶם 24 רוֹמּוּ מְּעַט וְאֵינֶנּוּ וְהֻמְּכוּ כַּכֹּל יִקָּפְצוּן וּכְרֹאשׁ שִׁבֹּלֶת יִמָּלוּ 25 וְאִם־לֹא אֵפוֹ מִי יַכְזִיבֵנִי וְיָשֵׂם לְאַל מִלָּתִי

1 וַיַּעַן בִּלְדַּד הַשֻּׁחִי וַיֹּאמַר

2 הַמְשֵׁל וָפַחַד עִמּוֹ עֹשֶׂה שָׁלוֹם בִּמְרוֹמָיו 3 הֲיֵשׁ מִסְפָּר לִגְדוּדָיו וְעַל־מִי לֹא־יָקוּם אוֹרֵהוּ 4 וּמַה־יִּצְדַּק אֱנוֹשׁ עִם־אֵל וּמַה־יִּזְכֶּה יְלוּד אִשָּׁה 5 הֵן עַד־יָרֵחַ וְלֹא יַאֲהִיל וְכוֹכָבִים לֹא־זַכּוּ בְעֵינָיו 6 אַף כִּי־אֱנוֹשׁ רִמָּה וּבֶן־אָדָם תּוֹלֵעָה

פרק כו

1 וַיַּעַן אִיּוֹב וַיֹּאמַר

2 מֶה־עָזַרְתָּ לְלֹא־כֹחַ הוֹשַׁעְתָּ זְרוֹעַ לֹא־עֹז 3 מַה־יָּעַצְתָּ לְלֹא חָכְמָה וְתוּשִׁיָּה לָרֹב הוֹדָעְתָּ

19 Drought and also heat dry up[16] the waters of snow. Sheol seizes[17] those who have sinned. 20 The womb will forget him. The worm finds him sweet.[18] He will not be remembered. Injustice will be broken as a tree. 21 He gets involved with a barren woman who will not give birth, and to the widow he does not do good. 22 He drags the mighty with his strength. He arises and does not believe in life. 23 He gives to him for security, and he is supported, and his eyes are on their ways. 24 They are exalted a little and he is gone. They are brought low, and like all they are gathered together, and like a head of grain they languish. 25 And if not, then who will prove me a liar, and make[19] my speech nothing?"[20] 25:1 Bildad the Shuhite answered and said, 2 "Exercising dominion and fear are with him. He makes peace in his heights. 3 Is there a number to his troops? And upon whom does his light not arise? 4 And how can man be righteous with God? Or how can one born of a woman be pure? 5 Behold, even the moon does not shine,[1] and the stars are not pure in his eyes. 6 How much less a man, who is a worm, and the son of man, who is a worm."[2] 26:1 Then Job answered and said, 2 "How have you helped without power? How[1] have you saved an arm without strength? 3 How have you counseled without wisdom, and declared sound wisdom for the multitude?

פרק כז

1 וַיֹּסֶף אִיּוֹב שְׂאֵת מְשָׁלוֹ וַיֹּאמַר

2 חַי־אֵל הֵסִיר מִשְׁפָּטִי וְשַׁדַּי הֵמַר נַפְשִׁי 3 כִּי־כָל־עוֹד נִשְׁמָתִי בִי וְרוּחַ אֱלוֹהַּ בְּאַפִּי 4 אִם־תְּדַבֵּרְנָה שְׂפָתַי עַוְלָה וּלְשׁוֹנִי אִם־יֶהְגֶּה רְמִיָּה 5 חָלִילָה לִּי אִם־אַצְדִּיק אֶתְכֶם עַד־אֶגְוָע לֹא־אָסִיר תֻּמָּתִי מִמֶּנִּי 6 בְּצִדְקָתִי הֶחֱזַקְתִּי וְלֹא אַרְפֶּהָ לֹא־יֶחֱרַף לְבָבִי מִיָּמָי 7 יְהִי כְרָשָׁע אֹיְבִי וּמִתְקוֹמְמִי כְעַוָּל 8 כִּי מַה־תִּקְוַת חָנֵף כִּי יִבְצָע כִּי יֵשֶׁל אֱלוֹהַּ נַפְשׁוֹ 9 הַצַעֲקָתוֹ יִשְׁמַע אֵל כִּי־תָבוֹא עָלָיו צָרָה 10 אִם־עַל־שַׁדַּי יִתְעַנָּג יִקְרָא אֱלוֹהַּ בְּכָל־עֵת 11 אוֹרֶה אֶתְכֶם בְּיַד־אֵל אֲשֶׁר עִם־שַׁדַּי לֹא אֲכַחֵד 12 הֵן־אַתֶּם כֻּלְּכֶם חֲזִיתֶם וְלָמָּה־זֶּה הֶבֶל תֶּהְבָּלוּ 13 זֶה חֵלֶק־אָדָם רָשָׁע עִם־אֵל וְנַחֲלַת עָרִיצִים מִשַּׁדַּי יִקָּחוּ 14 אִם־יִרְבּוּ בָנָיו לְמוֹ־חָרֶב וְצֶאֱצָאָיו לֹא יִשְׂבְּעוּ־לָחֶם 15 שְׂרִידָיו בַּמָּוֶת יִקָּבֵרוּ וְאַלְמְנֹתָיו לֹא תִבְכֶּינָה 16 אִם־יִצְבֹּר כֶּעָפָר כָּסֶף וְכַחֹמֶר יָכִין מַלְבּוּשׁ 17 יָכִין וְצַדִּיק יִלְבָּשׁ וְכֶסֶף נָקִי יַחֲלֹק 18 בָּנָה כָעָשׁ בֵּיתוֹ וּכְסֻכָּה עָשָׂה נֹצֵר 19 עָשִׁיר יִשְׁכַּב וְלֹא יֵאָסֵף עֵינָיו פָּקַח וְאֵינֶנּוּ 20 תַּשִּׂיגֵהוּ כַמַּיִם בַּלָּהוֹת לַיְלָה גְּנָבַתּוּ סוּפָה 21 יִשָּׂאֵהוּ קָדִים וְיֵלַךְ וִישָׂעֲרֵהוּ מִמְּקֹמוֹ 22 וְיַשְׁלֵךְ עָלָיו וְלֹא יַחְמֹל מִיָּדוֹ בָּרוֹחַ יִבְרָח 23 יִשְׂפֹּק עָלֵימוֹ כַפֵּימוֹ וְיִשְׁרֹק עָלָיו מִמְּקֹמוֹ

4 אֶת־מִי הִגַּדְתָּ מִלִּין וְנִשְׁמַת־מִי יָצְאָה מִמֶּךָּ 5 הָרְפָאִים יְחוֹלָלוּ מִתַּחַת מַיִם וְשֹׁכְנֵיהֶם 6 עָרוֹם שְׁאוֹל נֶגְדּוֹ וְאֵין כְּסוּת לָאֲבַדּוֹן 7 נֹטֶה צָפוֹן עַל־תֹּהוּ תֹּלֶה אֶרֶץ עַל־בְּלִי־מָה 8 צֹרֵר־מַיִם בְּעָבָיו וְלֹא־נִבְקַע עָנָן תַּחְתָּם 9 מְאַחֵז פְּנֵי־כִסֵּה פַּרְשֵׁז עָלָיו עֲנָנוֹ 10 חֹק־חָג עַל־פְּנֵי־מָיִם עַד־תַּכְלִית אוֹר עִם־חֹשֶׁךְ 11 עַמּוּדֵי שָׁמַיִם יְרוֹפָפוּ וְיִתְמְהוּ מִגַּעֲרָתוֹ 12 בְּכֹחוֹ רָגַע הַיָּם וּבִתְבוּנָתוֹ מָחַץ רָהַב 13 בְּרוּחוֹ שָׁמַיִם שִׁפְרָה חֹלֲלָה יָדוֹ נָחָשׁ בָּרִיחַ 14 הֶן־אֵלֶּה קְצוֹת דְּרָכָיו וּמַה־שֵּׁמֶץ דָּבָר נִשְׁמַע־בּוֹ וְרַעַם גְּבוּרֹתָיו מִי יִתְבּוֹנָן

4 To whom have you told words,[2] and whose spirit[3] has come out of you? 5 The dead writhe from beneath the waters and their inhabitants. 6 Sheol is naked in front of him, and there is no covering for Abaddon. 7 He stretches out the north over formlessness. He hangs the land over nothing.[4] 8 He binds up the waters in his clouds, and the cloud does not burst under them. 9 He encloses the face of the throne.[5] He spreads[6] his cloud upon it. 10 He draws a circle; a boundary[7] on the face of the waters, until the end of light with darkness.[8] 11 The pillars of heaven shake,[9] and they are astonished from his rebuke. 12 With his power he disturbs[10] the sea, and with his understanding he smites Rahab. 13 By his spirit the heavens are a beauty.[11] His hand pierced the fleeing serpent. 14 Behold, these are but the ends of his ways. And what whisper of a word is heard in it? But the thunder of his might,[12] who can understand?" 27:1 Job continued[1] to take up his discourse, and said, 2 "As long as God lives,[2] he has turned away my justice. And Shaddai—he has embittered my soul. 3 For as long as[3] my breath is in me, and the spirit of God is in my nose, 4 my lips will not speak injustice, and my tongue will not utter deceit.[4] 5 Far be it from me[5] if I should declare you as righteous. Until I die, I will not turn my integrity away from me. 6 To my righteousness I have taken hold and will not let it go. My heart does not reproach me for any of my days.[6] 7 May my enemy be like a wicked person, and the one rising up against me like an unrighteous person. 8 For what is the hope of the godless when he cuts it off; when God takes away[7] his soul? 9 Will God hear his cry when distress comes upon him? 10 Will he implore Shaddai? Will he call God in every moment? 11 I will teach you by the power[8] of God. That which is with Shaddai I will not conceal. 12 Behold, you, even all of you, have seen it. And why this breath that you breathe out? 13 This is the portion of a man who is wicked with God, and the inheritance of the ruthless that they receive from Shaddai. 14 If his children multiply, the sword is for them. And his offspring will not be satisfied with bread. 15 His survivors will be buried in the death.[9] His widows will not cry. 16 If he heaps up silver as dust, and like clay[10] he prepares attire—17 he prepares it, but the righteous will wear it—and silver, the innocent will divide. 18 He builds his house as the moth; as a booth that a watchman makes. 19 He lies down rich, but he will not be gathered. He opens his eyes, and he is not. 20 Terrors overtake him like the waters.[11] At night, a storm steals him away. 21 An east wind carries him away, and he departs; And it sweeps him from his place. 22 He shoots at him,[12] and does not spare. He surely flees from his power.[13] 23 He claps his hands at him, and hisses at him[14] from his place.

24

פרק כח

1 כִּי יֵשׁ לַכֶּסֶף מוֹצָא וּמָקוֹם לַזָּהָב יָזֹקּוּ 2 בַּרְזֶל מֵעָפָר יֻקָּח וְאֶבֶן יָצוּק נְחוּשָׁה 3 קֵץ שָׂם לַחֹשֶׁךְ וּלְכָל־תַּכְלִית הוּא חוֹקֵר אֶבֶן אֹפֶל וְצַלְמָוֶת 4 פָּרַץ נַחַל מֵעִם־גָּר הַנִּשְׁכָּחִים מִנִּי־רָגֶל דַּלּוּ מֵאֱנוֹשׁ נָעוּ 5 אֶרֶץ מִמֶּנָּה יֵצֵא־לָחֶם וְתַחְתֶּיהָ נֶהְפַּךְ כְּמוֹ־אֵשׁ 6 מְקוֹם־סַפִּיר אֲבָנֶיהָ וְעַפְרֹת זָהָב לוֹ 7 נָתִיב לֹא־יְדָעוֹ עָיִט וְלֹא שְׁזָפַתּוּ עֵין אַיָּה 8 לֹא־הִדְרִיכֻהוּ בְנֵי־שָׁחַץ לֹא־עָדָה עָלָיו שָׁחַל 9 בַּחַלָּמִישׁ שָׁלַח יָדוֹ הָפַךְ מִשֹּׁרֶשׁ הָרִים 10 בַּצּוּרוֹת יְאֹרִים בִּקֵּעַ וְכָל־יְקָר רָאֲתָה עֵינוֹ 11 מִבְּכִי נְהָרוֹת חִבֵּשׁ וְתַעֲלֻמָהּ יֹצִא אוֹר פ 12 וְהַחָכְמָה מֵאַיִן תִּמָּצֵא וְאֵי זֶה מְקוֹם בִּינָה 13 לֹא־יָדַע אֱנוֹשׁ עֶרְכָּהּ וְלֹא תִמָּצֵא בְּאֶרֶץ הַחַיִּים 14 תְּהוֹם אָמַר לֹא בִי־הִיא וְיָם אָמַר אֵין עִמָּדִי 15 לֹא־יֻתַּן סְגוֹר תַּחְתֶּיהָ וְלֹא יִשָּׁקֵל כֶּסֶף מְחִירָהּ 16 לֹא־תְסֻלֶּה בְּכֶתֶם אוֹפִיר בְּשֹׁהַם יָקָר וְסַפִּיר 17 לֹא־יַעַרְכֶנָּה זָהָב וּזְכוֹכִית וּתְמוּרָתָהּ כְּלִי־פָז 18 רָאמוֹת וְגָבִישׁ לֹא יִזָּכֵר וּמֶשֶׁךְ חָכְמָה מִפְּנִינִים 19 לֹא־יַעַרְכֶנָּה פִּטְדַת־כּוּשׁ בְּכֶתֶם טָהוֹר לֹא תְסֻלֶּה 20 וְהַחָכְמָה מֵאַיִן תָּבוֹא וְאֵי זֶה מְקוֹם בִּינָה 21 וְנֶעֶלְמָה מֵעֵינֵי כָל־חָי וּמֵעוֹף הַשָּׁמַיִם נִסְתָּרָה 22 אֲבַדּוֹן וָמָוֶת אָמְרוּ בְּאָזְנֵינוּ שָׁמַעְנוּ שִׁמְעָהּ 23 אֱלֹהִים הֵבִין דַּרְכָּהּ וְהוּא יָדַע אֶת־מְקוֹמָהּ 24 כִּי־הוּא לִקְצוֹת־הָאָרֶץ יַבִּיט תַּחַת כָּל־הַשָּׁמַיִם יִרְאֶה 25 לַעֲשׂוֹת לָרוּחַ מִשְׁקָל וּמַיִם תִּכֵּן בְּמִדָּה 26 בַּעֲשֹׂתוֹ לַמָּטָר חֹק וְדֶרֶךְ לַחֲזִיז קֹלוֹת 27 אָז רָאָהּ וַיְסַפְּרָהּ הֱכִינָהּ וְגַם־חֲקָרָהּ 28 וַיֹּאמֶר לָאָדָם הֵן יִרְאַת אֲדֹנָי הִיא חָכְמָה וְסוּר מֵרָע בִּינָה

פרק כט

1 וַיֹּסֶף אִיּוֹב שְׂאֵת מְשָׁלוֹ וַיֹּאמַר

2 מִי־יִתְּנֵנִי כְיַרְחֵי־קֶדֶם כִּימֵי אֱלוֹהַּ יִשְׁמְרֵנִי 3 בְּהִלּוֹ נֵרוֹ עֲלֵי רֹאשִׁי לְאוֹרוֹ אֵלֶךְ חֹשֶׁךְ 4 כַּאֲשֶׁר הָיִיתִי בִּימֵי חָרְפִּי בְּסוֹד אֱלוֹהַּ עֲלֵי אָהֳלִי 5 בְּעוֹד שַׁדַּי עִמָּדִי סְבִיבוֹתַי נְעָרָי 6 בִּרְחֹץ הֲלִיכַי בְּחֵמָה וְצוּר יָצוּק עִמָּדִי פַּלְגֵי־שָׁמֶן 7 בְּצֵאתִי שַׁעַר עֲלֵי־קָרֶת בָּרְחוֹב אָכִין מוֹשָׁבִי

28:1 For silver has a point of supply,[1] and a place for the gold which they refine. **2** Iron is taken from the dust of the land, and stone, one pours like copper. **3** He puts an end to darkness, and to every end he explores—stone, darkness, and gloom. **4** He breaks open a stream away from the sojourner. They are forgotten by the foot.[2] They languish. From men they totter. **5** A land from which[3] bread comes out; and under it, it is overturned as a fire. **6** A place where sapphires[4] are its stones; and it has dust of gold.[5] **7** A path that a bird of prey does not know,[6] and the eye of a falcon[7] has not seen.[8] **8** Wild animals[9] have not trodden it, nor has the lion passed on.[10] **9** He stretches out his hand against the flint. He overturns the mountains from the root. **10** He cleaves channels in the rocks, and every precious thing, his eye has seen. **11** He restrains the streams from weeping, and the secret thing he brings out to light. **12** But where then can wisdom be found, and where is a place of understanding? **13** Man does not know its value, and it is not found in the land of the living. **14** Deep says, 'It is not in me,' and Yamm says, 'It is not with me.' **15** Gold[11] is not given for it, and silver will not be measured for its price. **16** It cannot be weighed with the gold of Ophir, with the precious onyx,[12] or the sapphire. **17** Gold and glass do not compare with it, and its exchange is not[13] an object of fine gold. **18** Neither coral nor crystal is mentioned. The drawing up of wisdom is more valuable than rubies.[14] **19** The topaz of Cush does not compare with it.[15] It cannot be weighted with pure gold. **20** And wisdom, from where does it come, and where is a place of understanding? **21** It is concealed from the eyes of all of the living, and from the birds of the sky, it is hidden. **22** Abaddon and Death say, 'With our ears we heard its report.' **23** God understands its way, and he knows its place. **24** For he looks to the ends of the earth. All under the heavens, he sees—**25** making[16] weight for the wind, and waters that he meted out by a measure. **26** When he made[17] a decree for the rain, and a way for the lightning of the thunder,[18] **27** then he saw it and recounted it. He established it, and also examined it. **28** He said to man,[19] 'Behold, the fear of the Lord, that is wisdom; and to depart from evil is understanding.'" **29:1** Job continued[1] to take up his discourse, and said, **2** "If only I were like in the months of old, as in the days when God watched over me; **3** with the shining of his lamp[2] upon my head. By its light I walked in darkness. **4** Just as I was in the days of my youth, with the friendship[3] of God over my tent; **5** when Shaddai was still with me—when[4] my servants were still around me, **6** in the washing of my steps with cream,[5] and the rock poured out over me[6] streams of oil; **7** in my exiting the gate of the city,[7] in the open plaza I would establish my seat.

8 רָאוּנִי נְעָרִים וְנֶחְבָּאוּ וִישִׁישִׁים קָמוּ עָמָדוּ 9 שָׂרִים עָצְרוּ בְמִלִּים וְכַף יָשִׂימוּ לְפִיהֶם 10 קוֹל־נְגִידִים נֶחְבָּאוּ וּלְשׁוֹנָם לְחִכָּם דָּבֵקָה 11 כִּי אֹזֶן שָׁמְעָה וַתְּאַשְּׁרֵנִי וְעַיִן רָאֲתָה וַתְּעִידֵנִי 12 כִּי־אֲמַלֵּט עָנִי מְשַׁוֵּעַ וְיָתוֹם וְלֹא־עֹזֵר לוֹ 13 בִּרְכַּת אֹבֵד עָלַי תָּבֹא וְלֵב אַלְמָנָה אַרְנִן 14 צֶדֶק לָבַשְׁתִּי וַיִּלְבָּשֵׁנִי כִּמְעִיל וְצָנִיף מִשְׁפָּטִי 15 עֵינַיִם הָיִיתִי לַעִוֵּר וְרַגְלַיִם לַפִּסֵּחַ אָנִי 16 אָב אָנֹכִי לָאֶבְיוֹנִים וְרִב לֹא־יָדַעְתִּי אֶחְקְרֵהוּ 17 וָאֲשַׁבְּרָה מְתַלְּעוֹת עַוָּל וּמִשִּׁנָּיו אַשְׁלִיךְ טָרֶף 18 וָאֹמַר עִם־קִנִּי אֶגְוָע וְכַחוֹל אַרְבֶּה יָמִים 19 שָׁרְשִׁי פָתוּחַ אֱלֵי־מָיִם וְטַל יָלִין בִּקְצִירִי 20 כְּבוֹדִי חָדָשׁ עִמָּדִי וְקַשְׁתִּי בְּיָדִי תַחֲלִיף 21 לִי־שָׁמְעוּ וְיִחֵלּוּ וְיִדְּמוּ לְמוֹ עֲצָתִי 22 אַחֲרֵי דְבָרִי לֹא יִשְׁנוּ וְעָלֵימוֹ תִּטֹּף מִלָּתִי 23 וְיִחֲלוּ כַמָּטָר לִי וּפִיהֶם פָּעֲרוּ לְמַלְקוֹשׁ 24 אֶשְׂחַק אֲלֵהֶם לֹא יַאֲמִינוּ וְאוֹר פָּנַי לֹא יַפִּילוּן 25 אֶבְחַר דַּרְכָּם וְאֵשֵׁב רֹאשׁ וְאֶשְׁכּוֹן כְּמֶלֶךְ בַּגְּדוּד כַּאֲשֶׁר אֲבֵלִים יְנַחֵם

פרק ל

1 וְעַתָּה שָׂחֲקוּ עָלַי צְעִירִים מִמֶּנִּי לְיָמִים אֲשֶׁר־מָאַסְתִּי אֲבוֹתָם לָשִׁית עִם־כַּלְבֵי צֹאנִי 2 גַּם־כֹּחַ יְדֵיהֶם לָמָּה לִּי עָלֵימוֹ אָבַד כָּלַח 3 בְּחֶסֶר וּבְכָפָן גַּלְמוּד הָעֹרְקִים צִיָּה אֶמֶשׁ שׁוֹאָה וּמְשֹׁאָה 4 הַקֹּטְפִים מַלּוּחַ עֲלֵי־שִׂיחַ וְשֹׁרֶשׁ רְתָמִים לַחְמָם 5 מִן־גֵּו יְגֹרָשׁוּ יָרִיעוּ עָלֵימוֹ כַּגַּנָּב 6 בַּעֲרוּץ נְחָלִים לִשְׁכֹּן חֹרֵי עָפָר וְכֵפִים 7 בֵּין־שִׂיחִים יִנְהָקוּ תַּחַת חָרוּל יְסֻפָּחוּ 8 בְּנֵי־נָבָל גַּם־בְּנֵי בְלִי־שֵׁם נִכְּאוּ מִן־הָאָרֶץ 9 וְעַתָּה נְגִינָתָם הָיִיתִי וָאֱהִי לָהֶם לְמִלָּה 10 תִּעֲבוּנִי רָחֲקוּ מֶנִּי וּמִפָּנַי לֹא־חָשְׂכוּ רֹק 11 כִּי־יִתְרוֹ פִתַּח וַיְעַנֵּנִי וְרֶסֶן מִפָּנַי שִׁלֵּחוּ 12 עַל־יָמִין פִּרְחַח יָקוּמוּ רַגְלַי שִׁלֵּחוּ וַיָּסֹלּוּ עָלַי אָרְחוֹת אֵידָם 13 נָתְסוּ נְתִיבָתִי לְהַוָּתִי יֹעִילוּ לֹא עֹזֵר לָמוֹ 14 כְּפֶרֶץ רָחָב יֶאֱתָיוּ תַּחַת שֹׁאָה הִתְגַּלְגָּלוּ 15 הָהְפַּךְ עָלַי בַּלָּהוֹת תִּרְדֹּף כָּרוּחַ נְדִבָתִי וּכְעָב עָבְרָה יְשֻׁעָתִי 16 וְעַתָּה עָלַי תִּשְׁתַּפֵּךְ נַפְשִׁי יֹאחֲזוּנִי יְמֵי־עֹנִי

8 The young men saw me and hid themselves, and the aged rose up and stood. 9 Princes refrained words, and they placed a hand on their mouths.[8] 10 The voices of nobles was hidden,[9] and their tongues stuck to their palates.[10] 11 For an ear would hear me and call me happy; and an eye would see me and bear witness of me. 12 For I delivered the poor who cried out for help, and the orphan who had no helper.[11] 13 The blessing of a perishing man would come upon me, and the heart of the widow, I caused to sing for joy. 14 I wore righteousness and it wore me; my justice—like a robe and a turban. 15 Eyes I was to the blind, and feet I was to the lame. 16 Father I was to the to the needy, and the case I did not know, I investigated it. 17 I would break the fangs of the unjust and from his teeth I cast prey. 18 I said, 'With my nest, I will expire, and like the sand I will multiply days. 19 My root will be opened up toward the waters, and dew will remain on my branch.[12] 20 My abundance will be new with me[13] and my bow will replace itself in my hand.' 21 To me, people listened, and they waited. They kept still for my counsel. 22 After my speech they did not speak again, and upon them my word would drop. 23 They waited for me as for the rain, and their mouths opened wide for the latter rain. 24 I smiled toward them. They did not believe; and the light of my face, they did not cause to fall. 25 I chose out their way and sat as the head. I dwelled as a king in the troop, just as one who comforts mourners. 30:1 But now they laugh at me—those younger than me in days[1]—whose fathers I rejected[2] to put with the dogs of my flock. 2 Also, the strength of their hands, what was it to me? Upon them, vigor perished. 3 In want and in strong[3] famine they flee to the desert.[4] In the night, there is devastation and desolation. 4 They pluck mallow by the bushes,[5] and the root of the broom shrub for their food. 5 From a community, they are driven out. They shout out against them like they would to the thief; 6 to dwell in the slopes of streams; to dwell in[6] holes of the ground and rocks. 7 Among the bushes they bray. Under the thistles they are joined together. 8 They are children of fools; also, children of those without a name. They were scoured out of the land. 9 But now, their song of mockery, I have become. I have become to them a byword. 10 They abhor me, they are far from me, and in my presence, they do not withhold spit. 11 For he loosened his cord and afflicted me. And the restraint they let loose from my face. 12 On the right, a mob[7] arises. They let loose my feet, and they built up against me the ways of their destruction. 13 They have broken[8] my path. They benefited from my destruction.[9] There is no helper for them. 14 As a wide breach they come. Under destruction they roll themselves. 15 Terrors have been turned[10] on me. It pursues my honor as the wind. And as a cloud my salvation has passed. 16 And now upon me my soul pours itself out. Days of affliction have taken hold of me.

לַיְלָה עֲצָמַי נִקַּר מֵעָלָי וְעֹרְקַי לֹא יִשְׁכָּבוּן 18 בְּרָב־כֹּחַ יִתְחַפֵּשׂ לְבוּשִׁי כְּפִי כֻתָּנְתִּי יַאַזְרֵנִי 19 הֹרָנִי לַחֹמֶר וָאֶתְמַשֵּׁל כֶּעָפָר וָאֵפֶר 20 אֲשַׁוַּע אֵלֶיךָ וְלֹא תַעֲנֵנִי עָמַדְתִּי וַתִּתְבֹּנֶן בִּי 21 תֵּהָפֵךְ לְאַכְזָר לִי בְּעֹצֶם יָדְךָ תִשְׂטְמֵנִי 22 תִּשָּׂאֵנִי אֶל־רוּחַ תַּרְכִּיבֵנִי וּתְמֹגְגֵנִי תֻּשִׁיָּה 23 כִּי־יָדַעְתִּי מָוֶת תְּשִׁיבֵנִי וּבֵית מוֹעֵד לְכָל־חָי 24 אַךְ לֹא־בְעִי יִשְׁלַח־יָד אִם־בְּפִידוֹ לָהֶן שׁוּעַ 25 אִם־לֹא בָכִיתִי לִקְשֵׁה־יוֹם עָגְמָה נַפְשִׁי לָאֶבְיוֹן 26 כִּי טוֹב קִוִּיתִי וַיָּבֹא רָע וַאֲיַחֲלָה לְאוֹר וַיָּבֹא אֹפֶל 27 מֵעַי רֻתְּחוּ וְלֹא־דָמּוּ קִדְּמֻנִי יְמֵי־עֹנִי 28 קֹדֵר הִלַּכְתִּי בְּלֹא חַמָּה קַמְתִּי בַקָּהָל אֲשַׁוֵּעַ 29 אָח הָיִיתִי לְתַנִּים וְרֵעַ לִבְנוֹת יַעֲנָה 30 עוֹרִי שָׁחַר מֵעָלָי וְעַצְמִי־חָרָה מִנִּי־חֹרֶב 31 וַיְהִי לְאֵבֶל כִּנֹּרִי וְעֻגָבִי לְקוֹל בֹּכִים

פרק לא

1 בְּרִית כָּרַתִּי לְעֵינָי וּמָה אֶתְבּוֹנֵן עַל־בְּתוּלָה 2 וּמֶה חֵלֶק אֱלוֹהַּ מִמָּעַל וְנַחֲלַת שַׁדַּי מִמְּרֹמִים 3 הֲלֹא־אֵיד לְעַוָּל וְנֵכֶר לְפֹעֲלֵי אָוֶן 4 הֲלֹא־הוּא יִרְאֶה דְרָכָי וְכָל־צְעָדַי יִסְפּוֹר 5 אִם־הָלַכְתִּי עִם־שָׁוְא וַתַּחַשׁ עַל־מִרְמָה רַגְלִי 6 יִשְׁקְלֵנִי בְמֹאזְנֵי־צֶדֶק וְיֵדַע אֱלוֹהַּ תֻּמָּתִי 7 אִם תִּטֶּה אַשֻּׁרִי מִנִּי הַדָּרֶךְ וְאַחַר עֵינַי הָלַךְ לִבִּי וּבְכַפַּי דָּבַק מְאוּם 8 אֶזְרְעָה וְאַחֵר יֹאכֵל וְצֶאֱצָאַי יְשֹׁרָשׁוּ 9 אִם־נִפְתָּה לִבִּי עַל־אִשָּׁה וְעַל־פֶּתַח רֵעִי אָרָבְתִּי 10 תִּטְחַן לְאַחֵר אִשְׁתִּי וְעָלֶיהָ יִכְרְעוּן אֲחֵרִין 11 כִּי־הִיא זִמָּה וְהוּא עָוֹן פְּלִילִים 12 כִּי אֵשׁ הִיא עַד־אֲבַדּוֹן תֹּאכֵל וּבְכָל־תְּבוּאָתִי תְשָׁרֵשׁ 13 אִם־אֶמְאַס מִשְׁפַּט עַבְדִּי וַאֲמָתִי בְּרִבָם עִמָּדִי 14 וּמָה אֶעֱשֶׂה כִּי־יָקוּם אֵל וְכִי־יִפְקֹד מָה אֲשִׁיבֶנּוּ 15 הֲלֹא־בַבֶּטֶן עֹשֵׂנִי עָשָׂהוּ וַיְכֻנֶנּוּ בָּרֶחֶם אֶחָד 16 אִם־אֶמְנַע מֵחֵפֶץ דַּלִּים וְעֵינֵי אַלְמָנָה אֲכַלֶּה 17 וְאֹכַל פִּתִּי לְבַדִּי וְלֹא־אָכַל יָתוֹם מִמֶּנָּה 18 כִּי מִנְּעוּרַי גְּדֵלַנִי כְאָב וּמִבֶּטֶן אִמִּי אַנְחֶנָּה 19 אִם־אֶרְאֶה אוֹבֵד מִבְּלִי לְבוּשׁ וְאֵין כְּסוּת לָאֶבְיוֹן 20 אִם־לֹא בֵרֲכוּנִי חֲלָצָיו וּמִגֵּז כְּבָשַׂי יִתְחַמָּם

---

17 At night it pierces my bones from upon me and my gnawing pains do not rest. 18 With great strength, it hides itself in my clothing. Like the opening[11] of my tunic it encompasses me. 19 He has thrown me into the clay. I have become like dust and ashes. 20 I cry out to you, and you do not answer me. I stand up, and you direct your attention at me. 21 You have turned yourself cruel to me. With the power of your hand you harass me. 22 You lift me up to the wind and cause me to ride. You dissolve me in the storm.[12] 23 For I know that you will return me to death, and to the house of meeting for all of the living. 24 However, not even in a heap of ruins will he stretch out his hand. If he is in calamity, is there a cry of help for them?[13] 25 Did I not weep for the one in difficulty?[14] My soul grieved[15] for the needy. 26 For I hoped for good, and evil came. I waited for light; darkness came. 27 My inner parts have been boiled, and they are not still. Days of affliction have come before me. 28 Mourning[16] I walk, without sun; I stand up in the assembly and cry out. 29 I have become a brother to jackals, and a companion to ostriches. 30 My skin has become black upon me,[17] and my being burns from heat. 31 My harp has turned into mourning, and my flute into the sound of criers. 31:1 I made a covenant with my eyes, and how could I look at a young woman? 2 And what is the portion from God above, and the inheritance of Shaddai from the heights? 3 Is it not calamity for the unjust, and disaster for the workers of iniquity? 4 Does he not see my ways, and does he not count all my steps? 5 If I have walked with deception, and my foot has hastened upon deceit, 6 let him weigh me with the balances of righteousness, and may God know my integrity. 7 If my step has turned from the way, and if my heart has gone after my eyes, if a blemish has stuck to my hands, 8 then may I sow, and another eat. And my produce[1]—may it be uprooted. 9 If my heart has been enticed unto a woman, and upon the door of my friend I have lain in wait, 10 then may my wife grind for another, and upon her may others bow down. 11 For that is a wicked act, and iniquity to judges; 12 for it is a fire that consumes unto destruction, and all of my yield, it uproots. 13 If I have rejected the justice of my male servant and of my female servant in their dispute with me, 14 then what[2] will I do when God rises up? And when he visits, what will I respond to him? 15 Did my maker in the womb not make him? Did he not establish us in the one womb? 16 If I have withheld the poor from a desire, and the eyes of the widow I have caused to fail, 17 and I have eaten my morsel alone, and the orphan did not eat of it—18 for from my youth he grew up with me[3] like a father, and from the womb of my mother, I guided her—19 if I have seen one perishing without clothing, and seen[4] that there was no covering for the needy; 20 if his loins[5] have not blessed me, and from the fleece of my lambs he warms himself;

²¹ אִם־הֲנִיפוֹתִי עַל־יָתוֹם יָדִי כִּי־אֶרְאֶה בַשַּׁעַר עֶזְרָתִי ²² כְּתֵפִי מִשִּׁכְמָה תִפּוֹל וְאֶזְרֹעִי מִקָּנָה תִשָּׁבֵר ²³ כִּי פַחַד אֵלַי אֵיד אֵל וּמִשְּׂאֵתוֹ לֹא אוּכָל ²⁴ אִם־שַׂמְתִּי זָהָב כִּסְלִי וְלַכֶּתֶם אָמַרְתִּי מִבְטַחִי ²⁵ אִם־אֶשְׂמַח כִּי־רַב חֵילִי וְכִי־כַבִּיר מָצְאָה יָדִי ²⁶ אִם־אֶרְאֶה אוֹר כִּי יָהֵל וְיָרֵחַ יָקָר הֹלֵךְ ²⁷ וַיִּפְתְּ בַּסֵּתֶר לִבִּי וַתִּשַּׁק יָדִי לְפִי ²⁸ גַּם־הוּא עָוֹן פְּלִילִי כִּי־כִחַשְׁתִּי לָאֵל מִמָּעַל ²⁹ אִם־אֶשְׂמַח בְּפִיד מְשַׂנְאִי וְהִתְעֹרַרְתִּי כִּי־מְצָאוֹ רָע ³⁰ וְלֹא־נָתַתִּי לַחֲטֹא חִכִּי לִשְׁאֹל בְּאָלָה נַפְשׁוֹ ³¹ אִם־לֹא אָמְרוּ מְתֵי אָהֳלִי מִי־יִתֵּן מִבְּשָׂרוֹ לֹא נִשְׂבָּע ³² בַּחוּץ לֹא־יָלִין גֵּר דְּלָתַי לָאֹרַח אֶפְתָּח ³³ אִם־כִּסִּיתִי כְאָדָם פְּשָׁעָי לִטְמוֹן בְּחֻבִּי עֲוֺנִי ³⁴ כִּי אֶעֱרוֹץ הָמוֹן רַבָּה וּבוּז־מִשְׁפָּחוֹת יְחִתֵּנִי וָאֶדֹּם לֹא־אֵצֵא פָתַח ³⁵ מִי יִתֶּן־לִי שֹׁמֵעַ לִי הֶן־תָּוִי שַׁדַּי יַעֲנֵנִי וְסֵפֶר כָּתַב אִישׁ רִיבִי ³⁶ אִם־לֹא עַל־שִׁכְמִי אֶשָּׂאֶנּוּ אֶעֶנְדֶנּוּ עֲטָרוֹת לִי ³⁷ מִסְפַּר צְעָדַי אַגִּידֶנּוּ כְּמוֹ־נָגִיד אֲקָרֲבֶנּוּ ³⁸ אִם־עָלַי אַדְמָתִי תִזְעָק וְיַחַד תְּלָמֶיהָ יִבְכָּיוּן ³⁹ אִם־כֹּחָהּ אָכַלְתִּי בְלִי־כָסֶף וְנֶפֶשׁ בְּעָלֶיהָ הִפָּחְתִּי ⁴⁰ תַּחַת חִטָּה יֵצֵא חוֹחַ וְתַחַת־שְׂעֹרָה בָאְשָׁה

תַּמּוּ דִּבְרֵי אִיּוֹב

¹ וַיִּשְׁבְּתוּ שְׁלֹשֶׁת הָאֲנָשִׁים הָאֵלֶּה מֵעֲנוֹת אֶת־אִיּוֹב כִּי הוּא צַדִּיק בְּעֵינָיו ² וַיִּחַר אַף אֱלִיהוּא בֶן־בַּרַכְאֵל הַבּוּזִי מִמִּשְׁפַּחַת רָם בְּאִיּוֹב חָרָה אַפּוֹ עַל־צַדְּקוֹ נַפְשׁוֹ מֵאֱלֹהִים ³ וּבִשְׁלֹשֶׁת רֵעָיו חָרָה אַפּוֹ

פרק לב

21 if I have shaken my hand against the fatherless, because I saw my help in the gate, 22 then may my shoulder blade fall from the shoulder, and may my arm be broken from the joint.[6] 23 For the calamity of God is a terror to me, and because of his majesty, I can do nothing.[7] 24 If I have placed my confidence in gold, and to the gold I have said, 'My confidence;'[8] 25 If I have rejoiced because my wealth was great, and because my hand has found much; 26 If I have seen the sun when it shined, and the moon that is precious, moving, 27 and if[9] my heart has been secretly enticed, and my hand has kissed my mouth, 28 also this is a judgeable iniquity; for I would have denied the God who is above. 29 If I have rejoiced at the ruin of my hater, and was excited because evil found him— 30 and I have not permitted my palate to sin by demanding[10] his soul with a curse; 31 if the men of my tent have not said, 'If only one is not satisfied from his meat?' 32 (The sojourner did not spend the night in the outdoors. My doors I have opened to the traveler.) 33 If I have covered my transgression like Adam by hiding my iniquity in my bosom, 34 because I dreaded the great multitude,[11] and the contempt of families terrified me, I remained still and did not go out of the doorway. 35 If only I had someone listening to me! Behold, my mark! May Shaddai answer me! May my accuser write an indictment![12] 36 Surely, on my shoulder I would carry it, and I would bind it to me as a crown.[13] 37 The number of my steps I would declare to him; as a prince I would approach him. 38 If my land has cried out against me, and together its furrows cried; 39 if its produce I have eaten without money, and the soul of its owners I have caused them to breath out, 40 then instead of wheat may a thorn go forth, and instead of barley, stinkweed." Completed are the words of Job. **32:1** These three men ceased from answering Job, because he was righteous in his eyes. 2 Then the anger of Elihu the son of Barachel, the Buzite, of the family of Ram, burned against Job. His anger burned on account of his justifying his soul more than God. 3 And against his three friends his anger burned

פרק לג

עַל אֲשֶׁר לֹא־מָצְאוּ מַעֲנֶה וַיַּרְשִׁיעוּ אֶת־אִיּוֹב ³ וֶאֱלִיהוּ חִכָּה אֶת־אִיּוֹב בִּדְבָרִים כִּי זְקֵנִים־הֵמָּה מִמֶּנּוּ לְיָמִים ⁵ וַיַּרְא אֱלִיהוּא כִּי אֵין מַעֲנֶה בְּפִי שְׁלֹשֶׁת הָאֲנָשִׁים וַיִּחַר אַפּוֹ ⁶ וַיַּעַן אֱלִיהוּא בֶן־בַּרַכְאֵל הַבּוּזִי

צָעִיר אֲנִי לְיָמִים וְאַתֶּם יְשִׁישִׁים עַל־כֵּן זָחַלְתִּי וָאִירָא מֵחַוֺּת דֵּעִי אֶתְכֶם ⁷ אָמַרְתִּי יָמִים יְדַבֵּרוּ וְרֹב שָׁנִים יֹדִיעוּ חָכְמָה

⁸ אָכֵן רוּחַ־הִיא בֶאֱנוֹשׁ וְנִשְׁמַת שַׁדַּי תְּבִינֵם ⁹ לֹא־רַבִּים יֶחְכָּמוּ וּזְקֵנִים יָבִינוּ מִשְׁפָּט ¹⁰ לָכֵן אָמַרְתִּי שִׁמְעָה־לִּי אֲחַוֶּה דֵּעִי אַף־אָנִי ¹¹ הֵן הוֹחַלְתִּי לְדִבְרֵיכֶם אָזִין עַד־תְּבוּנֹתֵיכֶם עַד־תַּחְקְרוּן מִלִּין ¹² וְעָדֵיכֶם אֶתְבּוֹנָן וְהִנֵּה אֵין לְאִיּוֹב מוֹכִיחַ עוֹנֶה אֲמָרָיו מִכֶּם ¹³ פֶּן־תֹּאמְרוּ מָצָאנוּ חָכְמָה אֵל יִדְּפֶנּוּ לֹא־אִישׁ ¹⁴ וְלֹא־עָרַךְ אֵלַי מִלִּין וּבְאִמְרֵיכֶם לֹא אֲשִׁיבֶנּוּ ¹⁵ חַתּוּ לֹא־עָנוּ עוֹד הֶעְתִּיקוּ מֵהֶם מִלִּים ¹⁶ וְהוֹחַלְתִּי כִּי־לֹא יְדַבֵּרוּ כִּי עָמְדוּ לֹא־עָנוּ עוֹד ¹⁷ אַעֲנֶה אַף־אֲנִי חֶלְקִי אֲחַוֶּה דֵעִי אַף־אָנִי ¹⁸ כִּי מָלֵתִי מִלִּים הֱצִיקַתְנִי רוּחַ בִּטְנִי ¹⁹ הִנֵּה־בִטְנִי כְּיַיִן לֹא־יִפָּתֵחַ כְּאֹבוֹת חֲדָשִׁים יִבָּקֵעַ ²⁰ אֲדַבְּרָה וְיִרְוַח־לִי אֶפְתַּח שְׂפָתַי וְאֶעֱנֶה ²¹ אַל־נָא אֶשָּׂא פְנֵי־אִישׁ וְאֶל־אָדָם לֹא אֲכַנֶּה ²² כִּי לֹא יָדַעְתִּי אֲכַנֶּה כִּמְעַט יִשָּׂאֵנִי עֹשֵׂנִי

¹ וְאוּלָם שְׁמַע־נָא אִיּוֹב מִלָּי וְכָל־דְּבָרַי הַאֲזִינָה ² הִנֵּה־נָא פָּתַחְתִּי פִי דִּבְּרָה לְשׁוֹנִי בְחִכִּי ³ יֹשֶׁר־לִבִּי אֲמָרָי וְדַעַת שְׂפָתַי בָּרוּר מִלֵּלוּ ⁴ רוּחַ־אֵל עָשָׂתְנִי וְנִשְׁמַת שַׁדַּי תְּחַיֵּנִי ⁵ אִם־תּוּכַל הֲשִׁיבֵנִי עֶרְכָה לְפָנַי הִתְיַצָּבָה ⁶ הֵן־אֲנִי כְפִיךָ לָאֵל מֵחֹמֶר קֹרַצְתִּי גַם־אָנִי ⁷ הִנֵּה אֵמָתִי לֹא תְבַעֲתֶךָּ וְאַכְפִּי עָלֶיךָ לֹא־יִכְבָּד ⁸ אַךְ אָמַרְתָּ בְאָזְנָי וְקוֹל מִלִּין אֶשְׁמָע ⁹ זַךְ אֲנִי בְּלִי פָשַׁע חַף אָנֹכִי וְלֹא עָוֺן לִי ¹⁰ הֵן תְּנוּאוֹת עָלַי יִמְצָא יַחְשְׁבֵנִי לְאוֹיֵב לוֹ ¹¹ יָשֵׂם בַּסַּד רַגְלָי יִשְׁמֹר כָּל־אָרְחֹתָי ¹² הֶן־זֹאת לֹא־צָדַקְתָּ אֶעֱנֶךָּ כִּי־יִרְבֶּה אֱלוֹהַּ מֵאֱנוֹשׁ ¹³ מַדּוּעַ אֵלָיו רִיבוֹתָ כִּי כָל־דְּבָרָיו לֹא־יַעֲנֶה ¹⁴ כִּי־בְאַחַת יְדַבֶּר־אֵל וּבִשְׁתַּיִם לֹא יְשׁוּרֶנָּה ¹⁵ בַּחֲלוֹם חֶזְיוֹן לַיְלָה בִּנְפֹל תַּרְדֵּמָה עַל־אֲנָשִׁים בִּתְנוּמוֹת עֲלֵי מִשְׁכָּב

---

3 because[1] they did not find a response, and they condemned Job. 4 But Elihu waited to have words with Job[2] because they were elder than him in days.[3] 5 Elihu saw that there was no response in the mouth of these three men, and his anger burned. 6 Elihu the son of Barachel the Buzite answered and said, "I am young in days,[4] and you are aged. Therefore, I withdrew and was afraid of declaring my opinion to you.[5] 7 I said, 'Those older in days[6] should speak, and a multitude of years will make wisdom known.'[7] 8 Indeed, a spirit is in mankind,[8] and the breath of Shaddai gives them understanding. 9 Not many people[9] are wise, nor do the old understand justice. 10 Therefore I said, 'Listen to me. I—even I—will declare my opinion.' 11 Behold, I waited for your words, and I gave ear even to your understandings, until you investigated words. 12 Unto you, I directed my attention, but behold there was none who reproved Job.[10] There was none[11] who answered his utterances from among you.[12] 13 In case[13] you say, 'We have found wisdom. God will drive him away, not man.' 14 But he has not arranged words against me, and with your utterances I will not respond to him. 15 They are dismayed. They do not answer anymore. Their words have moved away from them. 16 I waited until they no longer spoke—until they stood still. They answered no more. 17 I will answer—even I—my part. I—even I—will declare my opinion. 18 For I am full[14] of words. The wind of my belly constrains me. 19 Behold, my belly is like wine that has not been opened; like a new wineskin that will burst.[15] 20 I will speak, and it will be relief for me.[16] I will open my lips, and I will answer. 21 May I not show partiality to anyone,[17] and to a man give an honorary title. 22 For I do not know how to give an honorary title.[18] If I did, quickly my maker would carry me off. 33:1 However,[1] Job, hear now my word, and to all of my words give ear. 2 Behold now, I opened my mouth. My tongue spoke in my palate. 3 My utterances are the uprightness of my heart, and knowledge my lips spoke purely.[2] 4 The Spirit of God made me, and the breath of Shaddai gives me life. 5 If you can, respond to me. Arrange words before me.[3] Take a stand. 6 Behold, I am just like you to God.[4] From clay I was pinched off—even I. 7 Behold, my terror will not terrify you, and my pressure upon you will not be heavy. 8 Surely you uttered in my ears, and the sound of words I have heard, 9 'I am pure, without transgression. I am clean, and I do not have iniquity.[5] 10 Behold, he finds grounds for opposition[6] against me. He accounts me an enemy to him.[7] 11 He puts my feet in the stocks. He watches all of my ways.' 12 Behold this, you are not righteous. I will answer you. For God is greater than mankind. 13 Why do you complain that all of his words he does not answer? 14 For once God speaks, and twice he does not regard it. 15 In a dream, a vision of the night, when deep sleep falls on men in slumber[8] on a couch;

29

פרק לד

אָז יִגְלֶה אֹזֶן אֲנָשִׁים וּבְמֹסָרָם יַחְתֹּם 16 לְהָסִיר אָדָם מַעֲשֶׂה וְגֵוָה מִגֶּבֶר יְכַסֶּה 17 יַחְשֹׂךְ נַפְשׁוֹ מִנִּי שָׁחַת וְחַיָּתוֹ מֵעֲבֹר בַּשָּׁלַח 18 וְהוּכַח בְּמַכְאוֹב עַל מִשְׁכָּבוֹ וְרֹב עֲצָמָיו אֵתָן 19 וְזִהֲמַתּוּ חַיָּתוֹ לָחֶם וְנַפְשׁוֹ מַאֲכַל תַּאֲוָה 20 יִכֶל בְּשָׂרוֹ מֵרֹאִי וְשֻׁפּוּ עַצְמוֹתָיו לֹא רֻאּוּ 21 וַתִּקְרַב לַשַּׁחַת נַפְשׁוֹ וְחַיָּתוֹ לַמְמִתִים 22 אִם יֵשׁ עָלָיו מַלְאָךְ מֵלִיץ אֶחָד מִנִּי אָלֶף לְהַגִּיד לְאָדָם יָשְׁרוֹ 23 וַיְחֻנֶּנּוּ וַיֹּאמֶר פְּדָעֵהוּ מֵרֶדֶת שָׁחַת מָצָאתִי כֹפֶר 24 רֻטֲפַשׁ בְּשָׂרוֹ מִנֹּעַר יָשׁוּב לִימֵי עֲלוּמָיו 25 יֶעְתַּר אֶל אֱלוֹהַּ וַיִּרְצֵהוּ וַיַּרְא פָּנָיו בִּתְרוּעָה וַיָּשֶׁב לֶאֱנוֹשׁ צִדְקָתוֹ 26 יָשֹׁר עַל אֲנָשִׁים וַיֹּאמֶר חָטָאתִי וְיָשָׁר הֶעֱוֵיתִי וְלֹא שָׁוָה לִי 27 פָּדָה נַפְשִׁי מֵעֲבֹר בַּשָּׁחַת וְחַיָּתִי בָּאוֹר תִּרְאֶה 28 הֶן כָּל אֵלֶּה יִפְעַל אֵל פַּעֲמַיִם שָׁלוֹשׁ עִם גָּבֶר 29 לְהָשִׁיב נַפְשׁוֹ מִנִּי שָׁחַת לֵאוֹר בְּאוֹר הַחַיִּים 30 הַקְשֵׁב אִיּוֹב שְׁמַע לִי הַחֲרֵשׁ וְאָנֹכִי אֲדַבֵּר 31 אִם יֵשׁ מִלִּין הֲשִׁיבֵנִי דַּבֵּר כִּי חָפַצְתִּי צַדְּקֶךָּ 32 אִם אַיִן אַתָּה שְׁמַע לִי הַחֲרֵשׁ וַאֲאַלֶּפְךָ חָכְמָה 33

1 וַיַּעַן אֱלִיהוּא וַיֹּאמַר 2 שִׁמְעוּ חֲכָמִים מִלָּי וְיֹדְעִים הַאֲזִינוּ לִי 3 כִּי אֹזֶן מִלִּין תִּבְחָן וְחֵךְ יִטְעַם לֶאֱכֹל 4 מִשְׁפָּט נִבְחֲרָה לָּנוּ נֵדְעָה בֵינֵינוּ מַה טּוֹב 5 כִּי אָמַר אִיּוֹב צָדַקְתִּי וְאֵל הֵסִיר מִשְׁפָּטִי 6 עַל מִשְׁפָּטִי אֲכַזֵּב אָנוּשׁ חִצִּי בְלִי פָשַׁע 7 מִי גֶבֶר כְּאִיּוֹב יִשְׁתֶּה לַּעַג כַּמָּיִם 8 וְאָרַח לְחֶבְרָה עִם פֹּעֲלֵי אָוֶן וְלָלֶכֶת עִם אַנְשֵׁי רֶשַׁע 9 כִּי אָמַר לֹא יִסְכָּן גָּבֶר בִּרְצֹתוֹ עִם אֱלֹהִים 10 לָכֵן אַנְשֵׁי לֵבָב שִׁמְעוּ לִי חָלִלָה לָאֵל מֵרֶשַׁע וְשַׁדַּי מֵעָוֶל 11 כִּי פֹעַל אָדָם יְשַׁלֶּם לוֹ וּכְאֹרַח אִישׁ יַמְצִאֶנּוּ 12 אַף אָמְנָם אֵל לֹא יַרְשִׁיעַ וְשַׁדַּי לֹא יְעַוֵּת מִשְׁפָּט 13 מִי פָקַד עָלָיו אָרְצָה וּמִי שָׂם תֵּבֵל כֻּלָּהּ 14 אִם יָשִׂים אֵלָיו לִבּוֹ רוּחוֹ וְנִשְׁמָתוֹ אֵלָיו יֶאֱסֹף 15 יִגְוַע כָּל בָּשָׂר יָחַד וְאָדָם עַל עָפָר יָשׁוּב 16 וְאִם בִּינָה שִׁמְעָה זֹּאת הַאֲזִינָה לְקוֹל מִלָּי 17 הַאַף שׂוֹנֵא מִשְׁפָּט יַחֲבוֹשׁ וְאִם צַדִּיק כַּבִּיר תַּרְשִׁיעַ

16 then he uncovers the ear of men, and in their discipline, he seals them 17 to turn a man away from an evil deed. He covers pride that comes from a man.[9] 18 He withholds his soul from the pit, and his life from passing over the water channel. 19 And he is reproved with pain on his couch—but many[10] of his bones are enduring. 20 His life abhors[11] bread, and his soul tasty food.[12] 21 His flesh wastes away from sight. His bones were laid bare.[13] They were not seen. 22 His soul comes near to the pit, and his life to the executioners.[14] 23 If there is upon him an angel, one mediator out of a thousand, to declare to man that he is upright,[15] 24 he will show favor to him and say, 'Redeem him[16] from going down to the pit. I have found a ransom.' 25 His flesh has grown fatter[17] than that of a youth. He returns to the days of his youthful vigor. 26 He prays to God, and he accepts him. He sees his face with a shout of joy. He restores to man his righteousness. 27 He watches men, and says, 'I have sinned, and a right person I caused to go astray, and it was not appropriate for me. 28 He has redeemed my soul[18] from crossing over into the pit, and my life[19] will see in the light.' 29 Behold, all of these things God does—twice, three times—with a man, 30 to bring back his soul from the pit, that he may be lit up with the light of the living. 31 Give attention, Job, listen to me. Be silent and I will speak. 32 If there are words, respond to me. Speak, for I am pleased to justify you. 33 If there are not, listen to me. Be quiet, and I will teach you wisdom." **34:1** Elihu answered and said, 2 "Hear, wise men, my words. And you who know,[1] give ear to me. 3 For an ear examines words, as[2] a palate tastes food.[3] 4 Let us choose justice for ourselves. Let us know between us what is good. 5 For Job has said, 'I am in the right, but God has turned away my justice. 6 About my justice, will I lie? My arrow is incurable. I am without transgression.' 7 What man like Job drinks derision like water, 8 and journeys for company[4] with workers of iniquity, walking[5] with men of wickedness? 9 For he has said, 'It does not profit a man to be pleased with God.'[6] 10 Therefore, men of understanding,[7] listen to me. Far be God from wickedness, and Shaddai from iniquity.[8] 11 For the work of a man he will pay to him, and according to the way, he causes a man to find it. 12 Surely,[9] God will not act wickedly,[10] and Shaddai will not pervert justice.[11] 13 Who appointed unto him the land,[12] and who placed upon him[13] the entire world?[14] 14 If he set his heart toward it, his spirit and his breath he would gather to himself; 15 all flesh would die together, and man would return to dust.[15] 16 And if now you have understanding, hear this; give ear to the voice of my words. 17 Would indeed a hater of justice bind up,[16] and will you condemn as guilty the righteous mighty one

30

פרק לה

¹ וַיַּעַן אֱלִיהוּא וַיֹּאמַר

² הֲזֹאת חָשַׁבְתָּ לְמִשְׁפָּט אָמַרְתָּ צִדְקִי מֵאֵל ³ כִּי־תֹאמַר מַה־יִּסְכָּן־לָךְ מָה־אֹעִיל מֵחַטָּאתִי ⁴ אֲנִי אֲשִׁיבְךָ מִלִּין וְאֶת־רֵעֶיךָ עִמָּךְ ⁵ הַבֵּט שָׁמַיִם וּרְאֵה וְשׁוּר שְׁחָקִים גָּבְהוּ מִמֶּךָּ ⁶ אִם־חָטָאתָ מַה־תִּפְעָל־בּוֹ וְרַבּוּ פְשָׁעֶיךָ מַה־תַּעֲשֶׂה־לּוֹ ⁷ אִם־צָדַקְתָּ מַה־תִּתֶּן־לוֹ אוֹ מַה־מִיָּדְךָ יִקָּח ⁸ לְאִישׁ־כָּמוֹךָ רִשְׁעֶךָ וּלְבֶן־אָדָם צִדְקָתֶךָ ⁹ מֵרֹב עֲשׁוּקִים יַזְעִיקוּ יְשַׁוְּעוּ מִזְּרוֹעַ רַבִּים ¹⁰ וְלֹא־אָמַר אַיֵּה אֱלוֹהַּ עֹשָׂי נֹתֵן זְמִרוֹת בַּלָּיְלָה ¹¹ מַלְּפֵנוּ מִבַּהֲמוֹת אָרֶץ וּמֵעוֹף הַשָּׁמַיִם יְחַכְּמֵנוּ ¹² שָׁם יִצְעֲקוּ וְלֹא יַעֲנֶה מִפְּנֵי גְּאוֹן רָעִים ¹³ אַךְ־שָׁוְא לֹא־יִשְׁמַע אֵל וְשַׁדַּי לֹא יְשׁוּרֶנָּה ¹⁴ אַף כִּי־תֹאמַר לֹא תְשׁוּרֶנּוּ דִּין לְפָנָיו וּתְחוֹלֵל לוֹ ¹⁵ וְעַתָּה כִּי־אַיִן פָּקַד אַפּוֹ וְלֹא־יָדַע בַּפַּשׁ מְאֹד ¹⁶ וְאִיּוֹב הֶבֶל יִפְצֶה־פִּיהוּ בִּבְלִי־דַעַת מִלִּין יַכְבִּר

¹⁸ הַאֲמֹר לְמֶלֶךְ בְּלִיָּעַל רָשָׁע אֶל־נְדִיבִים ¹⁹ אֲשֶׁר לֹא־נָשָׂא פְּנֵי שָׂרִים וְלֹא נִכַּר־שׁוֹעַ לִפְנֵי־דָל כִּי־מַעֲשֵׂה יָדָיו כֻּלָּם ²⁰ רֶגַע יָמֻתוּ וַחֲצוֹת לָיְלָה יְגֹעֲשׁוּ עָם וְיַעֲבֹרוּ וְיָסִירוּ אַבִּיר לֹא בְיָד ²¹ כִּי־עֵינָיו עַל־דַּרְכֵי־אִישׁ וְכָל־צְעָדָיו יִרְאֶה ²² אֵין־חֹשֶׁךְ וְאֵין צַלְמָוֶת לְהִסָּתֶר שָׁם פֹּעֲלֵי אָוֶן ²³ כִּי לֹא עַל־אִישׁ יָשִׂים עוֹד לַהֲלֹךְ אֶל־אֵל בַּמִּשְׁפָּט ²⁴ יָרֹעַ כַּבִּירִים לֹא־חֵקֶר וַיַּעֲמֵד אֲחֵרִים תַּחְתָּם ²⁵ לָכֵן יַכִּיר מַעְבָּדֵיהֶם וְהָפַךְ לַיְלָה וְיִדַּכָּאוּ ²⁶ תַּחַת־רְשָׁעִים סְפָקָם בִּמְקוֹם רֹאִים ²⁷ אֲשֶׁר עַל־כֵּן סָרוּ מֵאַחֲרָיו וְכָל־דְּרָכָיו לֹא הִשְׂכִּילוּ ²⁸ לְהָבִיא עָלָיו צַעֲקַת־דָּל וְצַעֲקַת עֲנִיִּים יִשְׁמָע ²⁹ וְהוּא יַשְׁקִט וּמִי יַרְשִׁעַ וְיַסְתֵּר פָּנִים וּמִי יְשׁוּרֶנּוּ וְעַל־גּוֹי וְעַל־אָדָם יָחַד ³⁰ מִמְּלֹךְ אָדָם חָנֵף מִמֹּקְשֵׁי עָם ³¹ כִּי־אֶל־אֵל הֶאָמַר נָשָׂאתִי לֹא אֶחְבֹּל ³² בִּלְעֲדֵי אֶחֱזֶה אַתָּה הֹרֵנִי אִם־עָוֶל פָּעַלְתִּי לֹא אֹסִיף ³³ הַמֵעִמְּךָ יְשַׁלְמֶנָּה כִּי־מָאַסְתָּ כִּי־אַתָּה תִבְחַר וְלֹא־אָנִי וּמַה־יָּדַעְתָּ דַבֵּר ³⁴ אַנְשֵׁי לֵבָב יֹאמְרוּ לִי וְגֶבֶר חָכָם שֹׁמֵעַ לִי ³⁵ אִיּוֹב לֹא־בְדַעַת יְדַבֵּר וּדְבָרָיו לֹא בְהַשְׂכֵּיל ³⁶ אָבִי יִבָּחֵן אִיּוֹב עַד־נֶצַח עַל־תְּשֻׁבֹת בְּאַנְשֵׁי־אָוֶן ³⁷ כִּי יֹסִיף עַל־חַטָּאתוֹ פֶשַׁע בֵּינֵינוּ יִסְפּוֹק וְיֶרֶב אֲמָרָיו לָאֵל

---

18 who says[17] to a king, 'Worthless,' and to nobles, 'Wicked'—19 who does not show partiality to princes and does not regard the rich before the poor, because they all are all the work of his hands? 20 In a moment they die, and in middle of the night. The people are shaken and pass away.[18] The mighty remove them without strength.[19] 21 For his eyes are on the ways of a man, and all of his steps, he sees. 22 There is no darkness, and there is no deep gloom, to hide themselves there for the workers of iniquity.[20] 23 For he does not pay attention[21] to a man anymore, that goes[22] to God in the judgment. 24 He breaks mighty men with no investigation, and establishes others in their place. 25 Therefore, he recognizes their works.[23] He overturns the night, and they are crushed. 26 Instead of the wicked he slaps them in a place of spectators[24]— 27 who, therefore, turned away from after him, and to all of his ways, they did not give attention; 28 to bring to him[25] the cry of the poor so that he can hear the cry of the poor.[26] 29 But if he makes quiet, who can agitate? If he hides his face, who can see him? He is over a nation[27] and over a man alike, 30 to keep a godless man from reigning and from being snares to the people.[28] 31 For to God has anyone[29] said, 'I endured. I will no longer act corruptly. 32 Apart from what I see, you teach me. If I have done iniquity, I will not do it again.' 33 According to you[30] will he recompense it, because you are fed up? For you choose, and not I; and what you know, speak. 34 Men of understanding will tell me, and a wise man listens to me. 35 'Job speaks without knowledge,[31] and his words are not with considering insight.' 36 Would that[32] Job be tried forever,[33] concerning his answers that are like[34] those of wicked men. 37 For he adds transgression upon his sin. He claps his hands among us and multiplies his words against God." 35:1 Elihu answered and said, 2 "Did you think this was for justice? You said, 'My righteousness is greater than God's.' 3 For you say, 'What benefit will it be to you? What do I profit from my sin?'[1] 4 I will respond to you with words, and to your companions with you. 5 Look at the heavens and see. Consider[2] the skies that are higher than you. 6 If you have sinned, what have you done against him? If your transgressions are many, what do you do to him? 7 If you are righteous, what do you give to him? Or, what from your hand does he take? 8 For a man like you is your wickedness, and for another person[4] is your 'righteousness.' 9 From an abundance of oppressions, they cry out. Many cry for help from power.[5] 10 But no one says,[6] 'Where is God my Maker,[7] giver of songs in the night?' 11 He teaches us[8] more than the animals of the earth, and makes us wiser than the birds of the sky.[9] 12 There they cry out, but he does not answer, because of the pride of evil people. 13 Surely, God will not hear emptiness, and Shaddai will not regard it.[10] 14 Even if you say you do not see him, a plea is before him, and you wait for him. 15 And now, because he has not visited[11] with his anger, and he does not know transgression[12] very much, 16 Job[13] opens his mouth with wind. Without knowledge, words he multiplies."[14]

פרק לו

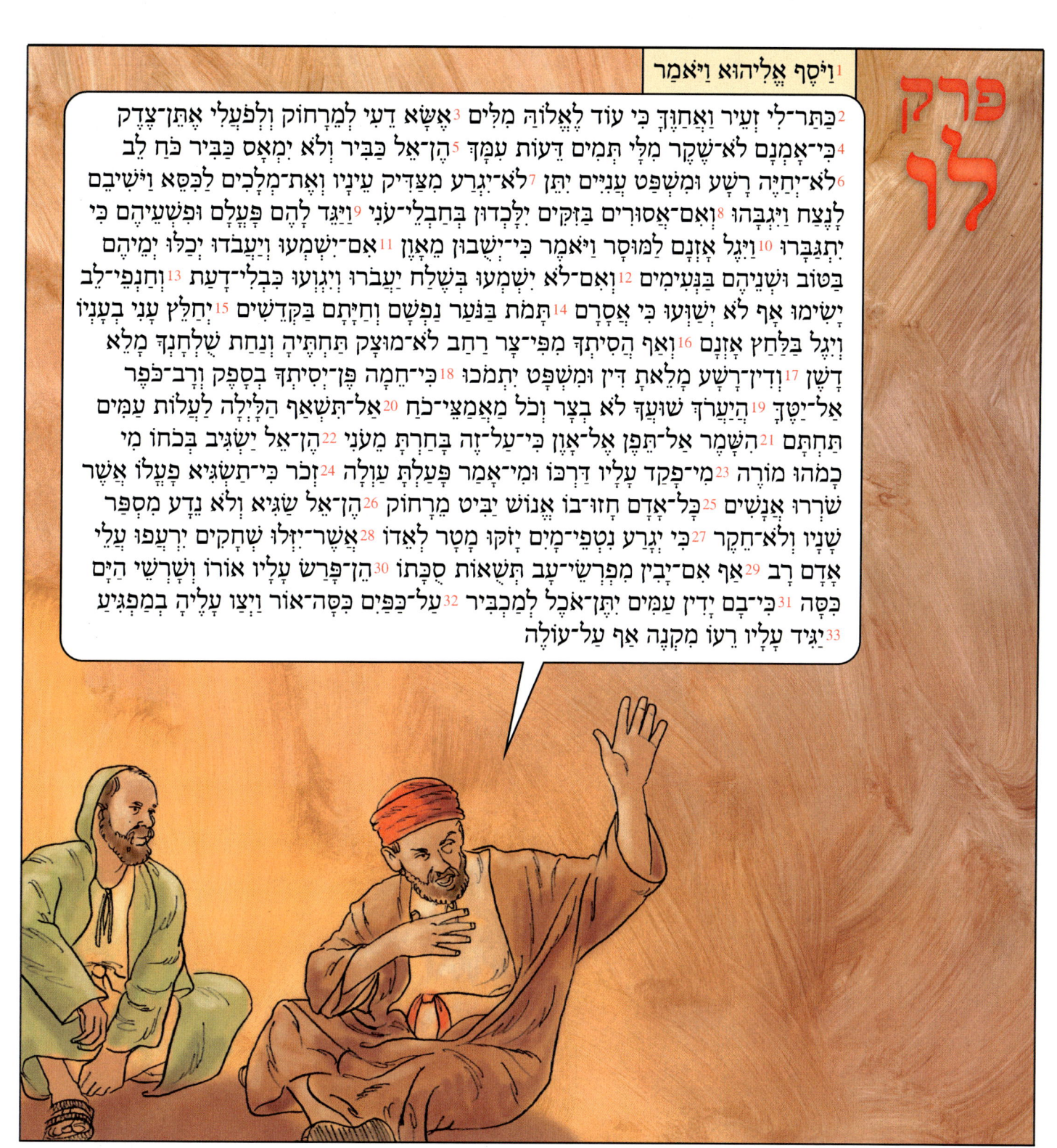

וַיֹּסֶף אֱלִיהוּא וַיֹּאמַר

2 כַּתַּר־לִי זְעֵיר וַאֲחַוֶּךָּ כִּי עוֹד לֶאֱלוֹהַּ מִלִּים 3 אֶשָּׂא דֵעִי לְמֵרָחוֹק וּלְפֹעֲלִי אֶתֵּן־צֶדֶק 4 כִּי־אָמְנָם לֹא־שֶׁקֶר מִלָּי תְּמִים דֵּעוֹת עִמָּךְ 5 הֶן־אֵל כַּבִּיר וְלֹא יִמְאָס כַּבִּיר כֹּחַ לֵב 6 לֹא־יְחַיֶּה רָשָׁע וּמִשְׁפַּט עֲנִיִּים יִתֵּן 7 לֹא־יִגְרַע מִצַּדִּיק עֵינָיו וְאֶת־מְלָכִים לַכִּסֵּא וַיֹּשִׁיבֵם לָנֶצַח וַיִּגְבָּהוּ 8 וְאִם־אֲסוּרִים בַּזִּקִּים יִלָּכְדוּן בְּחַבְלֵי־עֹנִי 9 וַיַּגֵּד לָהֶם פָּעֳלָם וּפִשְׁעֵיהֶם כִּי יִתְגַּבָּרוּ 10 וַיִּגֶל אָזְנָם לַמּוּסָר וַיֹּאמֶר כִּי־יְשֻׁבוּן מֵאָוֶן 11 אִם־יִשְׁמְעוּ וְיַעֲבֹדוּ יְכַלּוּ יְמֵיהֶם בַּטּוֹב וּשְׁנֵיהֶם בַּנְּעִימִים 12 וְאִם־לֹא יִשְׁמְעוּ בְּשֶׁלַח יַעֲבֹרוּ וְיִגְוְעוּ כִּבְלִי־דָעַת 13 וְחַנְפֵי־לֵב יָשִׂימוּ אָף לֹא יְשַׁוְּעוּ כִּי אֲסָרָם 14 תָּמֹת בַּנֹּעַר נַפְשָׁם וְחַיָּתָם בַּקְּדֵשִׁים 15 יְחַלֵּץ עָנִי בְעָנְיוֹ וְיִגֶל בַּלַּחַץ אָזְנָם 16 וְאַף הֲסִיתְךָ מִפִּי־צָר רַחַב לֹא־מוּצָק תַּחְתֶּיהָ וְנַחַת שֻׁלְחָנְךָ מָלֵא דָשֶׁן 17 וְדִין־רָשָׁע מָלֵאתָ דִּין וּמִשְׁפָּט יִתְמֹכוּ 18 כִּי־חֵמָה פֶּן־יְסִיתְךָ בְסָפֶק וְרָב־כֹּפֶר אַל־יַטֶּךָּ 19 הֲיַעֲרֹךְ שׁוּעֲךָ לֹא בְצָר וְכֹל מַאֲמַצֵּי־כֹחַ 20 אַל־תִּשְׁאַף הַלָּיְלָה לַעֲלוֹת עַמִּים תַּחְתָּם 21 הִשָּׁמֶר אַל־תֵּפֶן אֶל־אָוֶן כִּי־עַל־זֶה בָּחַרְתָּ מֵעֹנִי 22 הֶן־אֵל יַשְׂגִּיב בְּכֹחוֹ מִי כָמֹהוּ מוֹרֶה 23 מִי־פָקַד עָלָיו דַּרְכּוֹ וּמִי־אָמַר פָּעַלְתָּ עַוְלָה 24 זְכֹר כִּי־תַשְׂגִּיא פָעֳלוֹ אֲשֶׁר שֹׁרְרוּ אֲנָשִׁים 25 כָּל־אָדָם חָזוּ־בוֹ אֱנוֹשׁ יַבִּיט מֵרָחוֹק 26 הֶן־אֵל שַׂגִּיא וְלֹא נֵדָע מִסְפַּר שָׁנָיו וְלֹא־חֵקֶר 27 כִּי יְגָרַע נִטְפֵי־מָיִם יָזֹקּוּ מָטָר לְאֵדוֹ 28 אֲשֶׁר־יִזְּלוּ שְׁחָקִים יִרְעֲפוּ עֲלֵי אָדָם רָב 29 אַף אִם־יָבִין מִפְרְשֵׂי־עָב תְּשֻׁאוֹת סֻכָּתוֹ 30 הֵן־פָּרַשׂ עָלָיו אוֹרוֹ וְשָׁרְשֵׁי הַיָּם כִּסָּה 31 כִּי־בָם יָדִין עַמִּים יִתֶּן־אֹכֶל לְמַכְבִּיר 32 עַל־כַּפַּיִם כִּסָּה־אוֹר וַיְצַו עָלֶיהָ בְמַפְגִּיעַ 33 יַגִּיד עָלָיו רֵעוֹ מִקְנֶה אַף עַל־עוֹלֶה

36:1 Elihu continued further and said, **2** "Wait for me a little, and I will declare to you; for God still has words.[1] **3** I lift up my opinion from afar,[2] and to my Maker I will give righteousness. **4** For truly my words are not a lie. A person complete of knowledge[3] is with you. **5** Behold, God is mighty, and does not despise. He is mighty in strength of understanding. **6** He does not give the wicked life, but justice to the poor he gives. **7** He does not withdraw his eyes from a righteous person. He sets kings on the throne forever and he exalts it.[4] **8** And if they are bound in the fetters—caught in the cords of affliction— **9** he declares to them their deeds, and their transgressions because they behaved proudly. **10** He uncovers their ears[5] to discipline, and says that they return from iniquity. **11** If they listen and serve, they will complete their days in prosperity,[6] and their years in delights.[7] **12** But if they do not listen, they will pass over the water channel.[8] They will expire as if without knowledge. **13** But the godless of heart put on anger. They do not cry out for help though he binds them. **14** Their soul dies in youth,[9] and their life among the male prostitutes. **15** He rescues the afflicted in their affliction, and opens their ear in oppression;[10] **16** and indeed allured you from the mouth of distress, to an expanse where there is no distress;[11] and the comfort of your table is full of abundance.[12] **17** But you are full of the judgment of the wicked. Judgment and justice lay hold of you. **18** For wrath—it might allure you[13] with an abundance,[14] but may a great ransom not turn you away. **19** Will your cry for help set things in order and not in distress? And even all of the efforts of strength? **20** Do not long for the night, when people ascend in their place.[15] **21** Be guarded! Do not turn to iniquity. For you chose this[16] rather than affliction. **22** Behold, God is exalted in his power. Who, like him, is a teacher? **23** Who laid upon him[17] his way? And who said, 'You have done injustice?' **24** Remember that you magnify his work, which men have sung. **25** Every man[18] has beheld it. Mankind considers from a distance. **26** Behold, God is great, but we do not know. The number of his years is without investigation.[19] **27** For he withdraws drops of water that purify rain for its mist, **28** that the skies trickle. They drip on man exceedingly. **29** Does one really understand the spreading of the clouds,[20] or the thunderings of his booth? **30** Behold, he spreads his light upon him, and the roots of the sea[21] he covers. **31** For by them he judges nations. He gives food in abundance.[22] **32** Upon palms he covers light, and commands it when attacking.[23] **33** It declares his roar to him.[24] It also announces what rises to the cattle.[25]

פרק לז

1 אַף־לְזֹאת יֶחֱרַד לִבִּי וְיִתַּר מִמְּקוֹמוֹ 2 שִׁמְעוּ שָׁמוֹעַ בְּרֹגֶז קֹלוֹ וְהֶגֶה מִפִּיו יֵצֵא 3 תַּחַת־כָּל־הַשָּׁמַיִם יִשְׁרֵהוּ וְאוֹרוֹ עַל־כַּנְפוֹת הָאָרֶץ 4 אַחֲרָיו יִשְׁאַג־קוֹל יַרְעֵם בְּקוֹל גְּאוֹנוֹ וְלֹא יְעַקְּבֵם כִּי־יִשָּׁמַע קוֹלוֹ 5 יַרְעֵם אֵל בְּקוֹלוֹ נִפְלָאוֹת עֹשֶׂה גְּדֹלוֹת וְלֹא נֵדָע 6 כִּי לַשֶּׁלֶג יֹאמַר הֱוֵא אָרֶץ וְגֶשֶׁם מָטָר וְגֶשֶׁם מִטְרוֹת עֻזּוֹ 7 בְּיַד־כָּל־אָדָם יַחְתּוֹם לָדַעַת כָּל־אַנְשֵׁי מַעֲשֵׂהוּ 8 וַתָּבֹא חַיָּה בְמוֹ־אָרֶב וּבִמְעוֹנֹתֶיהָ תִשְׁכֹּן 9 מִן־הַחֶדֶר תָּבוֹא סוּפָה וּמִמְּזָרִים קָרָה 10 מִנִּשְׁמַת־אֵל יִתֶּן־קָרַח וְרֹחַב מַיִם בְּמוּצָק 11 אַף־בְּרִי יַטְרִיחַ עָב יָפִיץ עֲנַן אוֹרוֹ 12 וְהוּא מְסִבּוֹת מִתְהַפֵּךְ בְּתַחְבּוּלֹתָו לְפָעֳלָם כֹּל אֲשֶׁר יְצַוֵּם עַל־פְּנֵי תֵבֵל אָרְצָה 13 אִם־לְשֵׁבֶט אִם־לְאַרְצוֹ אִם־לְחֶסֶד יַמְצִאֵהוּ 14 הַאֲזִינָה זֹּאת אִיּוֹב עֲמֹד וְהִתְבּוֹנֵן נִפְלְאוֹת אֵל 15 הֲתֵדַע בְּשׂוּם־אֱלוֹהַּ עֲלֵיהֶם וְהוֹפִיעַ אוֹר עֲנָנוֹ 16 הֲתֵדַע עַל־מִפְלְשֵׂי־עָב מִפְלְאוֹת תְּמִים דֵּעִים 17 אֲשֶׁר־בְּגָדֶיךָ חַמִּים בְּהַשְׁקִט אֶרֶץ מִדָּרוֹם 18 תַּרְקִיעַ עִמּוֹ לִשְׁחָקִים חֲזָקִים כִּרְאִי מוּצָק 19 הוֹדִיעֵנוּ מַה־נֹּאמַר לוֹ לֹא נַעֲרֹךְ מִפְּנֵי־חֹשֶׁךְ 20 הַיְסֻפַּר־לוֹ כִּי אֲדַבֵּר אִם־אָמַר אִישׁ כִּי יְבֻלָּע 21 וְעַתָּה לֹא רָאוּ אוֹר בָּהִיר הוּא בַּשְּׁחָקִים וְרוּחַ עָבְרָה וַתְּטַהֲרֵם 22 מִצָּפוֹן זָהָב יֶאֱתֶה עַל־אֱלוֹהַּ נוֹרָא הוֹד 23 שַׁדַּי לֹא־מְצָאנֻהוּ שַׂגִּיא־כֹחַ וּמִשְׁפָּט וְרֹב־צְדָקָה לֹא יְעַנֶּה 24 לָכֵן יְרֵאוּהוּ אֲנָשִׁים לֹא־יִרְאֶה כָּל־חַכְמֵי־לֵב

פרק לח

1 וַיַּעַן־יְהוָה אֶת־אִיּוֹב מִן הַסְּעָרָה וַיֹּאמַר

2 מִי זֶה מַחְשִׁיךְ עֵצָה בְמִלִּין בְּלִי־דָעַת 3 אֱזָר־נָא כְגֶבֶר חֲלָצֶיךָ וְאֶשְׁאָלְךָ וְהוֹדִיעֵנִי

37:1 Even at this my heart trembles, and springs from its place. **2** Hear, hear[1] the raging of his thunder, and the growling coming out his mouth. **3** Under the whole sky he lets it loose, and his lightning upon the wings of the land.[2] **4** After it, a voice roars. He thunders with the voice of his exaltation and does not hold back—for his voice is heard. **5** God thunders marvelously[3] with his voice. He does great things and we do not understand. **6** For to the snow he says, 'Fall[4] on the earth,' and to a shower of rain—and the shower of the rains of his strength.[5] **7** By the hand of every man he seals, to know all the men of his work. **8** An animal enters into a den, and in its habitations, it dwells. **9** From the chamber comes a storm, and from winds[6]—cold. **10** From the breath of God, he gives ice,[7] and the expanse of the waters is frozen.[8] **11** Indeed, the cloud is burdened with moisture. He scatters the cloud of his lightning. **12** And it turns in circles by his guidance,[9] for them to do[10] all that he commands them on the face of the land of the earth[11]— **13** whether for the rod, or for his land, or for lovingkindness, he causes it to come.[12] **14** Listen to this, Job. Stand and consider the marvelous things of God. **15** Do you know how God lays a duty upon them,[13] and causes the lightning of his cloud to shine? **16** Do you know about the spreading of the clouds,[14] the marvelous things of the one complete of knowledge?[15] **17** Do you know[16]— you whose garments are hot, in the quieting of the land from the south wind? **18** Will you spread out the skies with him? They are strong like a cast mirror. **19** Teach us! What will we say to him? For we cannot arrange words against him[17] because of darkness. **20** Will it be told to him that I would speak? Did a man say that he would be swallowed? **21** But now they do not see light. It is bright in the skies, but wind passes through and cleanses them. **22** From the north comes gold. Awesome majesty is upon God. **23** We could not find Shaddai. He is great in power and justice—and great righteousness he will not afflict. **24** Therefore men fear him. He does not see any of the wise of heart." **38:1** Then Adonai answered Job out of the whirlwind and said, **2** "Who is this who darkens counsel by words without knowledge? **3** Gird, now, your lions like a man, for I will ask you, and you will inform me!

33

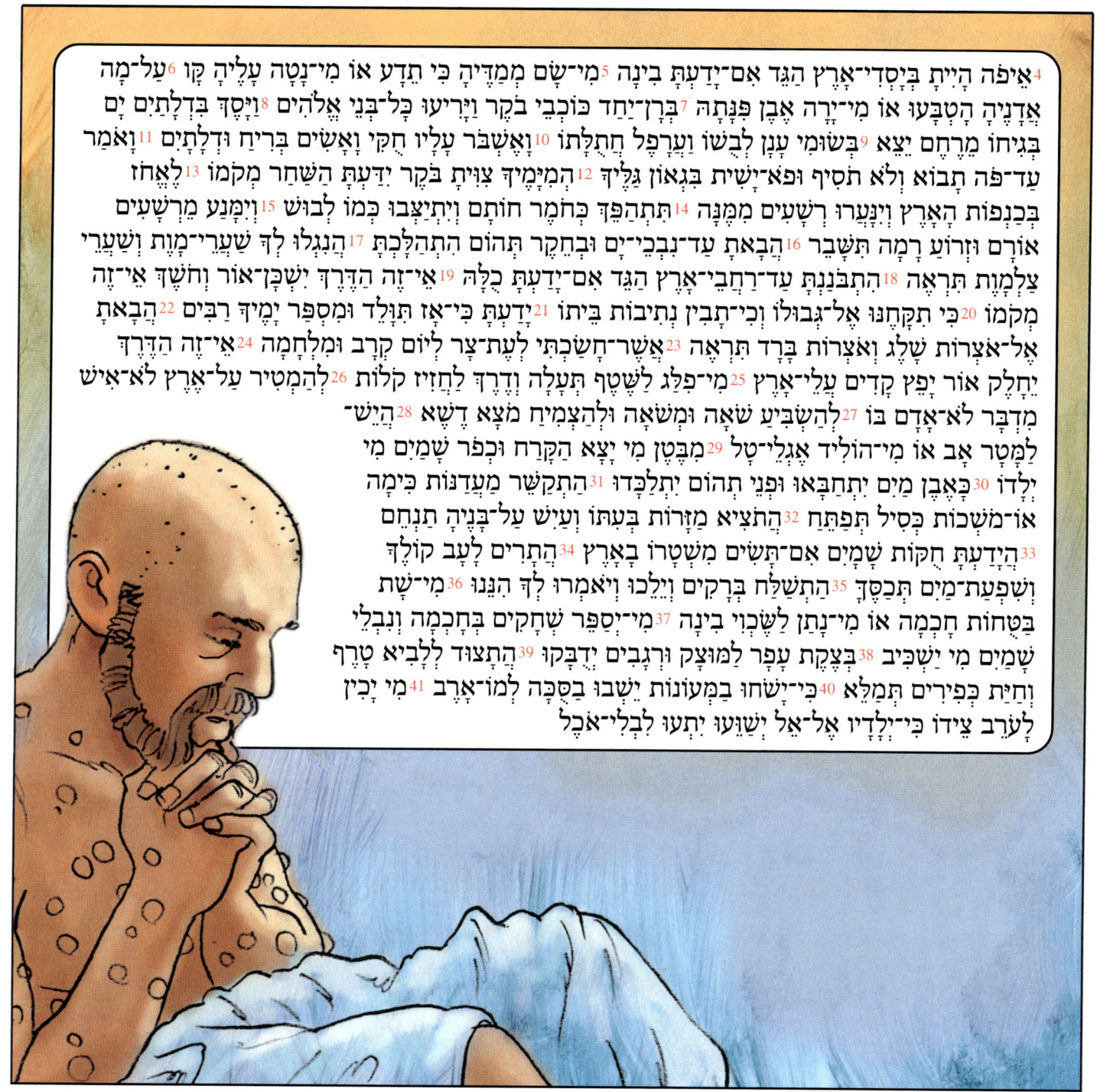

⁴ אֵיפֹה הָיִיתָ בְּיָסְדִי־אָרֶץ הַגֵּד אִם־יָדַעְתָּ בִינָה ⁵ מִי־שָׂם מְמַדֶּיהָ כִּי תֵדָע אוֹ מִי־נָטָה עָלֶיהָ קָּו ⁶ עַל־מָה אֲדָנֶיהָ הָטְבָּעוּ אוֹ מִי־יָרָה אֶבֶן פִּנָּתָהּ ⁷ בְּרָן־יַחַד כּוֹכְבֵי בֹקֶר וַיָּרִיעוּ כָּל־בְּנֵי אֱלֹהִים ⁸ וַיָּסֶךְ בִּדְלָתַיִם יָם בְּגִיחוֹ מֵרֶחֶם יֵצֵא ⁹ בְּשׂוּמִי עָנָן לְבֻשׁוֹ וַעֲרָפֶל חֲתֻלָּתוֹ ¹⁰ וָאֶשְׁבֹּר עָלָיו חֻקִּי וָאָשִׂים בְּרִיחַ וּדְלָתָיִם ¹¹ וָאֹמַר עַד־פֹּה תָבוֹא וְלֹא תֹסִיף וּפֹא־יָשִׁית בִּגְאוֹן גַּלֶּיךָ ¹² הֲמִיָּמֶיךָ צִוִּיתָ בֹּקֶר יִדַּעְתָּה שַׁחַר מְקֹמוֹ ¹³ לֶאֱחֹז בְּכַנְפוֹת הָאָרֶץ וְיִנָּעֲרוּ רְשָׁעִים מִמֶּנָּה ¹⁴ תִּתְהַפֵּךְ כְּחֹמֶר חוֹתָם וְיִתְיַצְּבוּ כְּמוֹ לְבוּשׁ ¹⁵ וְיִמָּנַע מֵרְשָׁעִים אוֹרָם וּזְרוֹעַ רָמָה תִּשָּׁבֵר ¹⁶ הֲבָאתָ עַד־נִבְכֵי־יָם וּבְחֵקֶר תְּהוֹם הִתְהַלָּכְתָּ ¹⁷ הֲנִגְלוּ לְךָ שַׁעֲרֵי־מָוֶת וְשַׁעֲרֵי צַלְמָוֶת תִּרְאֶה ¹⁸ הִתְבֹּנַנְתָּ עַד־רַחֲבֵי־אָרֶץ הַגֵּד אִם־יָדַעְתָּ כֻלָּהּ ¹⁹ אֵי־זֶה הַדֶּרֶךְ יִשְׁכָּן־אוֹר וְחֹשֶׁךְ אֵי־זֶה מְקֹמוֹ ²⁰ כִּי תִקָּחֶנּוּ אֶל־גְּבוּלוֹ וְכִי־תָבִין נְתִיבוֹת בֵּיתוֹ ²¹ יָדַעְתָּ כִּי־אָז תִּוָּלֵד וּמִסְפַּר יָמֶיךָ רַבִּים ²² הֲבָאתָ אֶל־אֹצְרוֹת שָׁלֶג וְאֹצְרוֹת בָּרָד תִּרְאֶה ²³ אֲשֶׁר־חָשַׂכְתִּי לְעֶת־צָר לְיוֹם קְרָב וּמִלְחָמָה ²⁴ אֵי־זֶה הַדֶּרֶךְ יֵחָלֶק אוֹר יָפֵץ קָדִים עֲלֵי־אָרֶץ ²⁵ מִי־פִלַּג לַשֶּׁטֶף תְּעָלָה וְדֶרֶךְ לַחֲזִיז קֹלוֹת ²⁶ לְהַמְטִיר עַל־אֶרֶץ לֹא־אִישׁ מִדְבָּר לֹא־אָדָם בּוֹ ²⁷ לְהַשְׂבִּיעַ שֹׁאָה וּמְשֹׁאָה וּלְהַצְמִיחַ מֹצָא דֶשֶׁא ²⁸ הֲיֵשׁ־לַמָּטָר אָב אוֹ מִי־הוֹלִיד אֶגְלֵי־טָל ²⁹ מִבֶּטֶן מִי יָצָא הַקָּרַח וּכְפֹר שָׁמַיִם מִי יְלָדוֹ ³⁰ כָּאֶבֶן מַיִם יִתְחַבָּאוּ וּפְנֵי תְהוֹם יִתְלַכָּדוּ ³¹ הַתְקַשֵּׁר מַעֲדַנּוֹת כִּימָה אוֹ־מֹשְׁכוֹת כְּסִיל תְּפַתֵּחַ ³² הֲתֹצִיא מַזָּרוֹת בְּעִתּוֹ וְעַיִשׁ עַל־בָּנֶיהָ תַנְחֵם ³³ הֲיָדַעְתָּ חֻקּוֹת שָׁמָיִם אִם־תָּשִׂים מִשְׁטָרוֹ בָאָרֶץ ³⁴ הֲתָרִים לָעָב קוֹלֶךָ וְשִׁפְעַת־מַיִם תְּכַסֶּךָּ ³⁵ הַתְשַׁלַּח בְּרָקִים וְיֵלֵכוּ וְיֹאמְרוּ לְךָ הִנֵּנוּ ³⁶ מִי־שָׁת בַּטֻּחוֹת חָכְמָה אוֹ מִי־נָתַן לַשֶּׂכְוִי בִינָה ³⁷ מִי־יְסַפֵּר שְׁחָקִים בְּחָכְמָה וְנִבְלֵי שָׁמַיִם מִי יַשְׁכִּיב ³⁸ בְּצֶקֶת עָפָר לַמּוּצָק וּרְגָבִים יְדֻבָּקוּ ³⁹ הֲתָצוּד לְלָבִיא טָרֶף וְחַיַּת כְּפִירִים תְּמַלֵּא ⁴⁰ כִּי־יָשֹׁחוּ בַמְּעוֹנוֹת יֵשְׁבוּ בַסֻּכָּה לְמוֹ־אָרֶב ⁴¹ מִי יָכִין לָעֹרֵב צֵידוֹ כִּי־יְלָדָיו אֶל־אֵל יְשַׁוֵּעוּ יִתְעוּ לִבְלִי־אֹכֶל

4 Where were you during my establishing[1] of the land? Tell, if you know understanding. 5 Who placed its measurements?[2] For, do you know? Or, who stretched a line upon it? 6 Whereupon were its pedestals sunk? Or who set its cornerstone, 7 when the stars of the morning sung for joy,[3] and the sons of God shouted out? 8 He shut off the sea with two doors, when it burst forth,[4] coming out of the womb; 9 when I placed[5] on a cloud its garment and a thick cloud its swaddling band, 10 I broke my boundary upon it, I set bars and two doors. 11 I said, 'Until here, you can come, and you will not go further.[6] And here,[7] he fixes your waves with pride.' 12 In your days[8] have you ever commanded the morning? Have you caused the dawn to know[9] its place; 13 to seize the wings of the earth,[10] so that wicked are shaken out of it? 14 It is changed[11] like a clay seal,[12] and they present themselves like a garment. 15 From the wicked, their light is withheld, and the raised arm is broken. 16 Have you come up to the sources of the sea?[13] Or have you walked about in the depth of the deep? 17 Have the gates of death been revealed to you? Or have you seen the gates of deep gloom? 18 Have you considered as far as the expanses of the land? Declare, if you know all of it. 19 Where is the way to where light dwells? And darkness, where is its place 20 that you can take it to its territory, and that you should understand the paths to its house? 21 You know, for then you are born, and the number of your days is great![14] 22 Have you entered the storehouses of snow, and the storehouses of hail, have you seen—23 which I have reserved for a time of distress; the day of battle and war? 24 Where is the way to where lightning is apportioned, that the east wind scatters upon the earth? 25 Who cleaved the channel for the flood water, and a way for the lighting of the thunder, 26 to send rain on a land without people[15]—a wilderness, in which there is no man[16]—27 to satiate the wasteland and desolate ground, and to cause the source of grass to grow? 28 Does the rain have a father?[17] Or who begot drops of dew?[18] 29 From the womb of whom did the ice come out? And the frost of the heavens, who gave birth to it? 30 The waters harden[19] like the stone, when the surface of the deep compacts together. 31 Can you bind the bands of the Pleiades, or loosen the cords[20] of Orion? 32 Can you bring out Mazzarot[21] in its season? And can you guide the Great Bear with her cubs?[22] 33 Do you know the statutes of the heavens? Can you establish its dominion on the earth? 34 Do you lift up your voice to the clouds[23] and an abundance of water covers you? 35 Do you send out lightning flashes, and they go? Do they say to you, 'Here we are'? 36 Who has put wisdom in the ibis, or who has given understanding to the rooster?[24] 37 Who counts the clouds with wisdom, and who tips the waterskins of the heavens, 38 when pouring dust[25] into the casting[26] of metal, and the clods of earth stick together? 39 Do you hunt prey for a lioness, and the life of the young lions,[27] do you fill them 40 when they crouch in their habitations,[28] and dwell in the thicket for an ambush? 41 Who prepares for the raven his provision, when his children[29] cry out to God and wander for lack of food?[30]

34

פרק לט

1 הֲיָדַעְתָּ עֵת לֶדֶת יַעֲלֵי־סָלַע חֹלֵל אַיָּלוֹת תִּשְׁמֹר 2 תִּסְפֹּר יְרָחִים תְּמַלֶּאנָה וְיָדַעְתָּ עֵת לִדְתָּנָה 3 תִּכְרַעְנָה יַלְדֵיהֶן תְּפַלַּחְנָה חֶבְלֵיהֶם תְּשַׁלַּחְנָה 4 יַחְלְמוּ בְנֵיהֶם יִרְבּוּ בַבָּר יָצְאוּ וְלֹא־שָׁבוּ לָמוֹ 5 מִי־שִׁלַּח פֶּרֶא חָפְשִׁי וּמֹסְרוֹת עָרוֹד מִי פִתֵּחַ 6 אֲשֶׁר־שַׂמְתִּי עֲרָבָה בֵיתוֹ וּמִשְׁכְּנוֹתָיו מְלֵחָה 7 יִשְׂחַק לַהֲמוֹן קִרְיָה תְּשֻׁאוֹת נוֹגֵשׂ לֹא יִשְׁמָע 8 יְתוּר הָרִים מִרְעֵהוּ וְאַחַר כָּל־יָרוֹק יִדְרוֹשׁ 9 הֲיֹאבֶה רֵּים עָבְדֶךָ אִם־יָלִין עַל־אֲבוּסֶךָ 10 הֲתִקְשָׁר־רֵים בְּתֶלֶם עֲבֹתוֹ אִם־יְשַׂדֵּד עֲמָקִים אַחֲרֶיךָ 11 הֲתִבְטַח־בּוֹ כִּי־רַב כֹּחוֹ וְתַעֲזֹב אֵלָיו יְגִיעֶךָ 12 הֲתַאֲמִין בּוֹ כִּי־יָשִׁיב זַרְעֶךָ וְגָרְנְךָ יֶאֱסֹף 13 כְּנַף־רְנָנִים נֶעֱלָסָה אִם־אֶבְרָה חֲסִידָה וְנֹצָה 14 כִּי־תַעֲזֹב לָאָרֶץ בֵּצֶיהָ וְעַל־עָפָר תְּחַמֵּם 15 וַתִּשְׁכַּח כִּי־רֶגֶל תְּזוּרֶהָ וְחַיַּת הַשָּׂדֶה תְּדוּשֶׁהָ 16 הִקְשִׁיחַ בָּנֶיהָ לְּלֹא־לָהּ לְרִיק יְגִיעָהּ בְּלִי־פָחַד 17 כִּי־הִשָּׁהּ אֱלוֹהַּ חָכְמָה וְלֹא־חָלַק לָהּ בַּבִּינָה 18 כָּעֵת בַּמָּרוֹם תַּמְרִיא תִּשְׂחַק לַסּוּס וּלְרֹכְבוֹ 19 הֲתִתֵּן לַסּוּס גְּבוּרָה הֲתַלְבִּישׁ צַוָּארוֹ רַעְמָה 20 הֲתַרְעִישֶׁנּוּ כָּאַרְבֶּה הוֹד נַחְרוֹ אֵימָה 21 יַחְפְּרוּ בָעֵמֶק וְיָשִׂישׂ בְּכֹחַ יֵצֵא לִקְרַאת־נָשֶׁק 22 יִשְׂחַק לְפַחַד וְלֹא יֵחָת וְלֹא־יָשׁוּב מִפְּנֵי־חָרֶב 23 עָלָיו תִּרְנֶה אַשְׁפָּה לַהַב חֲנִית וְכִידוֹן 24 בְּרַעַשׁ וְרֹגֶז יְגַמֶּא־אָרֶץ וְלֹא־יַאֲמִין כִּי־קוֹל שׁוֹפָר 25 בְּדֵי שֹׁפָר יֹאמַר הֶאָח וּמֵרָחוֹק יָרִיחַ מִלְחָמָה רַעַם שָׂרִים וּתְרוּעָה 26 הֲמִבִּינָתְךָ יַאֲבֶר־נֵץ יִפְרֹשׂ כְּנָפָיו לְתֵימָן 27 אִם־עַל־פִּיךָ יַגְבִּיהַּ נָשֶׁר וְכִי יָרִים קִנּוֹ 28 סֶלַע יִשְׁכֹּן וְיִתְלֹנָן עַל־שֶׁן־סֶלַע וּמְצוּדָה 29 מִשָּׁם חָפַר־אֹכֶל לְמֵרָחוֹק עֵינָיו יַבִּיטוּ 30 וְאֶפְרֹחָיו יְעַלְעוּ־דָם וּבַאֲשֶׁר חֲלָלִים שָׁם הוּא

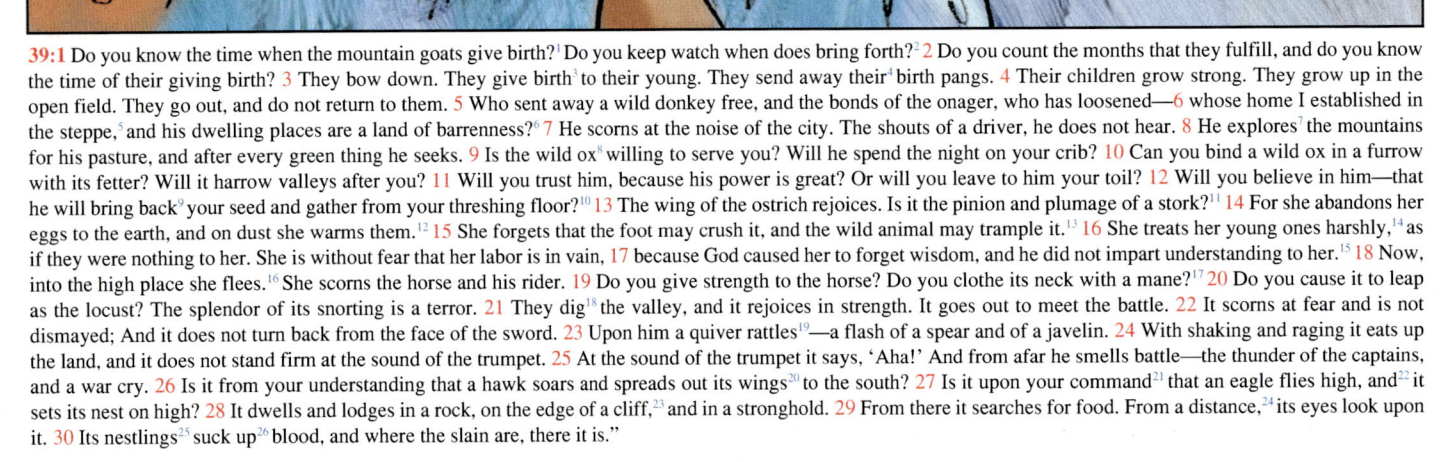

39:1 Do you know the time when the mountain goats give birth?[1] Do you keep watch when does bring forth?[2] **2** Do you count the months that they fulfill, and do you know the time of their giving birth? **3** They bow down. They give birth[3] to their young. They send away their[4] birth pangs. **4** Their children grow strong. They grow up in the open field. They go out, and do not return to them. **5** Who sent away a wild donkey free, and the bonds of the onager, who has loosened— **6** whose home I established in the steppe,[5] and his dwelling places are a land of barrenness?[6] **7** He scorns at the noise of the city. The shouts of a driver, he does not hear. **8** He explores[7] the mountains for his pasture, and after every green thing he seeks. **9** Is the wild ox[8] willing to serve you? Will he spend the night on your crib? **10** Can you bind a wild ox in a furrow with its fetter? Will it harrow valleys after you? **11** Will you trust him, because his power is great? Or will you leave to him your toil? **12** Will you believe in him—that he will bring back[9] your seed and gather from your threshing floor?[10] **13** The wing of the ostrich rejoices. Is it the pinion and plumage of a stork?[11] **14** For she abandons her eggs to the earth, and on dust she warms them.[12] **15** She forgets that the foot may crush it, and the wild animal may trample it.[13] **16** She treats her young ones harshly,[14] as if they were nothing to her. She is without fear that her labor is in vain, **17** because God caused her to forget wisdom, and he did not impart understanding to her.[15] **18** Now, into the high place she flees.[16] She scorns the horse and his rider. **19** Do you give strength to the horse? Do you clothe its neck with a mane?[17] **20** Do you cause it to leap as the locust? The splendor of its snorting is a terror. **21** They dig[18] the valley, and it rejoices in strength. It goes out to meet the battle. **22** It scorns at fear and is not dismayed; And it does not turn back from the face of the sword. **23** Upon him a quiver rattles[19]—a flash of a spear and of a javelin. **24** With shaking and raging it eats up the land, and it does not stand firm at the sound of the trumpet. **25** At the sound of the trumpet it says, 'Aha!' And from afar he smells battle—the thunder of the captains, and a war cry. **26** Is it from your understanding that a hawk soars and spreads out its wings[20] to the south? **27** Is it upon your command[21] that an eagle flies high, and[22] it sets its nest on high? **28** It dwells and lodges in a rock, on the edge of a cliff,[23] and in a stronghold. **29** From there it searches for food. From a distance,[24] its eyes look upon it. **30** Its nestlings[25] suck up[26] blood, and where the slain are, there it is."

35

פרק מ

וַיַּעַן יְהֹוָה אֶת־אִיּוֹב וַיֹּאמַר 1

2 הֲרֹב עִם־שַׁדַּי יִסּוֹר מוֹכִיחַ אֱלוֹהַּ יַעֲנֶנָּה

3 וַיַּעַן אִיּוֹב אֶת־יְהֹוָה וַיֹּאמַר

4 הֵן קַלֹּתִי מָה אֲשִׁיבֶךָּ יָדִי שַׂמְתִּי לְמוֹ־פִי 5 אַחַת דִּבַּרְתִּי וְלֹא אֶעֱנֶה וּשְׁתַּיִם וְלֹא אוֹסִיף

6 וַיַּעַן־יְהֹוָה אֶת־אִיּוֹב מִן סְעָרָה וַיֹּאמַר

7 אֱזָר־נָא כְגֶבֶר חֲלָצֶיךָ אֶשְׁאָלְךָ וְהוֹדִיעֵנִי 8 הַאַף תָּפֵר מִשְׁפָּטִי תַּרְשִׁיעֵנִי לְמַעַן תִּצְדָּק 9 וְאִם־זְרוֹעַ כָּאֵל לָךְ וּבְקוֹל כָּמֹהוּ תַרְעֵם 10 עֲדֵה נָא גָאוֹן וָגֹבַהּ וְהוֹד וְהָדָר תִּלְבָּשׁ 11 הָפֵץ עֶבְרוֹת אַפֶּךָ וּרְאֵה כָל־גֵּאֶה וְהַשְׁפִּילֵהוּ 12 רְאֵה כָל־גֵּאֶה הַכְנִיעֵהוּ וַהֲדֹךְ רְשָׁעִים תַּחְתָּם 13 טׇמְנֵם בֶּעָפָר יָחַד פְּנֵיהֶם חֲבֹשׁ בַּטָּמוּן 14 וְגַם־אֲנִי אוֹדֶךָּ כִּי־תוֹשִׁעַ לְךָ יְמִינֶךָ 15 הִנֵּה־נָא בְהֵמוֹת אֲשֶׁר־עָשִׂיתִי עִמָּךְ חָצִיר כַּבָּקָר יֹאכֵל 16 הִנֵּה־נָא כֹחוֹ בְמׇתְנָיו וְאֹנוֹ בִּשְׁרִירֵי בִטְנוֹ 17 יַחְפֹּץ זְנָבוֹ כְמוֹ־אָרֶז גִּידֵי פַחֲדָו יְשֹׂרָגוּ 18 עֲצָמָיו אֲפִיקֵי נְחוּשָׁה גְּרָמָיו כִּמְטִיל בַּרְזֶל 19 הוּא רֵאשִׁית דַּרְכֵי־אֵל הָעֹשׂוֹ יַגֵּשׁ חַרְבּוֹ 20 כִּי־בוּל הָרִים יִשְׂאוּ־לוֹ וְכׇל־חַיַּת הַשָּׂדֶה יְשַׂחֲקוּ־שָׁם 21 תַּחַת־צֶאֱלִים יִשְׁכָּב בְּסֵתֶר קָנֶה וּבִצָּה 22 יְסֻכֻּהוּ צֶאֱלִים צִלֲלוֹ יְסֻבּוּהוּ עַרְבֵי־נָחַל 23 הֵן יַעֲשֹׁק נָהָר לֹא יַחְפּוֹז יִבְטַח כִּי־יָגִיחַ יַרְדֵּן אֶל־פִּיהוּ 24 בְּעֵינָיו יִקָּחֶנּוּ בְּמוֹקְשִׁים יִנְקׇב־אָף 25 תִּמְשֹׁךְ לִוְיָתָן בְּחַכָּה וּבְחֶבֶל תַּשְׁקִיעַ לְשֹׁנוֹ 26 הֲתָשִׂים אַגְמוֹן בְּאַפּוֹ וּבְחוֹחַ תִּקּוֹב לֶחֱיוֹ 27 הֲיַרְבֶּה אֵלֶיךָ תַּחֲנוּנִים אִם־יְדַבֵּר אֵלֶיךָ רַכּוֹת 28 הֲיִכְרֹת בְּרִית עִמָּךְ תִּקָּחֶנּוּ לְעֶבֶד עוֹלָם 29 הַתְשַׂחֶק־בּוֹ כַּצִּפּוֹר וְתִקְשְׁרֶנּוּ לְנַעֲרוֹתֶיךָ 30 יִכְרוּ עָלָיו חַבָּרִים יֶחֱצוּהוּ בֵּין כְּנַעֲנִים 31 הַתְמַלֵּא בְשֻׂכּוֹת עוֹרוֹ וּבְצִלְצַל דָּגִים רֹאשׁוֹ 32 שִׂים־עָלָיו כַּפֶּךָ זְכֹר מִלְחָמָה אַל־תּוֹסַף

40:1 Adonai answered Job and said, 2 "Will one who disciplines, contend with Shaddai?[1] The one who reproves God, may he answer it." 3 Job answered Adonai and said, 4 "Behold, I am insignificant. What will I respond to you? My hand, I place on my mouth.[2] 5 Once I have spoken, and I will not answer; and twice—I will not do it again."[3] 6 Adonai answered Job out of the whirlwind and said, 7 "Gird, now, your loins like a man. I will ask you, and you will inform me. 8 Will you even frustrate my justice? Will you condemn me, so that you will be justified? 9 And do you have an arm like God?[4] And with a voice like him do you thunder? 10 Adorn yourself now with excellency and grandeur, and with splendor and majesty dress yourself. 11 Scatter the outbursts of your anger. See[5] every proud man, and bring him low. 12 See every proud man, and humble him. Crush[6] the wicked in their place. 13 Hide them in the dust together. Their faces—bind them in the darkness.[7] 14 And also, I will thank you; for your right hand will give victory to you. 15 Behold now, Behemoth, which I made along with you. It eats grass like the cattle. 16 Behold now, its strength is in its loins, and its power is in the muscles[8] of its belly. 17 It lowers[9] its tail like a cedar. The sinews of its thighs[10] are intertwined. 18 Its bones are tubes of bronze.[11] Its bones are like a rod of iron.[12] 19 It is the first of the ways of God. Let its maker[13] draw near with his sword. 20 For the mountains bear produce for it, and every animal of the field plays there.[14] 21 Under bushes,[15] it lies—in a hiding place with reed and swamp. 22 The bushes cover it with their shade. The willows of the wadi[16] surround it. 23 Behold, a river oppresses; he is not alarmed. It is confident when the Jordan bursts forth toward its mouth. 24 Will he capture it with his eyes? With snares, will he pierce its nose? 25 Will you drag Leviathan with a fishhook, and with a cord, will you press down on its tongue?[17] 26 Will you put bulrush[18] into its nose, and with a hook, will you pierce its jaw? 27 Will it increase to you its supplications? Will it speak to you soft words? 28 Will it make a covenant with you?[19] Will you take it for a servant forever? 29 Will you play with it like a bird[20] and will you bind it for your maidens? 30 Will partners in trade haggle over it? Will they divide it between the merchants? 31 Can you fill its skin with spears, and its head with a fish harpoon?[21] 32 Lay your palm on it. Remember the battle and do so no more.[22]

36

פרק מא

1 הֵן־תֹּחַלְתּוֹ נִכְזָבָה הֲגַם אֶל־מַרְאָיו יֻטָל 2 לֹא־אַכְזָר כִּי יְעוּרֶנּוּ וּמִי הוּא לְפָנַי יִתְיַצָּב 3 מִי הִקְדִּימַנִי וַאֲשַׁלֵּם תַּחַת כָּל־הַשָּׁמַיִם לִי־הוּא 4 לֹא־אַחֲרִישׁ בַּדָּיו וּדְבַר־גְּבוּרוֹת וְחִין עֶרְכּוֹ 5 מִי־גִלָּה פְּנֵי לְבוּשׁוֹ בְּכֶפֶל רִסְנוֹ מִי יָבוֹא 6 דַּלְתֵי פָנָיו מִי פִתֵּחַ סְבִיבוֹת שִׁנָּיו אֵימָה 7 גַּאֲוָה אֲפִיקֵי מָגִנִּים סָגוּר חוֹתָם צָר 8 אֶחָד בְּאֶחָד יִגַּשׁוּ וְרוּחַ לֹא־יָבוֹא בֵינֵיהֶם 9 אִישׁ־בְּאָחִיהוּ יְדֻבָּקוּ יִתְלַכְּדוּ וְלֹא יִתְפָּרָדוּ 10 עֲטִישֹׁתָיו תָּהֶל אוֹר וְעֵינָיו כְּעַפְעַפֵּי־שָׁחַר 11 מִפִּיו לַפִּידִים יַהֲלֹכוּ כִּידוֹדֵי אֵשׁ יִתְמַלָּטוּ 12 מִנְּחִירָיו יֵצֵא עָשָׁן כְּדוּד נָפוּחַ וְאַגְמֹן 13 נַפְשׁוֹ גֶּחָלִים תְּלַהֵט וְלַהַב מִפִּיו יֵצֵא 14 בְּצַוָּארוֹ יָלִין עֹז וּלְפָנָיו תָּדוּץ דְּאָבָה 15 מַפְּלֵי בְשָׂרוֹ דָבֵקוּ יָצוּק עָלָיו בַּל־יִמּוֹט 16 לִבּוֹ יָצוּק כְּמוֹ־אָבֶן וְיָצוּק כְּפֶלַח תַּחְתִּית 17 מִשֵּׂתוֹ יָגוּרוּ אֵלִים מִשְּׁבָרִים יִתְחַטָּאוּ 18 מַשִּׂיגֵהוּ חֶרֶב בְּלִי תָקוּם חֲנִית מַסָּע וְשִׁרְיָה 19 יַחְשֹׁב לְתֶבֶן בַּרְזֶל לְעֵץ רִקָּבוֹן נְחוּשָׁה 20 לֹא־יַבְרִיחֶנּוּ בֶן־קָשֶׁת לְקַשׁ נֶהְפְּכוּ־לוֹ אַבְנֵי־קָלַע 21 כְּקַשׁ נֶחְשְׁבוּ תוֹתָח וְיִשְׂחַק לְרַעַשׁ כִּידוֹן 22 תַּחְתָּיו חַדּוּדֵי חָרֶשׂ יִרְפַּד חָרוּץ עֲלֵי־טִיט 23 יַרְתִּיחַ כַּסִּיר מְצוּלָה יָם יָשִׂים כַּמֶּרְקָחָה 24 אַחֲרָיו יָאִיר נָתִיב יַחְשֹׁב תְּהוֹם לְשֵׂיבָה 25 אֵין־עַל־עָפָר מָשְׁלוֹ הֶעָשׂוּ לִבְלִי־חָת 26 אֶת־כָּל־גָּבֹהַּ יִרְאֶה הוּא מֶלֶךְ עַל־כָּל־בְּנֵי־שָׁחַץ

41:1 Behold, his hope is deceived. Will he also be cast down at the sight of it?[1] **2** There is no one so fierce[2] that he would arouse it; and who is it that will take a stand before me? **3** Who has confronted me, and I have restored him? Under all of the heavens—it is mine. **4** I will not[3] be silent about its members, and the matter of strength,[4] and the favor[5] of its value. **5** Who uncovers the face of its garment?[6] Who can enter into its double jaw? **6** Who can open the doors of its face? The surroundings of its teeth are a terror. **7** The furrows of its shields are its pride.[7] Closed up—it is a tight seal. **8** They draw near—one into another[8]—and wind cannot come between them. **9** They are joined to one another.[9] They grasp one another, and they will not be separated from each other. **10** Its sneeze[10] flashes forth light, and its eyes are like the break of dawn.[11] **11** From its mouth go torches. Sparks[12] of fire escape. **12** From its nostrils,[13] smoke goes like a fanned kettle and bulrush.[14] **13** Its breath sets coals ablaze, and a flame goes out of its mouth. **14** Strength lodges in its neck and before it, dismay dances.[15] **15** The folds of its flesh cling together. They are hardened on it. It will not slip. **16** Its heart is hardened like a stone and hardened like a lower millstone. **17** Gods fear from its exaltation[16]—from destructions, they are bewildered. **18** The one who reaches it—a sword will not stand. Neither will a spear, a dart, and a lance.[17] **19** It counts iron as straw;[18] and bronze as wood of rottenness.[19] **20** A son of a bow[20] does not make it flee. Sling stones[21] have turned into chaff for it. **21** Clubs[22] are counted as stubble, and it scorns at the shaking of a javelin. **22** Under it are sharp pieces[23] of potsherd. It spreads a channel upon the mud. **23** It boils the deep like a pot. It sets the sea like an ointment pot. **24** A path shines after him. One reckons the deep as a grey-haired person.[24] **25** There is nothing on dry land of its likeness that is made without fear.[25] **26** It sees everything that is high. It is king over all of the wild animals."[26]

37

42:1 Job answered Adonai and said, 2 "I know[1] that everything you are able to do, and that no purpose can be withheld from you.[2] 3 'Who is this that conceals counsel without knowledge?' Therefore, I have declared, but I did not understand—things too marvelous for me,[3] but I did not know. 4 'Listen, now, and I will speak. I will ask you, and you will inform me.' 5 For the hearing of an ear, I heard you; but now, my eye has seen you. 6 Therefore, I am fed up[4] and I am sorry[5] about dust and ashes." 7 And it came to pass after Adonai spoke these words to Job, Adonai said to Eliphaz the Temanite: "My wrath burns against you, and against your two friends, for you did not speak correctly about me like my servant Job. 8 And now, take for yourselves seven bulls and seven rams and go to my servant Job, and offer up a burnt offering for yourselves; and Job my servant will pray for you, for[7] I will lift up his face,[8] without doing something disgraceful to you.[9] For you did not speak correctly about me like my servant Job." 9 Eliphaz the Temanite, and Bildad the Shuhite, and Zophar the Naamathite went and did just as Adonai commanded to them. And Adonai lifted up the face of Job.

38

10 וַיהוָה שָׁב אֶת־שְׁבוּת אִיּוֹב בְּהִתְפַּלְלוֹ בְּעַד רֵעֵהוּ וַיֹּסֶף יְהוָה אֶת־כָּל־אֲשֶׁר לְאִיּוֹב לְמִשְׁנֶה 11 וַיָּבֹאוּ אֵלָיו כָּל־אֶחָיו וְכָל־אַחְיוֹתָיו וְכָל־יֹדְעָיו לְפָנִים וַיֹּאכְלוּ עִמּוֹ לֶחֶם בְּבֵיתוֹ וַיָּנֻדוּ לוֹ וַיְנַחֲמוּ אֹתוֹ עַל כָּל־הָרָעָה אֲשֶׁר־הֵבִיא יְהוָה עָלָיו וַיִּתְּנוּ־לוֹ אִישׁ קְשִׂיטָה אֶחָת וְאִישׁ נֶזֶם זָהָב אֶחָד 12 וַיהוָה בֵּרַךְ אֶת־אַחֲרִית אִיּוֹב מֵרֵאשִׁתוֹ וַיְהִי־לוֹ אַרְבָּעָה עָשָׂר אֶלֶף צֹאן וְשֵׁשֶׁת אֲלָפִים גְּמַלִּים וְאֶלֶף־צֶמֶד בָּקָר וְאֶלֶף אֲתוֹנוֹת 13 וַיְהִי־לוֹ שִׁבְעָנָה בָנִים וְשָׁלוֹשׁ בָּנוֹת 14 וַיִּקְרָא שֵׁם־הָאַחַת יְמִימָה וְשֵׁם הַשֵּׁנִית קְצִיעָה וְשֵׁם הַשְּׁלִישִׁית קֶרֶן הַפּוּךְ 15 וְלֹא נִמְצָא נָשִׁים יָפוֹת כִּבְנוֹת אִיּוֹב בְּכָל־הָאָרֶץ וַיִּתֵּן לָהֶם אֲבִיהֶם נַחֲלָה בְּתוֹךְ אֲחֵיהֶם

16 וַיְחִי אִיּוֹב אַחֲרֵי־זֹאת מֵאָה וְאַרְבָּעִים שָׁנָה וַיִּרְאֶה אֶת־בָּנָיו וְאֶת־בְּנֵי בָנָיו אַרְבָּעָה דֹּרוֹת 17 וַיָּמָת אִיּוֹב זָקֵן וּשְׂבַע יָמִים

10 And Adonai restored the fortune[10] of Job, when he prayed[11] on behalf of his friends. Adonai added twice as much to all there was to Job.[12] 11 All of his brothers, and all his sisters, and all those who had been his acquaintances from before came and ate bread with him in his house. They showed grief[13] for him and consoled him concerning all the evil that Adonai brought upon him. Everyone gave him a Kesitah[14] and everyone a ring of gold.[15] 12 And Adonai blessed the latter part of Job's life[16] more than his beginning. He had[17] fourteen thousand sheep and six thousand camels—one thousand yoke of oxen, and a thousand female donkeys. 13 He had[18] seven sons and three daughters. 14 He called the name of the first, Yemimah, and the name of the second, Ketziah, and the name of the third, Keren Happuch. 15 And there were not found[19] beautiful woman like the daughters of Job in all of the land. Their father gave to them an inheritance among their brothers.[20] 16 After this Job lived one hundred forty years,[21] and saw[22] his sons, and the sons of his sons—four generations. 17 Job died old and sated of days.

39

Endnotes

Chapter 1

1. Literally, וַיִּרָא "and he feared."

2. Literally, וַיְהִי מִקְנֵהוּ "his cattle was." The phrase consists of a singular verb and singular noun.

3. The word גָדוֹל "great" likely signifies wealth in this context.

4. Literally, בֵּית אִישׁ יוֹמוֹ "a house of a man, his day." It seems as if "his day" in the context of 1:4 is likely referring to each one of Job's children's birthdays.

5. Literally, this is the temporal clause וַיְהִי כִּי, "and it happened that…"

6. The root here is ברך, which is more frequently used to depict the act of blessing.

7. This is a specific day—not just any day. See, for example, how the phrase וַיְהִי הַיּוֹם is used in 1 Sam 1:4 (וַיְהִי הַיּוֹם וַיִּזְבַּח אֶלְקָנָה) and 2 Kings 4:8 (וַיְהִי הַיּוֹם וַיַּעֲבֹר אֱלִישָׁע אֶל־שׁוּנֵם וְשָׁם אִשָּׁה גְדוֹלָה).

8. Literally בְּנֵי הָאֱלֹהִים "the sons of God."

9. I have consistently translated the phrase הַשָּׂטָן as "the Satan," transliterating the noun alongside the comparable English-language definite article. The capitalization of the noun denotes the unique entity and role carried out by the figure in the prologue.

10. Literally, הֲשַׂמְתָּ לִבְּךָ "did you place your heart?" The phrase לשים לב is a frequently used idiom to indicate one paying attention, regarding, or considering something or someone else.

11. Literally, כָּל־אֲשֶׁר־לוֹ "all that is to him." See also 1:11–12.

12. See similar usage of פָּרַץ in Gen 30:30 (כִּי מְעַט אֲשֶׁר־הָיָה לְךָ לְפָנַי וַיִּפְרֹץ לָרֹב).

13. The phrase אִם־לֹא, is normally translated "if not" when followed by a verb. However, this phrase indicates certainty in this context.

14. Literally, מֵעִם פְּנֵי יְהוָה, "from with the face of the Lord."

15. Literally, עַל־יְדֵיהֶם "on the hands of theirs." The phrase עַל יד essentially means, "in close proximity."

16. The proper noun שְׁבָא denotes not only the particular area from which the term is derived, but also its inhabitants—hence, understood here as the "Sabeans" and not simply "Sheba."

17. Literally, לְפִי־חָרֶב, "to the mouth of [a/the] sword."

18. "Another" corresponds to the second time the demonstrative adjective זֶה appears in this verse (עוֹד זֶה מְדַבֵּר וְזֶה בָּא).

19. Literally, the particle הִנֵּה.

20. The phrase, "I came out," which is written as יָצָתִי is understood from the verb יצא. Occasionally, the א is not present when it is without a phonetic value (quiescent).

21. Literally, וְלֹא־נָתַן תִּפְלָה "and he did not give unseemliness."

Chapter 2

1. Literally, וַתְּסִיתֵנִי "and you incited me."

2. The exact significance of the idiom עוֹר בְּעַד־עוֹר is uncertain.

3. Literally, וְכֹל אֲשֶׁר לָאִישׁ "and all that is to a man."

4. "Life" is a translation of the Hebrew נֶפֶשׁ, which can also refer to the "soul."

5. See Exod 9:8–10. The word שְׁחִין is frequently translated as "boils," though it never appears in the plural in the Bible.

6. The Hebrew הַנְּבָלוֹת—usually translated "the foolish women"—likely means foolish in the sense of religious impiety and hence, "godless." Cf. Pss 14:1 (אָמַר נָבָל בְּלִבּוֹ אֵין אֱלֹהִים) and 53:2 (אָמַר נָבָל בְּלִבּוֹ אֵין אֱלֹהִים).

7. Literally, כְּדַבֵּר "as speaking."

8. The article of הַבָּאָה is used as a relative pronoun in this context.

9. Literally, וַיָּבֹאוּ אִישׁ מִמְּקֹמוֹ with an apparent discrepancy between the number of the verb and the subsequent singular noun as well as third person masculine singular possessive suffix. The verbal conjugation is reflecting the subsequent list of friends and is therefore in the plural. Additionally, the word אִישׁ can be used to indicate "each person."

10. There is a lack of subject verb agreement in the phrase וַיִּקְרְעוּ אִישׁ מְעִלוֹ. See note on וַיָּבֹאוּ אִישׁ מִמְּקֹמוֹ in 2:11.

11. "On the ground" is literally the phrase לָאָרֶץ "to the land" with a peculiar usage of the preposition ל. Nevertheless, the significance of this preposition is occasionally similar to that of על when utilized in a phrase with the verb ישב. See Isa 3:26; 47:1; Lam 2:10.

Chapter 3

1. Literally, יוֹמוֹ "his day."

Chapter 4

1. The third person pronoun הוּא seems to be functioning as a copula (a connecting word) and is expressing the verb "to be."

2. The Aramaic נתע should be read as the Hebrew cognate of נתץ "break down."

3. Literally, בִּנְפֹל תַּרְדֵּמָה "in the falling of deep sleep."

4. Literally, עַל־פְּנֵי—a phrase that with different object endings can simply mean "before someone/thing"—i.e., in the presence of. See Gen 32:22; Exod 20:3; 34:6; Deut 5:7.

5. The root סמר only appears one other time in a verbal form in the Bible. In Ps 119:20 it is used in a phrase similar to, but abbreviated from, the one in Job (סָמַר מִפַּחְדְּךָ בְשָׂרִי).

6. Literally, וָקוֹל אֶשְׁמָע "and a voice I heard."

7. The Hebrew word תָּהֳלָה is a *hapax legomenon* and generally understood to relate to some sort of mistake or error.

8. Literally, שֹׁכְנֵי בָתֵּי־חֹמֶר "dwellers of houses of clay."

9. The conjugation יְדַכְּאוּם appears to be an occasion in which the third person masculine plural with a vague personal subject assumes a passive voice.

10. This translation is from the difficult phrase מִבְּלִי מֵשִׂים in which the first two prepositions mean "without" —as in, without paying attention to (implied "them")—and the infinitive construct with the prefixed מִן is a shortened form of שִׂים לֵב "pay attention to."

11. Some read this יְתֵדָם and translate it more specifically relating to a "tent pin." However, יֶתֶר can also refer to a simple "cord."

12. The word בָּם is confusing. Perhaps, בָּם is an instrumental usage of the בְּ with the third person masculine plural pronominal suffix intended to indicate that "they" are essentially bringing about their own demise.

Chapter 5

1. The word כַּעַשׂ is a phonetic variation of כַּעַס "vexation, anger."

2. As in Aramaic, the direct object is indicated by the preposition לְ in the phrase כִּי־לֶאֱוִיל יַהֲרָג־כָּעַשׂ.

3. Literally, יְרַחֲקוּ "they distanced." Despite the fact that it is in the qal active paradigm, it seems to be taking on a passive sense. Cf. Mic 7:11

4. See the passive usage of דכא in 4:19 and note there.

5. Likely a personification of hunger. See 18:12.

2. The phrase יֹאבַד יוֹם אִוָּלֶד בּוֹ is language that reflects a curse (cf. Judg 5:31).

3. The phrase כִּמְרִירֵי יוֹם is difficult because the *hapax legomenon* *כַּמְרִיר is obscure. The translation "darkness of the day" is inferred from the parallels חֹשֶׁךְ וְצַלְמָוֶת in the first line of the verse.

4. This phrase עַפְעַפֵּי־שָׁחַר "eyelids of the morning" is only used one other time in the Bible (Job 41:10), and likely depicts the glimmering sun at the break of dawn.

5. The negative particle לֹא is implied from the first line of the verse.

6. The questioning resumes from verse 12, despite the absence of the interrogative particle.

7. The interrogative phrase "why was I not" is understood in light of the parallelism with the previous line.

8. The word רְשָׁעִים—commonly translated "wicked"—is translated as "restless" in light of the meaning of the verb רשע in Job 34:29. In 34:29, the verb appears in the hiphil paradigm to depict the act of agitating and is antithetically paralleled to שׁקט in the hiphil, which depicts the act of quieting.

9. The Hebrew phrase is literally יְגִיעֵי כֹחַ "the weary (pl.) of strength."

10. The word שָׁם does not appear in the Hebrew. However, it is understood based upon vv. 17, 19. All of that which Job depicts regarding post-mortem experience in vv. 13–19 is in the same location.

11. The personal pronoun הוּא appears as the last word of 19a, emphasizing the nominative—that is, the small and great as individual people.

12. The word שָׁם does not appear in the Hebrew but is once again supplied based upon context. Job is still describing one's experience in the same post-mortem location in this verse, but changes direction in v. 20.

13. The phrase לָמָּה יִתֵּן אוֹר is not in the Hebrew and is supplied from v. 20.

14. Literally, וַיָּסֶךְ אֱלוֹהַּ בַּעֲדוֹ "and God has placed a cover about him."

15. The subject of the verb וַיִּתְּכוּ is שַׁאֲגֹתִי which does not match in gender. This is an occasion in which a morphologically masculine plural verb appears with a feminine subject.

16. The verb שָׁלַוְתִּי may be from the original root שׁלוּ (see for example the noun שַׁלְוָה) and is related to שׁלה, "to be quiet, at ease."

Chapter 6

1. Reading הַוָּתִי from הַוָּה to mean "destruction" instead of הַיָּתִי.

2. This line is difficult because of the imperfect active masculine plural verb, evidently modifying the feminine singular הַוָּתִי. I have understood כַּעְשִׂי in the first line to be gapped in the second and, therefore, part of the subject of the verb. The passive understanding of the active conjugation may come as a result of the subject being indefinite. Supporting this idea is that the verb יִשְׂאוּ is in parallel with יִשָּׁקֵל—a passive in the niphal paradigm.

3. Job might be referring back to his anger כַּעְשִׂי with the masculine singular conjugation of the verb יִכְבָּד.

4. Understood in light of Prov 20:25, מוֹקֵשׁ אָדָם יָלַע קֹדֶשׁ it is likely that לוֹעַ relates to speaking rashly. Nevertheless, the words of Job are explicitly stated as that which have gone astray, and therefore, my translation indicates that Job's words are at fault (not passive) in carrying out carelessness.

5. The word בְּעוּתַי and the feminine בְּעָתָה are both derived from the more frequently attested verb בעת "to terrify."

6. Another more literal option for the phrase יַעַרְכוּנִי is understanding that the terrors of God בְּעוּתֵי אֱלוֹהַּ are setting Job in an array. However, the poetic imagery suggests that the inanimate fears are setting themselves in battle array against Job.

7. The donkey and the ox appear to be participating in the same type of action, given the parallelism of the two verses. However, both of the verbs נהק and געה are used infrequently in the Bible (elsewhere only in Job 30:7 and 1 Sam 6:2, respectively). Both of these words seemingly relate to audible sounds coming out of the mouth of the subject. I have translated along these lines.

8. The phrase בְּרִיר חַלָּמוּת is very difficult. Many translations understand the saying to refer to the "white of an egg"—with רִיר indicating the slimy part around the yolk. Understanding חַלָּמוּת as "yolk" is based upon the Aramaic חֶלְמוֹנָא. If this understanding of חַלָּמוּת is correct, then the phrase would be a descriptive way of depicting the slimy, tasteless portion surrounding the yolk.

9. This direct object is not technically stated but is implied based upon the third person masculine plural independent pronoun in the next line.

10. This independent pronoun does not have a clear antecedent. Since Job seems to be changing the subject from the previous verse, we assume he has begun speaking of his sufferings in general.

11. I understand the Hebrew root לחם in this context from the related words for "flesh" in Arabic and Aramaic.

6. This phrase אֲשֶׁר קְצִירוֹ is referring back to the אֱוִיל of v. 3 after a parenthetical statement about the fool's children in v. 4.

7. The phrase וְאֶל־מִצִּנִּים יִקָּחֵהוּ is difficult. Literally, "and to from thorns he takes it" does not make sense in this context. Understanding צֵן to mean "thorn,"—though it is only used one other time in the Bible (Prov 22:5)—I have left the prefixed preposition מִן untranslated.

8. Probably relating back to the אֱוִיל.

9. "Surely" seems to be the right translation of כִּי here, since this line is introducing a conclusion after a phrase with לֹא.

10. The word יוּלָּד is difficult as one would expect the participle pointing, the qal passive imperfect pointing, or the ו to be between the ל and the ד indicating the passive.

11. Perhaps a reference to the West Semitic deity Resheph.

12. Literally, עַל־פְּנֵי "on the face of," which we see in the first half of the verse.

13. Literally, חוּצוֹת. See Ps 144:13 Jb 5:10 Pr 8:26 for the plural indicating the "outsides," or open areas.

14. Literally, לָשׂוּם "to set."

15. This word קדר literally has to do with making something dark but might be being used in the context metaphorically relating to mourning.

16. The qal of the verb שגב can also assume a passive/stative meaning. See Deut 2:36 (לֹא הָיְתָה קִרְיָה אֲשֶׁר שָׂגְבָה מִמֶּנּוּ).

17. Literally, מִידֵי חָרֶב "from hands of a sword."

18. Literally, the phrase בְּשׁוֹט לָשׁוֹן "in/with the whip of the tongue." However, ב is likely intended to be understood as the preposition מִן as we see in the word מִשֹּׁד in the very next line.

19. The noun חַיָּה is being used collectively here. See Gen 3:1 וְהַנָּחָשׁ הָיָה עָרוּם מִכֹּל חַיַּת הַשָּׂדֶה.

20. The negative particle אַל is used in this situation where we would expect לֹא.

21. In the phrase וְחַיַּת הַשָּׂדֶה הָשְׁלְמָה־לָךְ, the subject and the verbal conjugation are in the feminine singular. Yet, the singular translation "animal of the field will be at peace with you" does not seem to capture what Eliphaz is trying to get across. Eliphaz is striving to communicate total peace for the person who authentically makes his supplication before God (cf. 5:8). In this context, everything in Job's life will be at peace with Job if he turns to God in his trouble.

22. Literally, כַּעֲלוֹת "as going up." Metaphorically, this can be understood as piling up.

23. Literally, דַּע־לָךְ which is translated in the sense of the imperative similar to לֶךְ־לְךָ מֵאַרְצְךָ וּמִמּוֹלַדְתְּךָ in Gen 12:1.

Chapter 7

1. The third person plural takes on a passive sense because there is no explicitly mentioned agent functioning to carry out the action.

2. Literally, וְשָׂבַעְתִּי נְדֻדִים, "I am sated with 'tossings' (i.e., restlessness)."

3. Many translations render לבש in the passive, but this does not make sense, because there is no noun adjacent that agrees in both gender and number. The phrase לָבַשׁ בְּשָׂרִי seems to depict Job directing his complaint to God.

4. Literally, the singular רִמָּה, which can be understood as a collective.

5. The idea seems to be that the "lumps of dirt" are scabs. Job is observing his skin scabbing and then opening up and, perhaps, blood flowing. See Ps 58:8 where מאס in the niphal is used to describe flowing water.

6. The word תִּקְוָה can also mean "cord," (Jos 2:18, 21) which might be intended here to better fit the metaphor related to making fabric.

7. For this imagery, cf. 4:19–21. Job seems to be talking to Eliphaz, which is signaled by the imperative for him to remember זְכֹר.

8. See Zophar's comments about the eyes of the wicked failing in 11:20.

9. Literally, בִי "in me."

10. Bildad seems to respond to this in 8:18.

11. The phrase יִשָּׂא בְשִׂיחִי probably refers to the lightening of the Job's burden, though it is unusual that the verb נשא appear with a ב.

12. The word מַחֲנָק translated here as "strangling" is only used once in that Bible and is related to חנק "to strangle."

13. See usage of מאס in 9:21, 42:6.

14. Literally, חֲדַל מִמֶּנִּי "desist from me."

15. The phrase לָשִׁית לֵב means "to pay attention."

16. Literally, לַבְּקָרִים, "to mornings." Perhaps this is a distributive ל used with the plural form to suggest "every" or the construction is intended to suggest "on a certain number of…"

17. Literally, לִרְגָעִים "to moments." For similar language concerning humankind in Job 7:17–18, see Ps 8:5.

18. Job is either asking God a question, "Have I sinned?" or presenting a conditional statement, "If I have sinned…"

19. Literally, לֶעָפָר "to dust."

12. The phrase מִי־יִתֵּן—literally translated "who would/will give" (cf. Judg 9:29)—is frequently used in the Bible to express a strong desire.

13. Literally, וּתְהִי "and it (fem sing) will be." Job is likely referring back to his wish or hope—both feminine singular nouns.

14. The phrase וַאֲסַלְּדָה בְחִילָה is difficult—particularly because סלד is only used here as a verb in the Bible. The word חִילָה too only appears here in this feminine form. It is likely a poetic feminine form of the more frequently attested חִיל "anguish." Since the context of the verse seems to suggest that Job desires that God would "crush him" and "cut him off," it is reasonable to suggest that סלד should be understood to refer to Job rejoicing if God were to grant him what he is petitioning (cf. chapter 3).

15. The phrase כִּי־אַאֲרִיךְ נַפְשִׁי is literally translated as "that I will lengthen my soul." This is evidently a figure of speech metaphorically indicating patience.

16. This is the only time the word נָחוּשׁ appears in the Bible in this form. This is evidently a masculine form similar in meaning to the more frequently attested נְחֹשֶׁת and נְחוּשָׁה.

17. The ה of the word הַקְּדָרִים is likely a demonstrative usage of the article.

18. See translation of קדר in 5:11 and note there.

19. The meaning of the phrase בֹּשׁוּ כִּי־בָטָח is difficult to discern because of the unmentioned change of subject between the two verbs.

20. The third person feminine singular suffix of עָדֶיהָ seems to be referring to the scene of the scorched streams depicted in the preceding verses.

21. The infinitive absolute הוֹכֵחַ is functioning as the subject of the verb with the same root (יוֹכִיחַ).

22. The infinitive הוֹכֵחַ is apparently gapped from the first line of the verse.

23. Literally, the preposition here is a ל "to, for."

24. Literally, the preposition is עַל "upon."

25. The third person feminine singular suffix of בָהּ likely refers to the general idea of the previous sentence.

26. Literally, the preposition is ב "in, with."

27. The palate is used in Prov 24:13 to be able to discern good information (of the parent) from bad information. See also its usage in Job 20:13.

28. Literally, הַוּוֹת "destructions."

12. The conditional אִם is supplied from the preceding line.

13. "Bruise" for שׁוּף is dubious and mostly deduced from the parallel word פְּצָעַי in the subsequent line.

14. Literally, יַשְׂבִּעֵנִי "causes me to be sated."

15. Some translations render this as the abstract noun "bitterness" evidently understanding the morphological form מַמְרֹרִים to be a plural of abstraction.

16. Literally, וַיְעַקְּשֵׁנִי "he causes me to twist" (if read as a hiphil the pointing is dubious).

17. See usage of מאס in 7:16, 42:6.

18. Literally, אָמְרִי "my saying."

19. The context indicates that Job is likely talking about a sad face. See 1 Sam 1:18.

Chapter 10

1. Literally, אִם־כִּרְאוֹת אֱנוֹשׁ תִּרְאֶה "like seeing humankind, will you see?"

2. Literally, וּלְחַטָּאתִי תִדְרֹשׁ "and for my sin you investigate."

3. The preposition עַל can metaphorically mean "in addition" to something or the similar concept, "despite the fact."

4. This translation reflects understanding שְׂבַע to be an imperative and not a construct.

5. The antecedent to the verb וְיִגְאֶה is likely Job's head from the previous verse.

6. The phrase וְתָשֹׁב is likely a periphrasis for "again."

7. Literally, תִּתְפַּלָּא־בִי "you show yourself wonderful in me."

8. It appears as if אֶהְיֶה and אוּבָל should be understood with a jussive sense despite being imperfect forms.

9. This translation represents the *Ketiv* forms יחדל and ישית.

10. Literally, וְלֹא סְדָרִים "and without orders."

Chapter 11

1. Literally אִישׁ שְׂפָתָיִם "a man of two lips." Context suggests that a "boaster" is likely inferred by this phrase.

2. The phrase מִי־יִתֵּן expresses an English phrase like "if only" throughout Job (6:8; 11:5; 13:5; 14:4, 13; 19:23; 23:3; 31:31, 35).

3. Literally, כִפְלַיִם "two-fold."

4. Literally, מֵעֲוֹנֶךָ "from your iniquity."

5. The feminine singular antecedent is likely תּוּשִׁיָּה in v. 6.

Chapter 8

1. The phrase בְּיַד should be understood as "on account of." See Job 27:11 (אוֹרֶה אֶתְכֶם בְּיַד־אֵל).

2. Literally, תְּשַׁחֵר אֶל־אֵל "you seek to God."

3. The word יָעִיר likely refers to God protecting. See Deut 32:11.

4. The conjugation of the word יִשְׂגֶּה does not match in gender with the feminine noun אַחֲרִית that serves as its subject.

5. The phrase הֲלֹא is supplied from first line.

6. The word אָחוּ is an Egyptian loanword. It is a collective masculine singular.

7. There is an unmentioned change of subject from the godless to the righteous between v. 15 and v. 16.

8. Bildad seems to be responding to Job's comments in 7:10.

9. The word אַחֵר is apparently being used as a collective here.

Chapter 9

1. The idea here seems to be "if someone desires to take up a legal case against God…"

2. Literally, אַחַת מִנִּי־אָלֶף "one from a thousand."

3. The phrase חכם לב(ב) can also refer to someone who is has special skills.

4. Literally, this is the transitive verb הִקְשָׁה that lacks a direct object. Given the omitted direct object, the phrase מִי־הִקְשָׁה אֵלָיו could be understood to depict a person "hardening himself toward God."

5. The word יִתְפַּלָּצוּן is is only used here in the Bible. It is related to the more frequently used words פלצות and מפלצת—both of which depict shuddering.

6. Literally, הָאֹמֵר לַחֶרֶס, "the speaker to the sun."

7. See Job 1:10 and 3:23 for בַּעַד being used in the same time of manner in order to indicate that all of the objects affected by the verb are included in the action.

8. The phrase עַל־בָּמֳתֵי יָם, might literally mean "on the high places [e.g., waves] of the sea." For the definition "back" see 33:29.

9. The exact constellation to which this phrase refers is still up for debate.

10. Literally, the phrase עַד־אֵין "until there is no," which is used to suggest "beyond." The same phrase is used in v. 10b.

11. The particle הֵן might be used with the value of "if" in this context, as in Aramaic.

3. Literally, וְהוֹכֵחַ אֶל־אֵל אֶחְפָּץ "and to argue unto God, I desire."

4. Literally, וְאוּלָם "and but."

5. Literally, וּתְהִי לָכֶם לְחָכְמָה "and it will be to you for wisdom."

6. Literally, הֲפָנָיו תִּשָּׂאוּן "will you lift up his face?" The phrase נָשָׂא פָּנִים can mean "to show favoritism." See Lev 19:15; Deut 28:50; 1 Sam 25:35.

7. The fact that מִשְׁלֵי־אֵפֶר and לְגַבֵּי־חֹמֶר are paralleled leads to the idea that the word גַב "boss" is likely being used metaphorically, referring to aphorisms that the friends state in order to defend their view of retribution.

8. Literally, הַחֲרִישׁוּ מִמֶּנִּי "be silent from me."

9. Literally, וְיַעֲבֹר עָלַי מָה "and pass over upon me what."

10. Literally גַּם־הוּא־לִי לִישׁוּעָה, "also he [is] to me for salvation."

11. The word אַחֲוֶה is presumably from אָחֲוָה which is based on the known Hebrew root חוה "to tell, declare."

12. Literally, אֶצְדָּק "will be righteous."

13. The phrase כִּי־עַתָּה is an idiom that means "for then."

14. Literally, כַּמָּה לִי עֲוֺנוֹת וְחַטָּאוֹת "how many to me iniquities and sins."

15. As for מְרֹרוֹת, see Zophar's statements using a similar word in 20:14.

16. The phrase עַל־שָׁרְשֵׁי רַגְלַי תִּתְחַקֶּה is a bit confusing. This phrase seems to suggest that God is marking a line for himself upon Job's footsteps, through which God is able to follow him around or stalk him.

17. Perhaps Job is referring to himself in the third person here.

18. Literally, כְּבֶגֶד אֲכָלוֹ עָשׁ "like a garment—a moth ate it."

Chapter 14

1. Literally, וּשְׂבַע־רֹגֶז "sated of agitation."

2. Job is likely referring to himself with the 3rd person demonstrative pronoun.

3. Literally, חֲרוּצִים יָמָיו "his days are cut out."

4. Literally, וְעוֹד "and again."

5. Literally, יֶחֱרַב וְיָבֵשׁ "dries up and is dry."

6. Literally, וְאִישׁ "and a man."

7. Literally, תִּשְׁטֹף־סְפִיחֶיהָ "the its (f.s.) torrents (f.p.) wash off (f.s.)." Occasionally, plural feminine nouns take a singular verb, functioning as if they were collective nouns.

6. Literally, יְלָבֵב "he is 'hearted.'" This likely relates to someone being provided the ability to think.

7. The verb תָּעֻפָה is likely related to the substantive עֵיפָה "darkness."

8. The word מַפַּח is a noun from the verbal root נפח "to breathe" that only appears once in the Hebrew Bible. Zophar seems to make several allusions to Job's speech in 7:6–7 in 11:20 by using the words כָּלָה and תִּקְוָה.

Chapter 12

1. Literally, לֹא־נֹפֵל אָנֹכִי מִכֶּם relates the idea that Job is not inferior to his friends.

2. Literally, לַפִּיד "for the calamity."

3. The meaning of the *hapax legomenon* לְעַשְׁתּוּת is dubious.

4. Perhaps וּבַטֻּחוֹת is a plural of intensity or a plural of abstraction.

5. Literally, וְאוּלָם "and but."

6. Literally, the phrase כָּל־בְּשַׂר־אִישׁ "all of the flesh of a man."

7. Literally, אֹכֶל יִטְעַם־לוֹ "tastes food for it."

8. Literally, לוֹ "to him."

9. See Isa 24:22 for סָגַר עַל used to indicate "close (someone) in(to)" a particular location.

10. Literally, לוֹ "to him."

11. As for יוֹעֲצִים שׁוֹלָל, this appears to be an occasion in which the adjective is in a singular morphological form, modifying a plural substantive. The same phenomenon occurs with the word עָרוֹם in Job 24:7, 10.

12. The word מְזִיחַ only appears in this form once in the Bible. It is seemingly related to מֵזַח which is used elsewhere to signify a "girdle" or "belt."

13. The word אֲפִיקִים is a bit difficult in that it seems related to the root אפק "be strong" (only used in the hitpael paradigm). However, the context here and that in Job 41:7 seem to suggest that the word has to do with "protection."

14. This phrase וַיַּנְחֵם is likely referring to the nations being led into exile, as it does in 2 Kings 18:11.

15. Literally, וְלֹא־אוֹר "and without light."

Chapter 13

1. Literally, כְּדַעְתְּכֶם "like your knowledge."

2. This is a repetition of Job's statement in 12:3.

22. The jussive form וְיַשְׁלֵךְ does not have any collateral sense in this context.

23. Literally, אָהֳלֵי־שֹׁחַד "tents of a bribe."

Chapter 16

1. Literally, אַחְבִּירָה עֲלֵיכֶם בְּמִלִּים "I could unite upon you with words."

2. Literally, וְאָנִיעָה עֲלֵיכֶם בְּמוֹ רֹאשִׁי "I would shake upon you with my head."

3. The rare word נִיד is understood to be related to נוּד "to move to and fro." The movement of the lips can be viewed as some sort of verbal comfort.

4. The conditional word אִם is supplied from the first line.

5. Literally, חָרַק עָלַי בְּשִׁנָּיו "gnashes upon me with his teeth." The verb חרק takes the preposition עַל to indicate gnashing at someone.

6. Literally, עָלָי "upon me."

7. The phrase יִרְטֵנִי is difficult. It is disputed whether the verb comes from רטה, which could mean "wring out," or from ירט which is also used in Num 22:32 and means "cast [into something]."

8. Literally, פֶּרֶץ עַל־פְּנֵי־פָרֶץ "breach upon the face of breach."

9. Literally, יָרֻץ עָלָי "he runs upon me."

10. The word גִלְדִּי is understood to come from גֶּלֶד and means "skin." It appears only once in the Bible.

11. The word חֳמַרְמְרוּ (or perhaps חֳמַרְמְרָה) is difficult. The phrase likely has to do with the face changing color because of distress.

12. The phrase בַּמְּרוֹמִים is frequently translated "on high."

13. Literally, דָּלְפָה "drips."

14. This line וְיוֹכַח לְגֶבֶר עִם־אֱלוֹהַּ is difficult. The subject is not explicitly stated, and the ל preceding גֶּבֶר is not easily explicable. I have assumed that the subject of וְיוֹכַח is not explicitly stated.

15. Literally, שְׁנוֹת מִסְפָּר "years of a number."

16. Literally, וְאֹרַח לֹא־אָשׁוּב אֶהֱלֹךְ "and a path, I will not return, I will go."

Chapter 17

1. Reading the rare word זֹעֵךְ as if it were related to the more common דעך "to be extinguished."

2. The phrase אִם־לֹא literally, "if not" can also depict an emphatic affirmative.

Chapter 15

1. The word בָּם at the end of the line is a bit of an enigma since the closest potential antecedent מִלִּים is a feminine plural.

2. Probably an accusation that Job breaks off godly fear.

3. Literally, עֲרוּמִים in the plural. See a similar usage in Job 5:12.

4. The second line literally reads תָּבִין וְלֹא־עִמָּנוּ הוּא "you understand and not with us [is] it."

5. Literally, גַּם־שָׂב גַּם־יָשִׁישׁ "also grey-haired, also aged." The rare form שָׂב is related to the more common שֵׂיבָה "grey-haired."

6. Literally, בָּנוּ "in us."

7. Literally, כַּבִּיר מֵאָבִיךָ יָמִים "greater than your father days."

8. Literally, מִמֶּךָּ "from you."

9. Literally, וְדָבָר לָאַט "and a word of gentleness."

10. The difficult word יִרְזְמוּן is suspected to be related to the Hebrew רמז in which case it would indicate some sort of secretive action.

11. The demonstrative זֶה can also function as a relative pronoun.

12. Literally, וּמִסְפַּר שָׁנִים נִצְפְּנוּ "and the number of years are hidden." This is an occasion in which the predicate agrees with the genitive as opposed to the nomen regens of the construct chain.

13. The phrase תִּתְקְפֵהוּ does not have an explicit subject mentioned.

14. The word כִּידוֹר is a *hapax legomenon* and is dubious.

15. Literally, בְּצַוָּאר "with a neck." The context seems to depict an act of rebellion.

16. Literally, בָּתִּים לֹא־יָשְׁבוּ לָמוֹ "houses they do not dwell to them."

17. Literally, וְלֹא־יָקוּם חֵילוֹ "and his substance will not stand."

18. The word מִנְלָם is a *hapax legomenon* and its meaning is very dubious. The context suggests that a concept related to wealth is being depicted.

19. Literally, לָאָרֶץ "to the land."

20. The word תִּמָּלֵא is likely an impersonal usage of the predicate.

21. Literally, יַחְמֹס "he will treat violently."

Chapter 19

1. The phrase תַּהְכְּרוּ־לִי is difficult because of the rare word הכר. The dictionary definitions are diverse (e.g., "to wonder," "to astonish," "to reproach"). The translation here is based upon the context seemingly indicating that Job's friends are humiliating him with their words.

2. Literally, וְאַף־אָמְנָם "and even surely."

3. This reading understands the rare word מְשׁוּגָה from שגה "to err."

4. The phrase עָלַי תַּגְדִּילוּ, literally "upon me you will do great things" is likely a reference to doing something bad—though the infinitive indicating the negative action is not present.

5. Literally, וְתוֹכִיחוּ עָלַי חֶרְפָּתִי "and you reprove upon me my shame."

6. Literally, סָבִיב "in a circuit, from/on every side."

7. Literally, וַיַּחְשְׁבֵנִי לוֹ כְצָרָיו "he considers me to him like his adversaries."

8. Literally, מֵעָלַי "from upon me."

9. The third person feminine plural verb תַּחְשְׁבֻנִי is conjugated based upon the feminine plural subject אֲמָהֹתַי.

10. The phrase כָּל־מְתֵי סוֹדִי is likely referring to a close group of friends.

11. The word זֶה is being used as a collective noun in this context.

12. It appears as if Job is expressing the idea of being stuck based upon the comment in the previous line. The verbal root מלט is likely related to the noun מֶלֶט "mortar."

13. The phrase כְּמוֹ־אֵל can be understood as "like a god," "like G/god," or, "like El."

14. Literally, מִי־יִתֵּן אֵפוֹ וְיִכָּתְבוּן מִלָּי "if only, then, and my words were written."

15. Literally, בַסֵּפֶר "in the book."

16. The usages of the demonstrative in the line is difficult. I have translated it as if it were written בזאת and referencing the tool used to flay.

17. Literally, וּמִבְּשָׂרִי "and from my flesh."

18. Both the *Ketiv* שַׁדִּין and the *Qere* שַׁדּוּן are difficult in this context. This translation is based upon both of these words coming from the root דין with the prefixed relative particle שׁ.

3. Literally, וּבְהֵמְרוֹתָם "and in their being contentious."

4. The word תְּרֻמַּם is evidently a contracted form of תְּרוֹמֵם which is what might be expected in this context.

5. See Zophar's comments in 11:20.

6. Read as משל "to rule" instead of the more common "to use as a proverb."

7. Literally, וְתֹפֶת לְפָנִים אֶהְיֶה "but spit to a face I have become."

8. Literally, כֻּלָּם "all of them."

9. Literally, תָּשֻׁבוּ "you all will return." This is an imperfect understood in the sense of the imperative.

10. Literally, בָכֶם "in you all"

11. This reading of מוֹרָשֵׁי understands it to be from the Hebrew root ארש which is related to desire.

12. The root שׂים with a ל can mean "to make, transform."

13. Literally, יְצוּעָי "my beds."

Chapter 18

1. Literally, קִנְצֵי לְמִלִּין "ends of for words." Sometimes the construct state precedes a preposition in poetry.

2. The word נִטְמִינוּ is very difficult. This translation his based off of understanding טמה to be related to טמא "to be unclean."

3. The plural possessive suffix of בְּעֵינֵיכֶם is a point of difficulty since Bildad refers to himself and his friends and then speaks to more than one person.

4. The phrase וּמַלְכֻּדְתּוֹ could also be translated as "and a trap for him," as the Biblical Hebrew genitive is used to occasionally express the dative.

5. Literally, וַהֲפִיצָהוּ לְרַגְלָיו "they scatter him/it at his feet."

6. It could be that the feminine singular verbal conjugation is reflecting one of the בהלות from v. 11 or his עצה of v. 7 leading the wicked to a (the) King of Terrors.

7. The phrase מִבְּלִי־לוֹ is difficult but is likely negating the possession of something.

8. The masculine singular verb יְזֹרֶה is peculiarly paired with the feminine singular noun גָפְרִית.

9. Literally, וְלֹא־שֵׁם לוֹ עַל־פְּנֵי־חוּץ "and there will not be a name for him on the face of outside."

10. This is an occasion in which a third person plural active verb (יְנַדֻּהוּ) is translated as a singular passive.

8. The phrase כַּמָּה is supplied here and in the following verses. Context indicates that the questioning continues after 21:17.

9. "God" is not explicitly stated in the text and is added for clarity.

10. The word חֶבֶל can also be understood to be a measured portion—as in a "lot." This, too, makes sense in the context.

11. Literally, גְּנָבַתּוּ סוּפָה "a strong wind steals him."

12. "God" is not in the text of the second line. I have supplied it from the first line for the sake of clarity.

13. The word כִּידוֹ is a *hapax legomenon*. It is paralleled with the חֵמָה of Shaddai and, thus, refers to some sort of calamity.

14. Literally, וּמִסְפַּר חֳדָשָׁיו "and a number of his months."

15. The plural verb חָצְצוּ is conjugated in agreement with the genitive and not the nomen regens in this construct.

16. Literally, וְהוּא "and he."

17. The word רָמִים could also refer to elevated places, suggesting that God judges from "the heavens."

18. Literally, כֻּלּוֹ "all of him/it." In the context, the phrase indicates totality.

19. The unique word שַׁלְאֲנָן is understood in light of the similar word שַׁאֲנָן "at ease."

20. The *hapax legomenon* עֲטִין is notoriously difficult. The word likely refers to a body part that holds liquid or fat.

21. Literally, וּמֹחַ עַצְמוֹתָיו יְשֻׁקֶּה "and the marrow of his bones is watered."

22. Literally, עוֹבְרֵי דָרֶךְ "passersby of a way."

23. Literally, לְיוֹם אֵיד יֵחָשֶׂךְ רָע "to a day of calamity wicked is withheld."

24. Literally, לְיוֹם עֲבָרוֹת "to a day of indignations."

25. It appears as if the plural קְבָרוֹת "graves" refers to a place in which there are many individual graves (i.e., a necropolis).

26. Literally, וּתְשׁוּבֹתֵיכֶם נִשְׁאַר־מָעַל "and your answers remains faithlessness."

Chapter 22

1. This is one of the few times in the Bible in which the normally plural עָלֵימוֹ is singular.

2. Literally, לֹא־מַיִם עָיֵף תַּשְׁקֶה "no water a weary person you give drink to."

3. It is likely that the phrase אִישׁ זְרוֹעַ refers to a man of great strength or resources.

Chapter 20

1. It appears as if the phrase הֲזֹאת is introducing a rhetorical question to suggest that Job should know what Zophar is about to state.

2. Literally, מִקָּרוֹב "from near."

3. This is one of the few occasions in the Bible in which the Hebrew מָקוֹם is to be understood as a feminine noun and, thereby, as corresponding with the feminine verb תְּשׁוּרֶנּוּ.

4. The word אִם is normally used to express a possibility, but in this case, it represents a time in which the consequence of the action has already taken place.

5. The word אִם is supplied from the previous line.

6. The phrase אַל־יֵרֶא expresses an action that cannot or should not happen.

7. This is the literal translation of the difficult phrase אַל־יֵרֶא בִפְלַגּוֹת נַהֲרֵי נַחֲלֵי in which three constructs appear consecutively.

8. Literally, בַּחֲמוּדוֹ "in his desired thing."

9. Literally, יֵצֶר לוֹ "it will be narrow for him."

10. God is not explicitly stated. The word is supplied to provide clarity of the change of subject from the wicked to God between v. 22 and v. 23.

11. The word עָלֵימוֹ normally refers to a masculine plural, but in this case it is assuming a masculine singular meaning.

12. The word בָּרָק is likely referring to the shiny part of the weapon—namely, the blade.

13. The verb יָצָא is seemingly gapped. I have supplied it from the previous line.

14. Literally, אֵשׁ לֹא־נֻפָּח "a fire not breathed."

Chapter 21

1. Literally, תַּנְחוּמֹתֵיכֶם "your (pl.) consolations."

2. The independent personal pronoun preceding a noun with a possessive suffix evidently functions to strengthen the suffix (הֶאָנֹכִי לְאָדָם שִׂיחִי)

3. Literally, לֹא־תִקְצַר רוּחִי "my spirit not be short."

4. Literally, וְשִׂימוּ יָד עַל־פֶּה "and put (pl.) a hand on a mouth."

5. Literally, כַּצֹּאן "like the flock."

6. The word יִשְׂאוּ is likely short for the phrase נָשָׂא קוֹל "lift up a voice" (i.e., sing).

7. Literally, בַּטּוֹב "in the prosperity."

3. The word יָשִׂם in this verse could be short for the phrase שִׂים לֵב "to pay attention to," though it would be an anomaly for the phrase to take the preposition בְּ.

4. This phrase is supplied from the second line of the verse. The first line simply begins with שְׂמֹאול בַּעֲשֹׂתוֹ.

5. The literal phrase בְאֶחָד "in one" is difficult. Perhaps it is communicating "altogether," and/or "unique" or maybe even, "uniquely one."

6. The Hebrew of this line is וּמִפָּנַי כִּסָּה־אֹפֶל "and from my face darkness covered." This translation strives to represent all of the Hebrew words, though slightly reshuffled, with the addition of the negation לֹא from the first line.

Chapter 24

1. Literally, מְשַׁחֲרֵי לַטָּרֶף "seekers of for the prey."

2. Literally, עֲרָבָה לוֹ לֶחֶם לַנְּעָרִים "a steppe for them food for the children." The masculine singular לוֹ is likely being used collectively to refer to the מְשַׁחֲרֵי לַטָּרֶף.

3. The rare verbal form of לקשׁ is understood as the harvesting of the לֶקֶשׁ "spring crop," which comes as a result of the מַלְקוֹשׁ "spring rain."

4. The word עָרוֹם is morphologically singular but represents an unmentioned plural substantive (i.e., "they"). Hence, the plural verb יָלִינוּ.

5. See note in v. 7 for explanation of עָרוֹם taking a plural verb.

6. Literally, עֹמֶר "sheaf," which is a collective noun.

7. I understand the word יָשִׂים to be an abbreviated form of the phrase שִׂים לֵב "to pay attention to."

8. See usage of the rare word תִּפְלָה in 1:22 and note there.

9. Literally, הֵמָּה הָיוּ בְּמֹרְדֵי־אוֹר "they are among rebels of light."

10. The phrase לֹא־הִכִּירוּ דְרָכָיו וְלֹא יָשְׁבוּ בִּנְתִיבֹתָיו can also be translated, "They do not know his ways and they do not dwell in his paths," if God, instead of light, is assumed to be the antecedent of the possessive suffixes.

11. Perhaps this is a pleonastic use of the preposition בְּ. In light of the actions described in the preceding line, the phrase simply indicates that he will be a thief.

12. Literally, חִתְּמוּ־לָמוֹ "they seal up for themselves."

13. Literally, יַחְדָּו "all together."

14. Perhaps the masculine singular conjugation יַכִּיר is representing one of the evildoers depicted in v. 16. Alternation between second and third person subjects and verbs happens repeatedly throughout this chapter.

4. The phrase נָשָׂא פָנִים means to raise one's countenance. One's whose countenance has been lifted up evidently refers to one who has been shown favor.

5. The feminine plural subject זְרֹעוֹת evidently takes the masculine singular passive verb יְדֻכָּא.

6. Literally, וְחוּג שָׁמַיִם יִתְהַלָּךְ "and in a circle of the heavens he walks."

7. Literally, וְלֹא־עֵת "and not time."

8. Eliphaz is referring to Job's comments in 21:16.

9. The word *קִים is a *hapax legomenon*. It is frequently understood as being related to קוּם and to depict someone who rises up against another person. It might also refer to something that is elevated or, perhaps, "greatness."

10. Literally, בָּהֶם "by these" is, perhaps, a phrase that refers to the general idea of the previous sentence.

11. The verbal form תְּבוּאָתְךָ is a bit of an anomaly because of the ת preceding the pronominal suffix. The related noun תְּבוּאָתְךָ "product, yield" could also be read with a very minor emendation.

12. The word אִם is implied and inserted from the first line of 22:23.

13. See Zophar's advice in 11:14.

14. Only the proper noun אוֹפִיר appears in the Hebrew text. The name is likely a reference to gold that comes from this particular location. See 1 Kings 10:11 וְגַם אֳנִי חִירָם אֲשֶׁר־נָשָׂא זָהָב מֵאוֹפִיר.

15. This verse seems to be an encouragement for Job to give up his riches.

16. Literally, בְּצָרֶיךָ "your golds." This is the same word for gold (בֶּצֶר) that appears in 22:24.

17. The meaning of the word תּוֹעָפוֹת is dubious. It might relay the idea of the heights and thereby refer to eminence.

18. This translation renders גֵּוָה as "pride," which is related to the more familiar terms relating to this concept, גַּאֲוָה and גֵּאָה. Admittedly, the meaning of גֵּוָה is not totally clear in this context.

19. Literally, אִי־נָקִי "not clean."

Chapter 23

1. Some translations emend יָדִי to יָדוֹ "his hand" which is a translation that suggests that the hand of God is heavy on Job despite Job's groaning.

2. Literally, וְאֶמְצָאֵהוּ "and I will find him."

12. The singular גְּבוּרָתוֹ "his might" is the *Ketiv*. The *Qere* is literally גְּבוּרוֹתָיו "his strengths."

Chapter 27

1. Literally, וַיֹּסֶף "added to."

2. See note in v. 4 relating to the phrase חַי־אֵל.

3. The phrase כָּל־עוֹד literally "all still" is comparable to the English phrase "as long as." See, for example, the phrase כִּי־כָל־עוֹד נַפְשִׁי בִּי in 2 Sam 1:9.

4. The phrase חַי־אֵל in v. 2 combined with the word אִם in v. 4 is a phrase used to suggest that the speaker will not carry out a certain action "as long as the Lord shall live." See for example 2 Kings 2:2 in which Elijah promises not to abandon Elisha, saying, חַי־יְהוָה וְחֵי־נַפְשְׁךָ אִם־אֶעֶזְבֶךָּ וַיֵּרְדוּ בֵּית־אֵל.

5. Literally, חָלִילָה לִּי which is an idiom that portrays the idea of an action being reprehensible or profane to someone.

6. Literally, לֹא־יֶחֱרַף לְבָבִי מִיָּמָי "my heart does not reproach from my days." In context, it is possible that Job is once again claiming his innocence.

7. The word יֵשׁ is difficult. In light of the context of just retribution (מַה־תִּקְוַת חָנֵף כִּי יִבְצָע), it is reasonable to understand the phrase יֵשֶׁל אֱלוֹהַּ נַפְשׁוֹ to relate to the wicked being cut off.

8. Literally, בְּיַד־אֵל "in a hand of God." This is a phrase that portrays strength or power.

9. The fact that the phrase בָּמוֹת appears with the definite article seems to suggest that a specific terrible event is being referenced here.

10. Literally, וְכַחֹמֶר "and like the clay."

11. The phrase תַּשִּׂיגֵהוּ כַמַּיִם בַּלָּהוֹת is apparently an occasion in which a plural noun takes a feminine singular verb.

12. Literally, וְיַשְׁלֵךְ עָלָיו "he shoots upon him."

13. Literally, מִיָּדוֹ "from his hand."

14. The verb שׁרק takes the preposition עַל to portray someone being hissed at in derision.

Chapter 28

1. Literally, כִּי יֵשׁ לַכֶּסֶף מוֹצָא "for there is for silver a source."

2. Perhaps, מִנִּי־רָגֶל refers to those who travel by foot.

3. Literally, אֶרֶץ מִמֶּנָּה "a land, from it."

4. Literally, סַפִּיר is in the singular form but is translated in the plural as "sapphires" in order to harmonize with the plural אֲבָנֶיהָ.

15. Perhaps floating is the idea that is communicated by "light on the face of the waters."

16. Literally, יִגְזְלוּ "(they) seize."

17. The verb גזל "seize" is provided from the previous line.

18. Literally, מְתָקוֹ רִמָּה "a worm is sweet it." The challenging translation is coupled with an occasion in which the masculine singular verb מְתָקוֹ is evidently modified by a feminine plural noun רִמָּה.

19. The phrase שִׂים לְ means to make or transform one thing into something else.

20. The common word אַל is being used substantively in this phrase to indicate nothingness.

Chapter 25

1. The rare verb יַאֲהִיל seems to be related to the verb הלל "to shine"—particularly in this context in which it is paralleled with the verb זכה "to be bright."

2. The insect "worm" is expressed by two different Hebrew words in 25:6: רִמָּה and תּוֹלֵעָה.

Chapter 26

1. The interrogative מָה is provided from the first line of the verse.

2. The verb הִגִּיד is used with the direct object marker אֶת instead of the usual accompanying preposition לְ.

3. Literally, וְנִשְׁמַת־מִי "and the spirit of whom."

4. Literally, עַל־בְּלִי־מָה "on/over without what."

5. The translation of פְּנֵי־כִסֵּה as "face of a throne" depends on the word כֵּסֶה being related to כִּסֵּא "throne." It might also be related to כֶּסֶא or the related form כֵּסֶה "full moon."

6. This translation understands the enigmatic word פַּרְשֵׁז to be related to the common Hebrew word פָּרַשׂ, "spread."

7. Literally, חֹק־חָג "a boundary he draws round."

8. The phrase עַד־תַּכְלִית אוֹר עִם־חֹשֶׁךְ likely refers to the boundary between areas of light and darkness.

9. The word יְרוֹפָפוּ is understood as "shake" because of the immediate context of the divine rebuke, and in light of the similar phrase וְעַמּוּדֶיהָ יִתְפַּלָּצוּן in 9:6.

10. The verbal root רגע can mean "to disturb" and "to rest."

11. The word שִׁפְרָה is particularly difficult to decipher because it is only used elsewhere as a proper noun in Exodus 1:15. It is apparently related to another rare word שֶׁפֶר "beauty, goodliness."

10. Both "tongue" לָשׁוֹן and "palate" חֵךְ are in the singular in this verse.

11. Literally, וְיָתוֹם וְלֹא־עֹזֵר לוֹ "and an orphan and no helper for him."

12. Literally, וְטַל יָלִין בִּקְצִירִי "and dew will spend the night in my branch."

13. Perhaps the idea is that Job thought that his riches would continuously grow.

Chapter 30

1. Literally, צְעִירִים מִמֶּנִּי לְיָמִים "younger than me to/for days."

2. Literally, אֲשֶׁר־מָאַסְתִּי אֲבוֹתָם "which I rejected their fathers."

3. Literally, גַּלְמוּד "barren." Evidently, this word functions as a strong adjective portraying the severity of the famine.

4. Literally, הָעֹרְקִים צִיָּה "the fleeing ones, desert."

5. Literally, עֲלֵי־שִׂיחַ "upon a bush."

6. This phrase לִשְׁכֹּן בְּ is implied from the previous line.

7. The word פֹּרֵחַ is dubious and is only used one time in the Bible. Here it is understood be related to פרח "sprout" and to portray the uprising of a crowd. Hence, the tentative translation, "mob." If this is the case, the word must also be understood as a feminine collective, assuming that it takes a masculine plural verb יָקוּמוּ.

8. This translation is based upon understanding נִתְּסוּ as related to נתץ.

9. Literally, לְהַוָּתִי יֹעִילוּ "they benefit for my destruction."

10. This is an occasion in which a singular verb (הָהְפַּךְ) has a plural subject (בַּלָּהוֹת). Verbs can be rendered in the passive when this phenomenon occurs.

11. Literally, כְּפִי "like a mouth."

12. This translation is based upon reading the *Ketiv* תשוה as related to תְּשֻׁאָה "storm."

13. The second line of this verse is very difficult. The literal translation of אִם־בְּפִידוֹ לָהֶן שׁוּעַ is "if in his calamity to them (feminine plural) a cry for help."

14. Literally, לִקְשֵׁה־יוֹם "for difficult of a day." Job is evidently talking about those who were experiencing difficulty in life, based upon this phrase being paralleled with the אֶבְיוֹן in the next line.

15. The word עָגְמָה is a *hapax legomenon*. Since it is paralleled with the word בָּכִיתִי, it is certainly communicating some sort of despair.

5. Literally, וְעַפְרֹת זָהָב לוֹ "and dusts of gold are to it."

6. Literally, לֹא־יְדָעוֹ עָיִט "does not know it a bird of prey."

7. The word אַיָּה might also refer to a hawk.

8. Literally, וְלֹא שְׁזָפַתּוּ עֵין אַיָּה "and not seen it an eye of a falcon."

9. The term בְּנֵי־שָׁחַץ "sons of pride" is likely making reference to some sort of wild animal, as it is paralleled with the recognizable word שָׁחַל.

10. Literally, לֹא־עָדָה עָלָיו שָׁחַל "not passed on it a lion."

11. The word סָגוּר is translated as an abbreviated form of זָהָב סָגוּר "closed up (i.e., solid) gold."

12. The exact identity of the word שֹׁהַם is dubious.

13. The word לֹא is supplied from the first line of the verse.

14. The word פְּנִינִים might also refer to pearls. Wisdom being more valuable than precious jewels (וּמֶשֶׁךְ חָכְמָה מִפְּנִינִים) is understood in light of how מִפְּנִינִים is used in Prov 3:15, 8:11, and 31:10.

15. The phrase לֹא־יַעַרְכֶנָּה פִּטְדַת־כּוּשׁ is an occasion in which there is curiously no subject-verb gender agreement.

16. Literally לַעֲשׂוֹת "to make." It is best to understand this verse as a continuation of the previous statement.

17. Literally, בַּעֲשֹׂתוֹ "in his making."

18. Literally, קֹלוֹת "thunders."

19. Literally, לָאָדָם "to the man" or maybe "to Adam."

Chapter 29

1. Literally, וַיֹּסֶף "added to."

2. Literally, בְּהִלּוֹ נֵרוֹ "with his shining of his lamp."

3. Literally, בְּסוֹד "with the (secret) counsel."

4. The phrase בְּעוֹד is supplied from the previous line.

5. This translation is based upon the word חֵמָה being related to חֶמְאָה "curd."

6. Literally, עִמָּדִי "with me."

7. Literally, שַׁעַר עֲלֵי־קָרֶת "gate over the city."

8. Literally, וְכַף יָשִׂימוּ לְפִיהֶם "and a palm they placed to their mouth."

9. The word נֶחְבָּאוּ is either conjugated in the plural to reflect the multiple voices implied by the collective noun קוֹל, or it is an occasion in which the verb is conjugated to agree with the genitive and not the nomen regens.

6. Only the word יָמִים "days" is written, but it is translated as if it were a shortened form of the phrase זְקֵנִים לְיָמִים.

7. The lack of agreement in number between the subject and verb in the phrase וְרֹב שָׁנִים יֹדִיעוּ can be explained as an occasion in which the verb agrees with the genitive and not with the construct.

8. Literally, אָכֵן רוּחַ־הִיא בֶאֱנוֹשׁ "indeed, a spirit—that is in mankind."

9. This translation reflects and understanding that word רַבִּים is being used substantively to refer to many people.

10. Literally, אֵין לְאִיּוֹב מוֹכִיחַ "there was not to Job a reprover."

11. The word אֵין is understood from the previous line.

12. Literally, עֹנֶה אֲמָרָיו מִכֶּם "an answerer of his utterances from you."

13. Literally, פֶּן "lest." This word is likely intended to function as a warning against saying the statement that follows.

14. The word מָלֵתִי is from the root מלא. The quiescent א is not present.

15. Apparently, the morphologically plural phrase אֹבוֹת חֲדָשִׁים refers to a singular wineskin, which is evident through the singular verbal conjugation יִבָּקֵעַ.

16. Literally, וְיִרְוַח־לִי "and it will be spacious for me."

17. Literally, אֶשָּׂא פְנֵי־אִישׁ "I will lift up the face of a man." The phrase נָשָׂא פָּנִים is a figure of speech meaning "to show favoritism/partiality."

18. Literally, לֹא יָדַעְתִּי אֲכַנֶּה "I did not know, I will give an honorary title."

Chapter 33

1. Literally וְאוּלָם "but however."

2. "Clearly" בָּרוּר is a past participle of the verb ברר "to purify." The word does not correlate to those around it like one might expect of this morphological form being used as an adjective. It appears as if it should be understood as an adverb.

3. The object of the phrase עָרְכָה לְפָנַי should probably understood to be מִלִּים/מִלִּין. See 32:14.

4. Literally, אֲנִי כְפִיךָ לָאֵל "I am like your mouth (i.e., in proportion to you) to God."

5. Literally, וְלֹא עָוֹן לִי "and no iniquity to me."

6. Literally, just the word תְּנוּאוֹת "oppositions" is written.

7. Literally, יַחְשְׁבֵנִי לְאוֹיֵב לוֹ "he accounts me for an enemy to him."

16. See note on קדר in 5:11.

17. Literally, מֵעָלַי "from upon me," which perhaps suggests that Job's skin is depicted as falling off of him.

Chapter 31

1. Literally, "produce" is in the plural (וְצֶאֱצָאַי).

2. Literally, וּמָה "and what."

3. The accusative suffix on the verb גְּדָלַנִי is a bit anomalous. This phrase is translated as if it were written גָּדַל עִמִּי, or something comparable.

4. The verb ראה is supplied from the previous line.

5. Reading the plural חֲלָצָיו.

6. The word קָנֶה has multiple meanings. The meaning "joint" is derived from it being in parallel with מִשִּׁכְמָה.

7. Literally, וּמִשֵּׂאתוֹ לֹא אוּכָל "and from his elevation I am not able."

8. The two words for gold in this verse are זָהָב and כֶּתֶם respectively. The words for confidence are כֶּסֶל and מִבְטָח respectively.

9. The conditional word אִם is implied from the previous verses.

10. Literally, לִשְׁאֹל "to ask."

11. Given that הָמוֹן and the feminine singular adjective רַבָּה do not correspond in gender, it appears as if רַבָּה is functioning substantively in this context to indicate a large group of people.

12. Literally, וְסֵפֶר כָּתַב אִישׁ רִיבִי "and a scroll wrote a man of my dispute."

13. Literally, עֲטָרוֹת "crowns." The plural of this word is evidently intended to be understood as the singular עֲטָרָה on some occasions. See Zech 6:11, 14.

Chapter 32

1. Literally, עַל אֲשֶׁר "upon which."

2. Literally, חִכָּה אֶת־אִיּוֹב בִּדְבָרִים "he waited (for) Job with words."

3. Literally, זְקֵנִים־הֵמָּה מִמֶּנּוּ לְיָמִים "older they were than him for days."

4. Literally, צָעִיר אֲנִי לְיָמִים "young I am for days."

5. Literally, אֶתְכֶם "you" as the second person masculine plural direct object.

this, the phrase is more literally translated "far be for God from wickedness, and Shaddai, from iniquity."

9. Literally, אַף־אָמְנָם "even surely."

10. The verbal root רשע in the hiphil can also mean "to condemn as guilty." Thus, this phrase might mean "God does not condemn as guilty those who are innocent." See 9:20 and 34:17.

11. Reminiscent of Bildad in 8:3.

12. The directional ה at the end of the word אָרְצָה likely does not have its conventional meaning.

13. The prepositional phrase עָלָיו "upon him" is understood from the first half of the verse.

14. Literally, שָׂם תֵּבֵל כֻּלָּהּ "placed (upon him) the world, all of it."

15. Literally, עַל־עָפָר "upon dust."

16. Perhaps חבש "bind up" is being used here in the sense of "to comfort." See 5:18.

17. The interrogative ה is used here with the infinitive construct of אמר (הַאֲמֹר) indicating that the questioning continues.

18. Literally, וְיַעֲבֹרוּ "and they pass over," which is a euphemism for dying.

19. This translation reflects reading עָם and אַבִּיר as collective nouns that take plural verbs. Some might understand the phrase וְיָסִירוּ as passive, but this is not the morphological form in the received text. The phrase לֹא בְיָד which is literally rendered "not with/in a hand" should likely be understood figuratively to imply "without the use of force."

20. Literally, לְהִסָּתֶר שָׁם פֹּעֲלֵי אָוֶן "to hide themselves there, workers of iniquity."

21. This translation reflects understanding the phrase לֹא עַל־אִישׁ יָשִׂים to be abbreviated for לֹא עַל־אִישׁ יָשִׂים לֵב.

22. Literally, just the infinitive construct, לַהֲלֹךְ "to go."

23. The rare word *מַעְבָּד, "work" is understood to come from the root עבד "to work."

24. Literally, רֹאִים "seers, observers."

25. The prepositional phrase עָלָיו seems to be functioning as the phrase אֵלָיו in this context.

26. Literally, the second line of this verse reads וְצַעֲקַת עֲנִיִּים יִשְׁמָע "and a cry of the poor, he will hear." This phrase seems to express the purpose of the action described in the first line. The two words for "poor" in this verse are דַּל and עָנִי respectively.

8. Literally, תְּנוּמוֹת "slumbers."

9. Literally, וְגֵוָה מִגֶּבֶר יְכַסֶּה "and pride from a man he covers."

10. This translation reflects the *Qere* reading וְרֹב, though it is disputable as to whether this or the *Ketiv* וְרִיב "and strife" is the best reading.

11. Literally, וְזִהֲמַתּוּ חַיָּתוֹ "and his life abhors." The uncommon word זהם is understood to relate to "abhorring" or "loathing" based on similar words in cognate languages as well as context.

12. Literally, מַאֲכַל תַּאֲוָה "food of desire."

13. Reading the *Qere* וְשֻׁפּוּ "they were laid bare" as opposed to the *Ketiv* וּשְׁפִי "bareness."

14. Literally, לַמְמֻתִים "the (ones) who put to death."

15. Literally, יָשְׁרוֹ "his uprightness."

16. The root פדע only appears in this passage in the Hebrew Bible, and, therefore, its meaning is somewhat dubious. The context suggests it has a similar meaning to the phonetically similar פדה "to ransom, to redeem."

17. The *hapax legomenon* רֻטֲפַשׁ is very difficult. This translation reflects a meaning that understands רֻטֲפַשׁ to be a passive voice, quadriradical extension of the root טפש "to be fat."

18. This translation reflects the *Ketiv* נַפְשִׁי as opposed to the *Qere* נַפְשׁוֹ.

19. This translation reflects the *Ketiv* וְחִיָּתִי as opposed to the *Qere* וְחִיָּתוֹ.

Chapter 34

1. Literally, וְיֹדְעִים "and knowers."

2. The ו is used to make a comparison between the two lines.

3. Literally, וְחֵךְ יִטְעַם לֶאֱכֹל "and a palate tastes to eat." Near identical quote of 12:11.

4. The rare word חֶבְרָה is understood in light of the word חָבֵר "companion."

5. Literally, וְלָלֶכֶת "and to walk."

6. Literally, בִּרְצֹתוֹ עִם־אֱלֹהִים "in his being pleased with God."

7. Literally, אַנְשֵׁי לֵבָב "men of heart," with "heart" referring to the inner person.

8. Literally, חָלִלָה לָאֵל מֵרֶשַׁע וְשַׁדַּי מֵעָוֶל. The phrase חָלִלָה לְ is an idiom that portrays the idea of an action being reprehensible or profane to someone (cf. 27:5). Considering

12. The word פַּשׁ is a *hapax legomenon* and is commonly translated as "folly" based upon related Arabic cognates. In this context, פַּשׁ appears to reflect a similar meaning to פֶּשַׁע "transgression."

13. Literally, וְאִיּוֹב "and/but Job."

14. Literally, יַכְבִּר "he makes great."

Chapter 36

1. Literally, כִּי עוֹד לֶאֱלוֹהַּ מִלִּים "for still to God words."

2. Literally, לְמֵרָחוֹק "for from afar."

3. Literally, תְּמִים דֵּעוֹת "complete of knowledges," though it is not uncommon for abstract nouns to appear in plural morphological forms.

4. This verse poses numerous difficulties to translating literally. Nevertheless, a literal translation of the entire verse (לֹא־יִגְרַע מִצַּדִּיק עֵינָיו וְאֶת־מְלָכִים לַכִּסֵּא וַיֹּשִׁיבֵם לָנֶצַח וַיִּגְבָּהוּ) is "He does not withdraw his eyes from a righteous person and kings for the throne he seats them forever and he exalts it."

5. Literally, אָזְנָם "their ear."

6. Literally, בַּטּוֹב "in the prosperity."

7. Literally, בַּנְּעִימִים "with/in the delights."

8. Literally, בְּשֶׁלַח "in a water channel."

9. Literally, בַּנֹּעַר "in the youth."

10. Literally, בַּלַּחַץ "in the oppression."

11. There are two different words translated as "distress" in the first two lines of this verse—צַר and מוּצָק respectively. Also, the second line of the verse רַחַב לֹא־מוּצָק תַּחְתֶּיהָ is literally rendered "an expanse, no distress under it." My translation reflects understanding רַחַב to be a feminine noun.

12. My translation of וְנַחַת שֻׁלְחָנְךָ מָלֵא דָשֶׁן reflects understanding נחת as a masculine noun.

13. Literally, פֶּן־יְסִיתְךָ "lest it allure/incite you." This appears to be an occasion in which the gender of the subject חֵמָה and its corresponding verb יְסִיתְךָ do not agree.

14. This translation understands סֵפֶק to be related to שֶׂפֶק "surfeit, excess." An abundance of wealth might be the idea portrayed here. See Job 20:22.

15. The meaning of this line is particularly difficult. Literally, לַעֲלוֹת עַמִּים תַּחְתָּם "to go up, people, under them (in their place)."

16. Literally, כִּי־עַל־זֶה בָּחַרְתָּ "for upon this, you chose."

17. Literally, מִי־פָקַד עָלָיו "who appointed upon him?"

27. Literally, וְעַל־גּוֹי "and over a nation."

28. This verse מִמְּלֹךְ אָדָם חָנֵף מִמֹּקְשֵׁי עָם is difficult and is literally translated "from reigning a godless man, from snares of people."

29. There is not clear antecedent to the phrase הֶאָמַר and, therefore, I have translated the phrase with an impersonal pronoun.

30. Literally, הֲמֵעִמְּךָ "is it from with you?"

31. Literally, אִיּוֹב לֹא־בְדַעַת יְדַבֵּר "Job, not with/in knowledge, speaks."

32. Literally, אָבִי "my father." Perhaps this serves as an exclamation figuratively addressing a superior through which a wish is expressed.

33. Literally, עַד־נֶצַח "until perpetuity."

34. The ב in this context seems to be functioning more like a כ.

Chapter 35

1. The literal translation of this verse appears to be problematic because Job is never depicted as asking such a question. Perhaps the phrase might be best understood as Job asking, "What will I gain from not sinning?"

2. Literally, וְשׁוּר "and consider."

3. Reminiscent of Job 7:20.

4. Literally, וּלְבֶן־אָדָם "and for a son of man/Adam."

5. The word רַבִּים is apparently used substantively and functions as the masculine plural subject of the verbs יַזְעִיקוּ and יְשַׁוֵּעוּ.

6. Literally, וְלֹא־אָמַר "and/but no he/it said."

7. The literal rendering of עֹשָׂי is "my makers." The plural, "makers," seems to be a way to refer to God as maker. See Isa 54:5 and Ps 149:2.

8. The word מַלְּפֵנוּ "he teaches us" is understood to be a piel conjugation of the root אלף "to learn." The א has evidently elided.

9. Reminiscent of 12:8.

10. The antecedent to the feminine singular object suffix יְשׁוּרֶנָּה is not readily apparent. Perhaps the reader should understand שָׁוְא in the previous sentence to be an abbreviated form of a phrase similar to צַעֲקַת שָׁוְא (see יִצְעֲקוּ in the previous verse), which would provide the feminine singular antecedent to the pronominal suffix.

11. Literally, כִּי־אַיִן פָּקַד "for there is not, he visit(ed)."

12. The word יִמְצָאֵהוּ understood as "he causes it to come" represents an atypical usage of the root מצא which normally relates to finding.

13. This is a somewhat interpretive rendering of הֲתֵדַע בְּשׂוּם־אֱלוֹהַּ עֲלֵיהֶם which is literally translated "do you know in the putting of God upon them."

14. This is the only time *מפלש appears in the Bible. The phrase מִפְלְשֵׂי־עָב in this context is understood in light of the similar phrase מִפְרְשֵׂי־עָב (literally, "the spreadings of a cloud.") in 36:29.

15. Concerning the plural form דֵעִים in the phrase תְּמִים דֵעִים, see note concerning the related word דֵעָה in 36:4.

16. The phrase הֲתֵדַע is supplied based upon the context of the preceding verses.

17. The mention of the verb ערך in this context seems to be an abbreviation of the phrase עֲרָךְ מִלִּים. In this case, the full phrase would be נַעֲרָךְ אֵלָיו מִלִּים.

Chapter 38

1. Literally, בְּיָסְדִי־אָרֶץ "in my establishing/founding of the land."

2. The unique word *מֶמַד is understood in light of the similar and more frequently used word מִדָּה "measurement."

3. Literally, בְּרָן־יַחַד כּוֹכְבֵי בֹקֶר "in singing together stars of a morning." The phenomenon of the ב preceding an infinitive construct can indicate a temporal phrase. I have translated accordingly, using a finite verb in translation for the infinitive in Hebrew.

4. Literally, בְּגִיחוֹ "in its bursting forth."

5. Literally, בְּשׂוּמִי "in my placing."

6. Literally, וְלֹא תֹסִיף "and you will not add to doing (i.e., do more, again)."

7. This translation represents understanding the rare word פֹּא to have the same meaning as the phonetically similar פֹּה "here."

8. Literally, הֲמִיָּמֶיךָ "from your days?" Notice the unique pointing of the interrogative ה as הֲ opposed to the expected הַ.

9. This translation reflects the Qere יִדַּעְתָּ הַשַּׁחַר. The Ketiv is יִדַּעְתָּה שַּׁחַר.

10. See 37:3 and note concerning כַּנְפוֹת הָאָרֶץ there.

11. Literally, תִּתְהַפֵּךְ "overturns itself."

12. Literally, כְּחֹמֶר חוֹתָם "like clay of a seal."

18. The phrase כָּל־אָדָם "every man" should be understood as a collective phrase and the subject of the plural verb חָזוּ.

19. Literally, מִסְפַּר שָׁנָיו וְלֹא־חֵקֶר "number of his years, and without searching out."

20. Literally, מִפְרְשֵׂי־עָב "a spreadings of the cloud."

21. "Roots of the sea" is a literal translation of שָׁרְשֵׁי הַיָּם which likely refers to the deepest or bottom portion of the sea.

22. Literally, לְמַכְבִּיר "for abounding."

23. Literally, וַיְצַו עָלֶיהָ בְמַפְגִּיעַ "and commands (up) it in assailing/attacking." The phrase בְמַפְגִּיעַ in this context is a bit dubious.

24. Literally, עָלָיו "about him/it."

25. Literally, מִקְנֶה אַף עַל־עוֹלֶה "cattle, even upon what rises."

Chapter 37

1. "Hear, hear" is the translation of an imperative and an infinitive absolute which function to intensify the call to action (שִׁמְעוּ שָׁמוֹעַ).

2. The phrase עַל־כַּנְפוֹת הָאָרֶץ is literally translated "upon the wings of the land" but is used here in a figurative sense to represent the most distant parts imaginable.

3. Literally, נִפְלָאוֹת "wonderous things." See 5:9, 9:10, and 37:14. This word is apparently used adverbially in this context, though it could conceivably maintain its substantival meaning.

4. The word הֱוֵא is understood in light of the root הוה "to fall."

5. The is the literal translation of the uniquely repetitive phrase וְגֶשֶׁם מָטָר וְגֶשֶׁם מִטְרוֹת עֻזּוֹ.

6. Literally, וּמִמְּזָרִים "and from scatterers." Perhaps wind is to be understood in terms of something that scatters. This meaning seems to be inferred by the mention of the word סוּפָה in the previous line.

7. The phrase, יִתֶּן־קָרַח could also be understood as "it gives ice." The subject of this phrase is not explicitly stated.

8. Literally, בְּמוּצָק "in constraint." Apparently, the frozen water is depicted in terms of being in such dire restraint that it is not able to move.

9. "His guidance" represents the Ketiv בְּתַחְבּוּלָתוֹ which is a singular form. The Qere reading is the plural form בְּתַחְבּוּלֹתָיו.

10. Literally, לְפָעֳלָם "for their doing."

11. Literally, עַל־פְּנֵי תֵבֵל אָרְצָה "on the face of the land toward (the) earth."

5. Literally, אֲשֶׁר־שַׂמְתִּי עֲרָבָה בֵיתוֹ "which I placed, steppe, his home."

6. Literally, מְלֵחָה "saltness." Perhaps it is a shortened form of אֶרֶץ מְלֵחָה (Jer 17:6).

7. The word יָתוּר is translated as a third person masculine singular imperfect from תּוּר "to explore," despite the unique pointing.

8. The רֵים of this verse and 39:10 should be understood as the "wild ox," which is normally spelled רְאֵם.

9. This translation is based on the *Qere* יָשִׂיב. The *Ketiv* is יָשׁוּב.

10. Literally, וְגָרְנְךָ יֶאֱסֹף "and your threshing floor, gather."

11. Literally, אִם־אֶבְרָה חֲסִידָה וְנֹצָה "if pinion, stork, and plumage."

12. The masculine singular pronominal suffix on תְּחַמֵּם has a feminine singular antecedent (בֵּיצֶיהָ).

13. The third person feminine singular pronominal suffixes on תְּזוּרֶהָ and תְּדוּשֶׁהָ seemingly refer to the feminine plural antecedent בֵּיצֶיהָ.

14. The verbal conjugation הִקְשִׁיחַ is a morphologically masculine form. Perhaps the form should be understood as if it were written הִקְשִׁיחָה. The feminine singular pronominal suffix on the adjacent word בָּנֶיהָ suggests that the subject is still a female bird.

15. Literally, וְלֹא־חָלַק לָהּ בַּבִּינָה "and did not impart to her in the wisdom."

16. The meaning of the word תַּמְרִיא is particularly difficult to discern. This is the only time the root מרא appears in the hiphil paradigm. The context is a bit puzzling, and other Biblical Hebrew words lend very little insight into the meaning.

17. The meaning of the rare word רַעְמָה is dubious, but the context suggests that it is that which a horse wears on its neck—namely, a mane.

18. The masculine plural יַחְפְּרוּ "they dig" seems to be out of place in this context since a singular subject is the topic of discussion in this context. Several of the versions seem to be reading יַחְפֹּר "he/it digs."

19. The rare word תִּרְנָה is difficult. Context suggests that it might refer to a quiver rattling as weapons are pulled out of it.

20. This translation represents reading כְּנָפוֹ as כְּנָפָיו.

21. Literally, פִּיךָ "your mouth."

22. Literally, וְכִי "and for/that/when."

13. The phrase עַד־נִבְכֵי־יָם is understood in light of the understandable parallel phrase וּבְחֵקֶר תְּהוֹם. It appears as if both of these phrases depict the deepest part of the ocean.

14. In the phrase וּמִסְפַּר יָמֶיךָ רַבִּים the adjective רַבִּים is in agreement with the genitive (יָמִים).

15. Literally, עַל־אֶרֶץ לֹא־אִישׁ "upon a land, no man."

16. Literally, מִדְבָּר לֹא־אָדָם בּוֹ "wilderness, no man in it."

17. Literally, הֲיֵשׁ־לַמָּטָר אָב "is there, to the rain, a father?"

18. The phrase אֶגְלֵי־טָל is translated "drops of dew" in light of the parallel word מָטָר.

19. Literally, מַיִם יִתְחַבָּאוּ "(the) waters draw together."

20. The word *מֹשְׁכוֹת only appears once in the Bible. In this context, it is understood in light of the parallel term מַעֲדַנּוֹת which is also difficult, but likely means "bands."

21. The word מַזָּרוֹת only appears here in the Hebrew Bible. It seems as if the term is referring to a specific star constellation based upon it being set in parallel with עַיִשׁ and the third person masculine singular possessive suffix of the phrase בְּעִתּוֹ.

22. Literally, עַל־בָּנֶיהָ "upon her children."

23. Literally, לָעָב "to the cloud."

24. Both טֻחוֹת and the parallel שֶׂכְוִי are rare words. They can both mean a type of bird, and I have translated them accordingly to maintain the parallelism.

25. Literally, בְּצֶקֶת עָפָר "in the pouring of dust."

26. Literally, לַמּוּצָק "to the casting."

27. The phrase וְחַיַּת כְּפִירִים "life of young lions" might be understood to relate to the appetite.

28. Literally, בַּמְּעוֹנוֹת "in the habitations."

29. This translation reflects reading יְלָדָיו for the written text יְלָדוֹ.

30. Literally, לִבְלִי־אֹכֶל "for without food."

Chapter 39

1. Literally, עֵת לֶדֶת יַעֲלֵי־סָלַע "the time of the birthing of the wild goats of the cliff."

2. Literally, חֹלֵל אַיָּלוֹת "the bringing forth of does."

3. Literally, תְּפַלַּחְנָה "they cleave." The image is that of young ones emerging from an animal as it cleaves in childbirth.

4. The phrase חֶבְלֵיהֶם is an occasion in which the antecedent to the masculine plural pronominal suffix is a feminine plural noun.

19. Literally, הֲיִכְרֹת בְּרִית עִמָּךְ "will it cut a covenant with you."

20. Literally, כַּצִּפּוֹר "like the bird."

21. The meanings of both *שֶׂכָה and *צִלְצָל are dubious. By their usage, is appears as if they are referring to sharp weapons.

22. Literally, אַל־תּוֹסַף "do not add (to do)."

Chapter 41

1. Literally, אֶל־מַרְאָיו "to its sight."

2. Literally, just לֹא־אַכְזָר "no fierce (one)."

3. This is a translation of the *Ketiv* לֹא and not the *Qere* לוֹ.

4. Literally, גְּבוּרוֹת "strengths."

5. The word חִין is difficult, and the context does not provide a parallel word. This translation represents חִין to be similar to חֵן "favor."

6. Perhaps a reference to this creature's skin.

7. The phrase גַּאֲוָה אֲפִיקֵי מָגִנִּים likely makes reference to the scales on Leviathan's back. For this reason, some of the versions translate גַּאֲוָה as the phonetically similar word גֵּוָה "his back." This translation represents the written text with an addition of the possessive pronoun, "its."

8. Literally, אֶחָד בְּאֶחָד "one into one."

9. "One another" is the translation of Hebrew phrase אִישׁ אָחִיו.

10. Literally, עֲטִישֹׁתָיו "sneezes." This word (*עֲטִישָׁה), a *hapax legomenon*, appears to be in the plural but takes a feminine singular verb in this verse (תָּהֶל). The meaning of the word is mostly derived from related cognate words of other Semitic languages.

11. Literally, עַפְעַפֵּי־שָׁחַר "eyelids of the morning." See Job 3:9.

12. The word *כִּידוֹד is a *hapax legomenon*. The word's meaning is deduced from the context of the verse—particularly, because כִּידוֹד is set in parallel to לַפִּידִים.

13. The meaning of the word *נְחִיר has been deciphered by its usage in this context as well as other related Semitic language cognates.

14. The phrase כְּדוּד נָפוּחַ וְאַגְמֹן seems to be portraying a kettle being fanned over bulrush that is on fire and, therefore, producing smoke.

15. The word תָּדוּץ only appears here in the Bible. The meaning is taken from the Aramaic root דוץ "to dance."

23. Literally, עַל־שֶׁן־סֶלַע "on a tooth of a cliff."

24. Literally, לְמֵרָחוֹק "for from a distance."

25. The translation "its nestlings" is based off of the *Qere* וְאֶפְרֹחָיו "and its nestlings."

26. The word יְעַלְעוּ is a difficult *hapax legomenon*. The mentioning of baby birds in the context provokes the image of seeking after sustenance, making "suck up" a reasonable translation.

Chapter 40

1. Literally, הֲרֹב עִם־שַׁדַּי יִסּוֹר "contend with Shaddai, discipliner?"

2. Literally, לְמוֹ־פִי "to my mouth."

3. Literally, וּשְׁתַּיִם וְלֹא אוֹסִיף "but twice and I will not add."

4. Literally, וְאִם־זְרוֹעַ כָּאֵל לָךְ "and an arm like a god (or like God), to you?"

5. Literally, וּרְאֵה "and see."

6. Literally, וַהֲדֹךְ "and crush." The verb הדך is only used here in the Bible. Its meaning is understood to imply an injurious act by the context of the verse and a comparable Arabic cognate.

7. Literally, בַּטָּמוּן "in/with the hidden/concealed [thing/place]."

8. This word *שָׂרִיר is a *hapax legomenon* but is understood to relate to the Behemoth's strength mentioned in the verse.

9. The common meaning of the roots חפץ "to delight, take pleasure in" does not seem to make sense in this context. The meaning suggested here is derived from an Arabic cognate.

10. This translation reflects *Qere* פְּחָדָיו. The *Ketiv* is פחדו.

11. Literally, אֲפִיקֵי נְחוּשָׁה "channels of bronze."

12. The two words used for "bone" in this verse are עֶצֶם and גֶּרֶם respectively.

13. Literally, הָעֹשׂוֹ "the maker [of] it."

14. In the phrase וְכָל־חַיַּת הַשָּׂדֶה יְשַׂחֲקוּ־שָׁם the term חַיַּת הַשָּׂדֶה should be understood collectively, which is indicated by the plural verb יְשַׂחֲקוּ.

15. The exact plant of the word צֶאֱלִים remains under question. The English translation is in the plural because it is understood as a plural noun in the following verse.

16. Perhaps עַרְבֵי־נָחַל refers to the "poplars of a wadi."

17. Literally, תַּשְׁקִיעַ לְשֹׁנוֹ "cause his tongue to sink."

18. Perhaps the word אַגְמֹן refers to a rope made of bulrush.

on," see Ps 90:13 שׁוּבָה יְהוָה עַד־מָתָי וְהִנָּחֵם עַל־עֲבָדֶיךָ.

6. The phrase עָפָר וָאֵפֶר makes reference to the human condition. See Job 30:19.

7. Literally, כִּי אִם "for if."

8. Perhaps the phrase נָשָׂא פָנִים in this context means "to be gracious," or "hold in honor."

9. Literally, לְבִלְתִּי עֲשׂוֹת עִמָּכֶם נְבָלָה "without doing with you disgrace."

10. This translation reflects the Qere שְׁבוּת.

11. Literally, בְּהִתְפַּלְלוֹ "in his praying."

12. Literally, וַיֹּסֶף יְהוָה אֶת־כָּל־אֲשֶׁר לְאִיּוֹב לְמִשְׁנֶה "Adonai added all that was to Job for a double portion."

13. Literally, וַיָּנֻדוּ לוֹ which likely represents the subject showing grief by shaking the head as an act of sympathy.

14. A type of currency whose origin is difficult to identify.

15. "Everyone" is simply reflected through the Hebrew אִישׁ, indicating that each individual person gave Job the items mentioned.

16. The word אַחֲרִית can refer to the entire latter portion of a person's life. For example, see the phrase וְאַחֲרִיתְךָ in Job 8:7.

17. Literally, וַיְהִי־לוֹ "and it was to him."

18. Literally, וַיְהִי־לוֹ "and it was to him."

19. The subject of the singular verb נִמְצָא is evidently the plural נָשִׁים.

20. The reference is to the daughters despite the masculine plural possessive pronouns on לָהֶם, אֲבִיהֶם, אֲחֵיהֶם.

21. Literally, שָׁנָה "year."

22. Reading along with the Qere וַיִּרְאֶה.

16. The phrase מְשֻׁתוֹ is translated with the same meaning as the more common phrase שְׂאֵתוֹ.

17. The final two words מַסָּע and שִׁרְיָה are rare but are understood in context to have similar meanings to the more common words חֶרֶב and חֲנִית.

18. Literally, לְתֶבֶן "for straw."

19. Literally, לְעֵץ רִקָּבוֹן "for a tree of rottenness."

20. "A son of a bow" (בֶּן־קָשֶׁת) likely refers to an arrow.

21. Literally, אַבְנֵי־קָלַע "stones of slinging."

22. The word תּוֹתָח is a *hapax legomenon* and is understood in context to be an instrument of battle because it is set in parallel to the more common כִּידוֹן. Additionally, תּוֹתָח should likely be understood as a collective noun in light of the plural verb נֶחְשָׁבוּ.

23. The word *חַדּוּד is understood in light of the related word חַד and verbal root חדד to mean something sharp.

24. Literally, לְשֵׂיבָה "for a grey-haired person."

25. Literally, הֶעָשׂוּ לִבְלִי־חָת "the made without fear."

26. Literally, עַל־כָּל־בְּנֵי־שָׁחַץ "over all of the sons of pride." Cf. 28:8.

Chapter 42

1. Reading the Qere יָדַעְתִּי and not the Ketiv יָדַעְתָּ.

2. The subject of the verb יִבָּצֵר (masculine) is evidently מְזִמָּה (feminine).

3. Literally, נִפְלָאוֹת מִמֶּנִּי "marvelous things from me."

4. See Job 7:16 for an instance in which מאס appears without a direct object and should be understood to mean "to be fed up."

5. For נחם in the sense of "to have compassion on, take pity